Competing in

D1322092

Given the increasing prominence of Emerging markets, a sophisticated understanding of their perils and promises is crucial to the growth of companies, including those from within Emerging markets themselves. Thus, it is surprising that, in their quest to train managers, only a few academic institutions currently provide a systematic forum to generate a superior understanding of this important economic event.

This groundbreaking book provides an essential set of readings and case studies that will facilitate a much-needed fundamental rethinking about drivers of successful *as well as* unsuccessful firm conduct in these markets, and about the role of sophisticated but (usually) poorly-serving Western theories and ideas regarding competition and competitive traps and successes.

Although the book is intended primarily for Emerging markets courses, it can also be used for various other courses in International management or International strategy. It explores the following themes:

● The strategic and operational challenges companies face while competing in these relatively new (and, therefore, generally unfamiliar) markets
● The imperative to generate creative solutions in response to idiosyncratic challenges posed by Emerging markets.

Competing in Emerging Markets emphasizes both the unique challenges facing corporate managers who operate (or intend to operate) in Emerging markets, and the ways in which managers can efficiently and effectively respond to these competitive challenges. As one of the first comprehensive texts on this subject, *Competing in Emerging Markets* is certain to become a standard in the field.

Dr. Hemant Merchant is Associate Professor of International Strategy at Barry Kaye College of Business of Florida Atlantic University (USA). He has lived and worked in Emerging as well as non-Emerging markets, and chaired the Emerging markets track at the 2007 *Academy of International Business* conference. Dr. Merchant has published in several leading strategy and international business journals, and serves on the editorial boards of the *Strategic Management Journal, Thunderbird International Business Review, Canadian Journal of Administrative Sciences*. He is also the 'Strategy and Business Environment' editor at the *Journal of Asia Business Studies*. Dr. Merchant's research has earned several prestigious awards, including two Douglas C. Mackay Outstanding Paper Award(s) in International Business. Dr. Merchant has been nominated five times for the prestigious TD-Canada Trust Distinguished Teaching Award and has been recognized several times for his teaching in Bachelors, Masters, and Executive programs.

Competing in Emerging Markets

Cases and Readings

Edited by

Hemant Merchant

Routledge
Taylor & Francis Group

NEW YORK AND LONDON

First published 2008
by Routledge
270 Madison Ave, New York, NY 10016

Simultaneously published in the UK
by Routledge
2 Park Square, Milton Park, Abingdon, Oxon 0X14 4RN

Routledge is an imprint of the Taylor & Francis Group, an informa business

Typeset in Perpetua and Bell Gothic by
RefineCatch Limited, Bungay, Suffolk
Printed and bound in the United States of America on acid-free paper by
Edwards Brothers, Inc., Lillington, NC

Library of Congress Cataloging in Publication Data
A catalog record has been requested for this book

ISBN10: 0–415–39949–1 (hbk)
ISBN10: 0–415–39950–5 (pbk)

ISBN13: 978–0–415–39949–4 (hbk)
ISBN13: 978–0–415–39950–0 (pbk)

Dedication

To
the perseverance and optimism of the people in emerging markets
and
Mira, Maya, and Natasha, who love India

Contents

CASE STUDIES

READINGS

Preface

The phenomenon of emerging markets (EMs)—in relation to both competing *in* these markets and competition *from* these markets—does not warrant much introduction, if any at all. Indeed, it is now common to find cover stories about various aspects of these markets in leading business periodicals, for example. The era of EMs has arrived. It is widely expected to prevail, at least for the foreseeable future. Thus, it is surprising that, in their quest to train managers, only a few academic institutions currently provide a systematic forum to generate a superior understanding of this crucial economic event. Surely, we can—and must—do better. This book, perhaps the first of its kind, takes a small step in that direction.

This book was born out of a personal conviction that a serious study of how Western as well as domestic firms could compete in EMs was overdue. Also overdue was a much needed fundamental rethinking about drivers of successful *as well as* unsuccessful firm conduct in these markets, and about the role of sophisticated but (usually) poorly serving Western theories and ideas regarding competition and competitive traps and successes. Indeed, as many of us have begun to recognize, EMs must be viewed as being more than simply a convenient collection of nouveau developing countries.

The purpose of this book is to facilitate fresh thinking about how firms can (or might!) successfully compete in EMs worldwide. It tries to do so via the medium of real-life case studies of profit-seeking firms who have (and often still do) competed in these markets, sometimes with unflattering results. Thus, the book is primarily intended for a business school audience—undergraduates as well as graduates, including executives—particularly one that is interested in strategic management and international business issues. Nonetheless, students of public policy would also benefit from the use of this book. Needless to say, although the charge undertaken here is onerous, it is not without consequent benefits.

Framework and structure

Figure 1 provides a organizing framework to better realize this book's anticipated gains. This framework is simple, but not simplistic, and has been very well received in undergraduate and graduate classes. The framework invokes two elements—an "engagement" element that underscores the principal loci of firms' interface, and a "temporal" element that broadly indicates the phase of firms' entry into EMs.[1]

Figure 1 Competing in emerging markets: a conceptual framework
Note: The contents of each cell refer to case studies included in this book.

	Pre-market entry phase	**Post-market entry phase**
Interactions with institutions	Dell's Dilemma in Brazil Kmart De Mexico	Unicord PLC
Interactions with strategic partners	Nora-Sakari Red Star China	Hero Honda Motors (India)
Interactions with internal organizations	Strategic Crossroads at Matáv	Managing Pibrex Russia Olly Racela in Bangkok

Essentially, firms that operate (or contemplate operating) in EMs must contend with three types of non-mutually exclusive challenges—those arising from: (1) interactions with institutionally-entrenched legacies; (2) interactions with strategic partners, broadly defined; (3) firms' necessity to make internal decisions about competing efficiently *as well as* effectively in EMs. Firms must confront these challenges in anticipation of their entry into EMs or after they have committed themselves to these markets.

The case studies included in this book fit well in the above framework. They cover the entire spectrum defined by the two dimensions noted, thus permitting instructors to progress logically in their efforts to develop a comprehensive understanding of the competitive dynamic of EMs. To aid instructors in that objective, the book also includes practitioner-friendly readings. Each of these readings can be assigned to multiple case studies, as shown in Figure 2. Conversely, every case study has a set of readings to draw upon. This overlap is intentional: it enables cross-pollination of ideas across a range of case study decisions. The most promising problem-solving approaches often span two, sometimes more, domains.

With creativity, all readings included in this book can be reconstructed into useful templates, even toolkits. Some readings do this already; all lend themselves

Figure 2 Readings

Cases →	Dell's Dilemma in Brazil	Kmart De Mexico	Unicord PLC	Nora-Sakari	Red Star China	Hero Honda Motors	Strategic Crossroads at Matáv	Managing Pibrex Russia	Olly Racela
Readings									
Harnessing the Science of Persuasion	√√√	?		√√√	√√			√√	?
Distance Still Matters	√	√√√	√	?		√√√	√√√	√	√
Strategy Under Uncertainty	√√	√	√√				√√		√
Achieving Business Success in Confucian Societies	?		√	√	√√√	?			√√
The Role of Family Conglomerates in EMs			√√√	√	√	√√			
Transferring Management Knowledge to Russia	?	√				?	√	√√√	

to an "applied" adaptation which, experience repeatedly avers, students deeply appreciate.

Coverage and scope

Selecting a coherent set of case studies and readings for this book was itself a challenge. Though only a few cases studies emphasized the *essence* of competing in EMs, there still were too many interesting case studies to choose from. Putting together a coherent set of non-academic readings was harder, for many of these readings apparently were not intended for use in an EMs course. Fortunately, the above-mentioned challenges were mitigated by my multi-year, multi-level experience in teaching an EMs course at universities worldwide. The experience gave rise to the following criteria for selection of material included in this book.

- Above all, case studies had to fit with the "competing in emerging markets" theme. Cases that did not facilitate a superior understanding of this book's intended purpose were excluded. Cases that characterized EMs merely in terms of geography were also discarded.
- Cases and readings were selected for insights they provided and the depth of takeaways they had to offer. However, these takeaways had to tie in with the book's intended purpose.
- Cases had to be either decision-oriented, to facilitate managerial training, and/ or reflection-oriented to help uncover significant inter-relationships between a focal firm/decision-maker and its stakeholders, particularly those based in EMs. Cases that mostly described competitive conditions in EMs were excluded.
- Cases that met the above criteria were then required to be more or less evenly spread across various cells in the framework shown in Figure 1. Such balance is imperative to achieve a comprehensive understanding of the competitive dynamic in EMs.
- Moreover, the selected cases had to be geographically dispersed because EMs are not restricted to any single region of the world. Indeed, the nine cases included in this book highlight EM conditions in eight distinct EM contexts, which span North as well as South America, Southeast Asia as well as the rest of Asia, and Eastern Europe. All leading emerging markets (Brazil, Russia, India, and China) are represented in the cases included this book.
- Cases that focused on the following types of investment flows were deliberately selected: (1) developed-country firms entering into EMs; (2) firms from emerging markets entering into other EMs; (3) emerging market firms entering into developed markets, so reflecting the very current trend on "reverse" foreign direct investment.
- Cases and readings were selected from eight distinct sources (four sources each) to minimize possible institutional biases associated with each of these sources. Constructing such diversity is crucial—especially for a book like this one—because emerging markets are heterogeneous in several ways. Indeed,

many of the authors themselves reflect diverse ethnic backgrounds from emerging (and non-emerging) markets!

● The readings were selected to further a general understanding of EMs. Thus, the readings had to be broad in their approach and appeal.

● The selected readings had to be practitioner-friendly: they had to contain ideas, concepts, or tools—or the makings thereof—to facilitate a workable solution to case studies.

One welcome, and somewhat unexpected, consequence of applying the above-mentioned selection criteria was the *multi-dimensionality* reflected in the shortlisted case studies. In addition to the dimensions suggested previously, the cases vary along the following axes, as highlighted in Figure 3:

● strategic orientation (formulation; implementation)
● level of decision-making focus (macro; micro)
● governance structures (public companies; family-owned enterprises)
● industry sectors (manufacturing; non-manufacturing)
● teaching approach (discussion-based; role play-based)
● level of analysis (firm; alliance; personal)
● case protagonist (male; female)
● firm size (large; medium; small)
● data source (personal interviews; secondary data).

Needless to say, many fine cases and readings could not be included in the inaugural edition of this book. Perhaps they will appear in the book's future editions. Indeed, I will appreciate receiving comments and suggestions from all users (and non-users!) of this book to augment its intended purpose. These can be sent to me at: <merchant@fau.edu>.

Teaching notes

The case studies included in this book all have detailed teaching notes. The notes are available on the companion website for this book, www.routledge.com/textbooks/9780415399500, for those who adopt this book for use in courses. The use of these notes will help instructors develop a feel for how the case authors intended their cases to be used. Indeed, the teaching notes will serve as useful templates in class discussions.

Note

1   The usefulness of this dimension became apparent during a conversation with Paul Beamish.

Figure 3 Highlights of case studies

Cases → Dimension	Dell's Dilemma in Brazil	Kmart De Mexico	Unicord PLC	Nora-Sakari	Red Star China	Hero Honda Motors	Strategic Crossroads at Matáv	Managing Pibrex Russia	Olly Racela
EM setting	Brazil	Mexico	Thailand	Malaysia	China	India	Hungary	Russia	Thailand
Non-EM setting	USA	USA	USA	Finland	Singapore	Japan	Hungary	Sweden	USA
Investment flows	Developed→EM	D→EM	EM→D	D→EM	Within EM	D→EM	EM→EM	D→EM	Within EM
Primary focus	Decision	Decision	Reflection	Decision	Reflection	Decision	Decision	Decision	Decision
Strategic orientation	Implementation	Implementation	Formulation	Implementation	Implementation	Formul.	Formul.	Implementation	Implementation
Level of focus	Macro	Micro	Macro	Micro	Micro	Macro	Macro	Micro	Micro
Governance structure	Public	Public	Family, Public	Public	?	Family, Public	Public	Public	–
Sector	Manufacturing	Non-manufacturing	Manufacturing	Non-manufacturing	Non-manufacturing	Manufacturing	Non-manufacturing	Manufacturing	Non-manufacturing
Teaching approach	Discussion, Role play	Discussion	Discussion	Role play, Discussion	Role play, Discussion	Discussion	Discussion	Discussion, Role play	Discussion
Level of analysis	Firm	Firm	Firm	Alliance	Personal	Alliance	Firm	Firm	Personal
Protagonist	Male	Male	Male	Male	Male	Male	Male	Female	Female
Data source	Field	Field	Library	Field	Field	Library	Field	Field	Field

Acknowledgements

The merits of a book on "competing in emerging markets" were readily apparent to many stakeholders right from the start. I appreciate their confidence and am grateful for their support. Foremost among these supporters was Jacqueline Curthoys (then Routledge's Senior Commissioning Editor). Jacqueline's significant experience allowed her to "see" the book's appeal long before most others did. To Jacqueline, I am profoundly indebted. The anonymous reviewers of this book's proposal were equally encouraging. Although they recommended some caution about the ambitious nature of this book, none doubted the need for a deliberate attempt to systematize learning about how firms could compete in EMs.

Much of this learning—that of my students and, indeed, my own—took place in classrooms in North America and Europe. To my students, many themselves from emerging markets worldwide, go my sincere thanks. It is them from whom I have learned much—and continue to learn. I also learned about book writing during my conversations with Paul Beamish, who has been an inspiration to me and to many others. I am grateful to Paul for enabling me to experiment with my "emerging" ideas.

Finally, I am thankful to Nancy Hale, my editor at Routledge, as well as her assistant, Felisa Salvago-Keyes. Nancy's expertise came across in many ways; her understanding and patience helped make this book "stronger" than it might have been. Felisa has been understanding as well. I know she is waiting for this manuscript! I appreciate their kindness and continued guidance.

In the end, a book is only as good as its readers perceive it to be. Thus, the principal test of this book's value-added will be in classrooms worldwide. Certainly, there is enough substance in this book to dedicate an *entire* semester to the book's topic. I hope this book provides a useful—and much needed—structure for understanding a significant economic occurrence that, evidently, is shaping a new world order. The book will have made a small contribution to that understanding if, ultimately, it encourages you to distill what is "emerging" about emerging markets.

Hemant Merchant
Ft. Lauderdale (Florida, USA),
August, 2007
<merchant@fau.edu>

Abstracts for Case Studies and Readings

Case studies

1. Dell's Dilemma in Brazil: Negotiating at the State Level

Dell has recently concluded a site selection process in Brazil to determine where it will locate its manufacturing plant in that country; it will be its first manufacturing plant in Latin America. After a lengthy site selection process in the first half of 1998, involving five states in Brazil—São Paulo, Rio de Janeiro, Paraná, Minas Gerais, and Rio Grande do Sul—Dell has decided to locate the plant in the state of Rio Grande do Sul, Brazil. Although a number of factors influence Dell's decision, one of them is the generous incentives that Governor Antonio Britto of the relatively centrist Partido do Movimento Democratico Brasileiro (PMDB) has offered the company. However, after Dell makes this decision a new governor, Olivio Dutra of the Partido dos Trabalhadores (PT, or Workers' Party) is elected in October 1998 and takes office in January 1999. The PT is a socialist party. Having made an issue of what he considered to be overly generous incentives offered to transnational corporations during his campaign, Governor Dutra seems likely to rescind the incentives that the Britto government had offered.

Given this situation, Keith Maxwell, Dell's Senior Vice President for Worldwide Operations, must make a recommendation to Michael Dell. The case presents three possible options for Dell: (1) leave Brazil entirely; (2) move the plant to another state within Brazil; (3) try to renegotiate with Governor Dutra.

2. Kmart De México S.A. De C.V. (Abridged)

El Puerto de Liverpool, S.A. de C.V., one of Mexico's oldest and largest retail department store chains, has entered into an agreement with U.S. retail giant Kmart Corporation to open and operate a series of Super Kmart Centers throughout Mexico. The new CEO of Kmart de Mexico must create the new Mexican organization. He must consider all elements of the Mexican business environment and assess how, separately and collectively, these elements will impact the transferability of the U.S. retail concept. Specifically, he must consider issues of store layout and design, food, management hiring, training programs, and corporate culture.

3. Unicord PLC: The Bumble Bee Acquisition

This case pertains to a rags-to-riches-to-rags saga of a Thai firm whose acquisition of an American competitor both enabled it to become a global leader in the tuna fish processing industry and, shortly thereafter, led to its competitive demise. Although Unicord's acquisition was supported by an apparently sound logic, various changes in its internal, external, and managerial domains proved too much for the firm to handle. Less than five years after Unicord acquired Bumble Bee, the company filed for bankruptcy. Dr. Juanjai Ajanant, special advisor to Unicord's board, is charged with the daunting task of engineering Unicord's turnaround. However, to do so, he must first analyze what had gone so wrong for the firm. The case provides a detailed history of pre- and post-acquisition events that would assist Dr. Juanjai in his task.

4. Nora-Sakari: A Proposed JV in Malaysia (Revised)

This case presents the perspective of a Malaysian company, Nora Bhd, which was in the process of trying to establish a telecommunications joint venture with a Finnish firm, Sakari Oy. Negotiations have broken down between the firms, and students are asked to try to restructure a win-win deal. The case examines some of the most common issues involved in partner selection and design in international joint ventures.

5. Red Star China: Discovering the Essence of Guanxi (A)

Set in September 2002, this case revolves around Howard Zhao, Senior VP (Brokerage) of Red Star China Shipping Company. Howard's mandate is to secure future business with Nanjing ZP Chemical Company (NCC), a Sino-German joint venture. Howard believes he must first establish *guanxi* (i.e. a personal connection) with Pan Weidong, NCC's Director of Logistics, to compete successfully against SSK Shipping, which is also striving for NCC's lucrative business. If Red Star earns NCC's business, it will ensure its own future in China. If SSK obtains the business, it will open an office in Shanghai and probably win over Red Star China's existing customers. Howard therefore needs to build *guanxi* with someone influential at NCC in order to differentiate Red Star China from SSK. That way, if the two competitors' price and service levels are reasonably close to each other, the *guanxi* will favor Red Star.

Case A describes Howard's *guanxi*-building activities and suggests how *guanxi* can be used to offset a firm's strategic weaknesses. Just as the relationship between Howard and Pan seems secure, Pan is apparently demoted. Howard has to decide whether to: (1) continue building *guanxi* with Pan, who appears to have lost his usefulness for satisfying Howard's purposes; (2) switch his attention to NCC's new Director of Logistics, Hans Hol, who is a German; (3) start all over again by finding a new person at NCC to build *guanxi* with. Case B outlines developments that aggravate Howard's dilemma. After Howard makes his decision (above), Pan is re-transferred to NCC, albeit in a different role. Pan is visibly cold to Howard, who wonders how to repair the breach with Pan. Is such repair necessary to get NCC's business? Should Howard make an effort to reintegrate himself with Pan, or should he work with Hans or someone else at NCC?

6. *Hero Honda Motors (India) Ltd.: Is it* Honda *that Made it a* Hero?

The case focuses on a joint venture between Honda Motor Company (HMC) of Japan and the Hero Group, a conglomerate of Indian companies held by the Munjal family. Hero is the largest manufacturer of bicycles in the world and at that time had already dabbled in the motorized two-wheeler market with its mopeds. HMC entered into a 50/50 alliance with Hero to manufacture motorcycles for the Indian market. It assumed product design and technology transfer responsibilities, while Hero was in charge of manufacturing and marketing. The venture performed very well until the contract renewal period when Hero felt that HMC was slowing down its technology transfers. The agreement was extended for another ten years after protracted negotiations. Just as the relationship appeared to get better, HMC announced the setting up of a subsidiary in India to manufacture scooters. It said that the subsidiary would enter the motorcycle market in 2004. This grew from a split between Honda and its Indian partner in a venture that was manufacturing scooters. Having exited the venture, HMC wanted to go it alone. This caused serious concerns for Hero since HMC's entry into the motorcycle market would threaten its very survival. The case closes with a set of issues that face Hero, and sets the stage for exploring alternative paths that Hero could take in managing its future.

7. *Strategic Crossroads at Matáv: Hungary's Telecommunications Powerhouse*

In September 2004, four months after Hungary joined the European Union, the strategy group of Matáv—Hungary's largest communications company—is working on its mid-term strategic plan. Since being privatized from the state in 1993, the company has seen several changes in its strategy, structure and culture. Nearly 15 years later, the company is a fully integrated telecommunications company involved in a broad range of services including fixed-line telephony, mobile communications, Internet services, data transmission and outsourcing. The company's latest acquisition of a state-run telecommunications company is considered a success, and management believes that international expansion is necessary to realize dynamic growth as its domestic fixed-line business is declining. In addition, Hungary's mobile market is highly competitive and saturated, with 80 percent of the country having a mobile phone. The management team feels that Matáv is at a crossroads with three main options: (1) expansion in Hungary; (2) regional expansion; (3) focusing on organic growth in existing product lines. The team has to consider all of the lines of business in forming a strategy and whether Matáv's resources and organization are suitable for a healthy future.

8. Managing Pibrex Russia (A): New Crisis, Old Grievances

Pibrex is one of the world's largest developers of petrochemical-based polymers for the plastics market. The company has purchased a plant in Russia and after three years of serious operating losses has appointed a new general manager of the plant. The plant lacks a strong organizational culture; communications within and between departments are poor; inequity in wages, working conditions, and training exist but motivation and retention problems are prevalent; Pibrex headquarters is losing interest in the Russian operation, and two sub-cultures exist within the Pibrex Russia organization. The general manager must develop an action plan that can turn operations around with minimal expense to Pibrex.

9. Olly Racela in Bangkok

A recent MBA graduate describes the joys and frustrations of an expatriate life— both at personal and professional levels—as experienced by a young, single woman. She has been living in Bangkok for three years and is slowly adjusting to the local way of life when she receives a job offer that will relocate her back to her home in Hawaii. Reaching a decision, however, is not easy given career-related uncertainties in both countries, as well as the array of conflicting emotions that confront her. She must decide how to sort through these issues. Should she remain in Bangkok or return home? Her decision is complicated by the fact that she had not entertained the idea of returning to the United States.

Readings

10. Distance Still Matters: The Hard Reality of Global Expansion

Companies routinely overestimate the attractiveness of foreign markets. Dazzled by the sheer size of untapped markets, they lose sight of the difficulties of pioneering new, often very different territories. The problem is rooted in the analytic tools (the most prominent being country portfolio analysis, or CPA) that managers use to judge international investments. By focusing on national wealth, consumer income, and people's propensity to consume, CPA emphasizes potential sales, ignoring the costs and risks of doing business in a new market.

Most of these costs and risks result from the barriers created by distance. "Distance," however, does not refer only to geography; its other dimensions can make foreign markets considerably more or less attractive. The CAGE framework of distance presented here considers four attributes: cultural distance (religious beliefs, race, social norms, and language that are different for the target country and the country of the company considering expansion); administrative or political distance (colony–colonizer links, common currency, and trade arrangements); geographic distance (the physical distance between the two countries, the size of the target country, access to waterways and the ocean, internal topography, and transportation and communications infrastructures); and economic distance (disparities in the two countries' wealth or consumer income, and variations in the cost and quality of financial and other resources).

This framework can help to identify the ways in which potential markets may be distant from existing ones. The article explores how (and by how much) various types of distance can affect different types of industries, and shows how dramatically an explicit consideration of distance can change a company's picture of its strategic options.

11. Strategy Under Uncertainty

At the heart of the traditional approach to strategy lies the assumption that by applying a set of powerful analytic tools, executives can predict the future of any business accurately enough to allow them to choose a clear strategic direction. But what happens when the environment is so uncertain that no amount of analysis will allow us to predict the future? What makes for a good strategy in highly uncertain business environments?

The authors, consultants at McKinsey & Company, argue that uncertainty requires a new way of thinking about strategy. All too often, they say, executives take a binary view: either they underestimate uncertainty to come up with the forecasts required by their companies' planning or capital-budgeting processes, or they overestimate it, abandon all analysis, and go with their gut instinct.

The authors outline a new approach that begins by making a crucial distinction among four discrete levels of uncertainty that any company might face. They then explain how a set of generic strategies—shaping the market, adapting to it, or reserving the right to play at a later time—can be used in each of the four levels. And they illustrate how these strategies can be implemented through a combination of three basic types of actions: big bets, options, and no-regrets moves.

The framework can help managers determine which analytic tools can inform decision making under uncertainty—and which cannot. At a broader level, it offers executives a discipline for thinking rigorously and systematically about uncertainty and its implications for strategy.

12. Harnessing the Science of Persuasion

If leadership, at its most basic, consists of getting things done through others, then persuasion is one of the leader's essential tools. Many executives have assumed that this tool is beyond their grasp, available only to the charismatic and the eloquent. Over the past several decades, though, experimental psychologists have learned which methods reliably lead people to concede, comply, or change. Their research shows that persuasion is governed by several principles that can be taught and applied.

The first principle is that people are more likely to follow someone who is similar to them than someone who is not. Wise managers, then, enlist peers to help make their cases. Second, people are more willing to cooperate with those who are not only like them but who like them, as well. So it's worth taking the time to uncover real similarities and offer genuine praise. Third, experiments confirm the intuitive truth that people tend to treat you the way you treat them. It's sound policy to do a favor before seeking one. Fourth, individuals are more likely to keep promises they make voluntarily and explicitly. The message for managers here is to get commitments in writing. Fifth, studies show that people really do defer to experts. So before they attempt to exert influence, executives should take pains to establish their own expertise and not assume that it's self-evident. Finally, people want more of a commodity when it's scarce; it follows, then, that exclusive information is more persuasive than widely available data.

By mastering these principles—and, the author stresses, using them judiciously and ethically—executives can learn the elusive art of capturing an audience, swaying the undecided, and converting the opposition.

13. Achieving Business Success in Confucian Societies: The Importance of Guanxi (Connections)

The web of interpersonal connections plays a key role in East and Southeast Asia business dealings. New research shows why and how.

14. The Role of Family Conglomerates in Emerging Markets: What Western Companies Should Know

Large, diversified, family-owned businesses are dominant players in the economies of most emerging markets and can be excellent business partners for Western companies. This article highlights the evolutionary patterns of family conglomerates (FCs) and delineates principal drivers of their growth, expansion, and internationalization. Those aspects of FCs examined in this study include early mover advantages, foreign alliances, competitive market positioning, and diversification. Also discussed are entry-mode considerations for Western companies contemplating doing business in the fast-growth markets of East Asia, Latin America, and elsewhere.

15. Transferring Management Knowledge to Russia: A Culturally Based Approach

Russian managers entered the decade of the 1990s ill-prepared to manage their companies in the country's chaotic transition to a market economy. This article draws lessons for transferring Western management knowledge to Russian managers from programs conducted over a ten-year period by the Rayter Group, a cross-cultural training organization. The group's experience underscores the transitional nature of business values among Russian managers, including the need to recognize the barriers and potential opportunities that traditional culture and values can create, as well as the potential for newly developing ones to support the transfer of Western knowledge. These two sets of values must be understood and appreciated by those transferring knowledge through the design and execution of management education programs, as well as in other situations like joint ventures and parent–subsidiary operations. The lessons presented in this article are grounded in the context of a culturally based approach to transferring knowledge that includes the culture, values, attitudes, and behaviors of Russian managers. These factors affect the capabilities of both transferors and receivers of knowledge to engage in effective knowledge transfer. The article concludes with recommendations for knowledge transfer in Russia that may also be useful in other transitional economies.

Chapter 1

Dell's dilemma in Brazil

Negotiating at the state level

IN MID-MARCH 1999, Keith Maxwell, Senior Vice President for World-wide Operations, Dell Computer Corporation, looked out the window of his office at Dell's headquarters in Round Rock, Texas, and pondered the frustrating situation he faced in Brazil, where Dell had decided to locate its first manufacturing plant in Latin America.

In early 1998, Maxwell led the site selection team that visited five different states in Brazil in order to decide where Dell should locate its manufacturing plant.[1] In June 1998, after the team confirmed its initial findings and concluded its negotiations, Maxwell made the final recommendation to Michael Dell: the plant should be built in Brazil's southernmost state, Rio Grande do Sul. By mid-March 1999, Dell had already signed agreements with the local state government on the terms of the investment, the process of hiring local personnel to manage the plant had begun, and construction on the plant itself was scheduled to start soon.

Suddenly, however, the political climate in Rio Grande do Sul changed. A new governor, Olivio Dutra of the Partido dos Trabalhadores (Workers' Party),[2] took office in Rio Grande do Sul on January 1, 1999 and appeared likely to

THUNDERBIRD
SCHOOL OF GLOBAL MANAGEMENT

rescind the entire agreement. This was a setback, and Maxwell had to decide on a course of action to recommend: (1) leave Brazil entirely; (2) move the plant to another state; or (3) try to renegotiate with Governor Dutra.

Dell and the Brazilian computer market

As Maxwell considered the options, he reflected on the events that had led to this situation. Dell had begun the process of selecting a site for its manufacturing plant in Brazil in 1998, after the company had experienced a long period of astonishing growth. Founded in 1984 by Michael Dell in his University of Texas dorm room, by 1999 Dell Computer Corporation had annual revenue of over $23 billion and a market capitalization of $98 billion. In just 15 years, the revenues Dell generated were the second largest in the world for personal computer manufacturers, just behind Compaq, and the company was still one of the fastest growing PC makers in the industry.

Most of Dell's success could be attributed to its revolutionary business approach, which had become known as the Direct Model. Following the Direct Model, Dell shipped its products to its customers directly from the factory, without any intermediary retailers. Dell also set up its supply chain of parts and components using the latest just-in-time (JIT) methods, which allowed the company to maintain minimal inventory. These highly efficient practices enabled Dell not only to get its products to customers faster than its competitors could, but also to reduce its costs substantially. The resulting ability to pass on these savings directly to customers created a tremendous competitive edge that enabled the company to control 25% of the U.S. market for personal computers, and 11% of the market worldwide.[3]

In order to maintain its rapid growth, Dell adopted a strategy of emphasizing international expansion. From its headquarters in Round Rock, Texas, the company expanded its operations to the point that by the late 1990s, it had offices in 34 countries around the world, sales in over 170 countries and territories, and manufacturing facilities in five countries, including Ireland and China. Although the company outsourced some of its manufacturing to contract manufacturers in Mexico, it did not have any manufacturing facilities of its own in Latin America when, in early 1998, it began evaluating possible sites for the construction of its own manufacturing plant in Brazil.

Brazil was a logical place for a manufacturing plant. In the late 1990s, sales of personal computers were growing faster in Latin America than anywhere else in the world and Brazil, the largest Latin American country with a population of over 170 million, was a very attractive market for the company. Despite the maxi-devaluation of the Brazilian currency, the *real*, in January 1999, Dell had decided to continue with its plans to invest in Brazil as part of its long-term strategy. Dell executives realized that having a plant in Brazil would be essential if the company were to enter the Brazilian market successfully. Although in 1992 the Brazilian government had abandoned its market reserve policy of allowing only domestic manufacturers to make computers in the country, Brazil's protectionist barriers for imports were still high. Moreover, Brazil was a member of

Mercado Comun do Sul (Mercosul), the South American customs union t|
included Argentina, Uruguay, and Paraguay, with Chile and Bolivia as associ.
members. The benefit of Mercosul was that any company that produced at least
60% of a given product in any of the Mercosul countries would, with some
exceptions, be able to export the product to any of the other Mercosul countries
at zero tariffs. Clearly, Brazil's Mercosul membership was another plus for
putting the plant in Brazil.

Once Dell had selected Brazil, however, the question remained as to exactly
where the manufacturing plant would be located. Brazil had a federal system,
with 26 separate states—each with its own governor and state legislature, as
well as a federal district, and many of these states eagerly sought Dell's investment. Having chosen Brazil as the site for the new manufacturing plant in Latin
America, Dell's executives would have still another decision to make.

Maxwell and the others on Dell's site selection team visited five different
states in Brazil: São Paulo, Minas Gerais, Rio de Janeiro, Paraná, and Rio Grande
do Sul. All of these states essentially met the requirements for levels of education
and sufficient numbers of qualified personnel, adequate supply of electrical
energy, and quality of telecommunications and transportation infrastructure.
The main differences of interest to the Dell team were the special financial
incentives each state offered, and the nature of the agency with which the
company interacted when making the investment decision.

Competition between the states

The guerra fiscal

In their exuberance during Brazil's transition to democracy, politicians elected
to Brazil's Constituent Assembly approved a constitution in 1988 that gave
states considerably more power than before. Among other things, states were
authorized to collect state sales taxes, or Impostos sobre a Circulação de Merca-
dorias e Serviços (ICMS). Although the current average for these taxes was 12%,
states had some leeway to reduce these taxes in order to attract investment.

In theory, individual states could not change their ICMS tax rates unless
all states agreed to do so within the Conselho Nacional de Política Fazendária
(CONFAZ), the representative body for the states on finance and taxation
policy. Nevertheless, from the beginning, states made such changes without
CONFAZ approval. Since the early 1990s, the competition between the states to
lower their taxes and attract investment had become so fierce that journalists
called it the "guerra fiscal," or taxation war.

Taxation rates mattered to large transnational corporations trying to
decide where to invest. Competition among these companies was fierce, and
a difference in sales tax meant that companies could offer their products at
reduced costs without passing on the tax burden to consumers. Such incentives
also compensated for extra costs associated with investing outside of the more
industrialized and heavily populated locations of Brazil, especially the state of São
Paulo, which traditionally received, by far, the greatest proportion of Brazil's

foreign investment. Significantly, São Paulo itself did not offer this particular incentive—it did not need to do so.

But many in Brazil saw this policy as detrimental to the country's overall interests. Critics of the *guerra fiscal* argued that transnational corporations (TNCs) could use it to play one state against another for their own benefit, without concern for the welfare of the country as a whole. Poor Brazilian states, these critics maintained, were in no position to be giving tax concessions to large, wealthy transnational corporations.[4] Supporters of the policy, on the other hand, argued that without such incentives, the TNCs would not invest at all in states far from the more industrialized regions.[5] And as one supporter of the policy put it, "12% [the full taxation rate] of nothing is still nothing."[6]

The incentives Brazil's states could offer to attract foreign investment went beyond reductions in the ICMS. State governments could (and did, in many cases) also offer to provide free land on which to build infrastructure (usually roads or port facilities), and to provide government loans on highly concessional terms, including lengthy grace periods and low interest rates. As with the ICMS tax reductions, these incentives also came under harsh attack from critics. This was the environment that Maxwell and the Dell team had entered when they began their site selection process in Brazil.

Financial incentives and contrasting approaches to investment promotion

During the site selection process, one of the team's chief concerns had been to investigate the prospects for obtaining financial incentives in each state. Upon actually visiting each state, however, the site selection team's initial and most important contacts were with the agency responsible for investment promotion. The nature of the working relationships Maxwell and the rest of the team established with these agencies also turned out to play a major role in the decision-making process.

Each state in Brazil that the Dell executives visited had a unique approach to promoting foreign investment; and in every state, the investment promotion organization responsible for meeting with the Dell team had a slightly different organizational structure and style. With the sole exception of Pólo-RS, Agência de Desenvolvimento (Pólo), the independent, private, nonprofit investment promotion agency that collaborated with the state government of Rio Grande do Sul, all of the state agencies the Dell executives encountered were government agencies. This made a difference in how these agencies interacted with Dell. While other states such as Minas Gerais offered Dell similar financial incentives, only in Rio Grande do Sul did the Dell executives, working with Pólo as an intermediary, encounter an investment promotion agency that they felt had made a concerted effort to understand Dell's specific needs. In other states, in contrast, Dell executives perceived that the government officials they were dealing with either did not sufficiently understand Dell's unique requirements, or were not sufficiently committed to attracting high-technology investment.

São Paulo, for example, was a state that initially attracted Dell. It had a large pool of skilled labor and, because of its large, relatively prosperous population, it was the principal market for computers in Brazil. São Paulo's sheer market size was the main reason that in the final selection process, two possible sites in the state, one in the city of São Jose dos Campos and the other in Campinas, were ranked high on the list, although still below Rio Grande do Sul.[7] But the Dell site selection team formed a negative impression of São Paulo when harried state government officials appeared to be somewhat indifferent to Dell's specific concerns.[8] Moreover, the state, which already had significant investment, had a policy of not offering special financial incentives.[9]

In Rio de Janeiro, the team encountered a different situation. The head of the Companhia de Desenvolvimento Industrial do Estado do Rio de Janeiro (CODIN), Rio de Janeiro's investment promotion agency, was accustomed to long drawn-out negotiations with automobile firms that sometimes lasted for a year or more. Consequently, he made a very low initial offer for financial incentives to Dell, expecting the company to come back with a counter offer. He was stunned when the Dell executives, accustomed to making decisions on a much speedier basis, never returned.[10]

In Paraná, the state government was not able to offer Dell the same financial incentives that Rio Grande do Sul offered.[11] In addition to that, Maxwell and others on the Dell team also perceived that the state was giving the same sort of presentation to them that it gave to all companies, regardless of the specific sector the company represented.[12]

Other than São Paulo, which was ranked high principally because of the size of its market rather than its investment promotion efforts, only Minas Gerais came close to winning the competition with Rio Grande do Sul for Dell's investment. In Minas, the Dell executives met with state government officials from various agencies, as well as with *técnicos* from the Instituto de Desenvolvimento Industrial de Minas Gerais (INDI).

Created in 1968, INDI had a unique structure. It was financed partly by the Companhia Energética de Minas Gerais (CEMIG), the state energy company—a mixed enterprise, 70% state-owned, 30% private—and partly by the Banco de Desenvolvimento de Minas Gerais (BDMG), the state-owned Minas Gerais Development Bank. While INDI was a government institution, then, the partially private ownership of one of INDI's supporting institutions, CEMIG, gave INDI more flexibility in hiring personnel than it would have had if it were purely a state-owned institution.[13] As a result, at least some of INDI's staff also received salaries that were considerably higher than those working in regular government agencies.[14] In this way, INDI was able to recruit highly qualified staff that specialized in at least six broadly diversified industrial sectors—mining and metallurgy; chemicals and nonchemical materials; industry and tourism; agroindustries; textiles, garments, leather, footwear, furniture, and publishing; and mechanics, electroelectronics and computers—who might otherwise have taken jobs in the private sector.[15]

It is a testament to INDI's effectiveness that members of Dell's site selection team made three separate visits to Minas Gerais to meet with state government officials. The final proposal that INDI prepared was only slightly less favorable than that of Rio Grande do Sul—the state that ultimately won Dell's investment. Minas Gerais was able to offer Dell a 70% reduction in the ICMS tax for 10 years; a loan for R$20 million (20 million *reais*), with a four-year grace period and a four-year repayment period; and free land for the plant site.[16] But in the end, Dell chose Rio Grande do Sul.

INDI was in some ways a victim of its own success. The agency's past achievements in attracting companies from the mining, steel, and automobile sectors had made such an impact on the state that when the Dell site selection team arrived, they had the impression that this was the primary focus of the government's activities. Historically, of course, Minas Gerais had always had a strong mining sector. (Minas Gerais itself means "General Mines" in Portuguese.) INDI's later success in attracting foreign investment from companies in the heavy capital equipment and automobile sectors further contributed to the state's industrial development. Observing the results of this prior industrialization, however, the Dell executives came away with the impression that Minas Gerais, especially in the vicinity of the Fiat plant and the greater metropolitan region of Belo Horizonte, was a heavy-industry, rust-belt region. This reinforced their sense that the government officials they were dealing with in Minas had grown accustomed to working with the large, capital-intensive, heavy-industry firms that were common in the mining and automobile industries, and would not fully be able to appreciate Dell's specific needs as a fast-paced, just-in-time-oriented, knowledge-intensive company.[17] Fair impression or not, the INDI staff were unable to change this view during the Dell executives' time in Minas Gerais, and it had a strong influence on the company's decision not to invest there.

Rio Grande do Sul, the ultimate choice

Rio Grande do Sul had not even been on Dell's short list when representatives from Pólo and the state government visited the company in early 1998 and convinced Dell's senior executives that the state deserved a closer look. But by June 1998—less than six months after that initial visit—Maxwell and the team had made the recommendation that Dell should establish a plant in Rio Grande do Sul.

Certainly, Rio Grande do Sul had a lot to offer. It had a well-developed, modern infrastructure; and as the first state to privatize its telecommunications company, its telecommunications infrastructure was among the more efficient in the country. In fact, a quick analysis indicated that, even before factoring in any incentives the state government might offer, lower costs in Rio Grande do Sul for the plant's overall facilities would already compensate for the additional expense associated with shipping computers to customers elsewhere in Brazil.[18] And although customers in São Paulo, for example, would have to wait a day longer to receive their computers from a plant in Rio Grande do Sul than they would if the plant were located in São Paulo itself, previous studies had indicated that this would not be a serious problem.[19]

Security was another factor. In terms of security from hijackings and robbery, the main road from Rio Grande do Sul to São Paulo, Dell's principal market, appeared to be considerably safer than many of the roads within the state of São Paulo itself. In addition, the Dell executives felt personally safe in and around the vicinity of Porto Alegre, Rio Grande do Sul's capital, where the plant would be located. Expatriate executives and suppliers from out of town might not know which areas to avoid in a large, unfamiliar city, but this was not really a serious problem in the greater metropolitan region of Porto Alegre, where the crime rate was relatively low.

Home to a number of well-regarded universities, Rio Grande do Sul had a well-educated population. It was one of the most prosperous of Brazil's states, with a standard of living that some rated as the highest in Brazil. In the end, too, the Rio Grande do Sul state government was able to offer very generous terms: a 75% reduction in the ICMS tax for 12 years, plus a R$20 million loan (over USD $16 million at the prevailing exchange rate), with a five-year grace period, to be paid back over a 10-year period.[20]

While offering generous incentives, the state government made sure that Dell would be providing benefits to Rio Grande do Sul as well. In the contract that the government signed with the company, Dell promised to develop joint research and development projects with local universities, such as the Universidade Federal de Rio Grande do Sul (UFRGS) and the Pontifícia Universidade Católica (PUC).[21] In addition to the company's R$128 million investment in its plant (USD $108.5 million), which alone would create beneficial linkage effects in the local economy in its construction and continued operation, Dell also promised to hire 260 direct employees in the first year and 700 employees within five years. If it did not, the contract would be nullified.[22]

These potential benefits help to explain why so many states in Brazil considered Dell's investment to be such a prize, and why Rio Grande do Sul was willing to offer such attractive incentives. Nevertheless, without Pólo's intervention Dell would not even have considered the state. Because Pólo played such an instrumental role in this outcome, further background on the agency itself is in order.

The creation of Pólo

Pólo originated in the early 1990s within the Federação das Associacoes do Rio Grande do Sul (FEDERASUL), which represented commercial enterprises in the state, and the Federação das Industrias do Rio Grande do Sul (FIERGS), which represented industries. Leaders within these two organizations proposed creating an independent, private agency to promote foreign investment that would be more flexible and nimble than a government entity. Funding for the agency would come from the private sector, but Pólo would work in conjunction with the state government to promote economic development in Rio Grande do Sul by attracting direct foreign investment in the state. Representatives from FEDERASUL and FIERGS presented it to the two candidates for governor in the 1994 election: Olivio Dutra, a socialist from the Partido dos Trabalhadores (PT), and Antonio Britto, a pro-business moderate from the relatively centrist Partido do Movimento Democrático Brasileiro (PMDB). Although holding widely divergent political views, both candidates endorsed the idea, and thus Pólo was formally created in December 1995.

Pólo's founders sought to maintain a connection with the government by allowing the governor a key role in selecting the agency's president. This was done to ensure that the governor would maintain a close working relationship with the agency.[23] Ideally, both the government and the agency would work in concert to attract foreign investment that would contribute to the development of the state. However, this rule was changed in 1999, and the Board of Directors became solely responsible for selecting Pólo's president.[24]

The new high-technology emphasis

Antonio Britto, the pro-business moderate, won the 1994 gubernatorial campaign and took office in January 1995. Having campaigned on a promise to promote foreign investment in areas that would bring jobs and economic development to Rio Grande do Sul, Britto was, for the most part, able to follow through with his plans. Using tax and other incentives aggressively, he was able to land large investments.[25] In order to convince General Motors (GM) to establish a plant in the state, for example, Britto had offered substantial reductions in the ICMS state sales tax and generous loans at low interest rates, totalling hundreds of millions of dollars.[26]

José Cesar Martins, who became president of Pólo midway through Britto's administration in 1997, collaborated closely with the state government in an aggressive effort to attract more foreign investment like the GM plant. The agency maintained close contacts with several of what it called its "virtual" representatives: expatriate business people from Rio Grande do Sul working in New York City and San Francisco, who helped the agency by keeping tabs on investment trends and providing advice about how to deal with foreign investors. Martins also made sure that Pólo's staff participated in frequent investment forums and road shows around the world, in order to make contacts with potential investors and persuade them of the merits of investing in Rio Grande do Sul.

On one of these visits, Martins and other representatives from Pólo accompanied Governor Britto himself, as well as Nelson Proença, head of the Secretaria do Desenvolvimento e dos Assuntos Internacionais (SEDAI)—the state agency charged with attracting foreign investment to Rio Grande do Sul—to New York City for a series of meetings with potential investors. Marcelo Cabral, U.S. Managing Director for Banco Fator (a Brazilian investment bank) in New York City and one of Pólo's virtual agents in the U.S., had a substantial role in arranging this event.

A former equity analyst for Morgan Stanley, Cabral had extensive experience dealing with U.S. institutional investors who invested in Latin America, such as Scudder and Alliance Capital, and knew something about what made them tick. As an informal (virtual) advisor to Pólo, he explained to Martins that such investors would want to hear only briefly from the Governor and from Proença before speaking directly with managers of local companies looking for investment capital. To Cabral's surprise, Martins, a businessman himself, understood immediately and followed his suggestion.[27]

At the meeting, one of the investors that Cabral had invited argued that Rio Grande do Sul should seek to attract high-technology companies. Although Governor Britto was at first resistant to this idea, Nelson Proença, who had been an executive for IBM in Brazil for 10 years before working in the Britto government, was intrigued by this possibility. He reasoned that focusing on high-technology investment made a lot of sense given Rio Grande do Sul's unique characteristics: the large number of universities in the state already offering degrees in Computer Science and Electrical Engineering, and the overall high levels of education in the state's population as a whole.[28]

José Cesar Martins also thought the idea was worth pursuing. After discussing it further with Proença, Martins asked Cabral to help Pólo find a consultant in the area of high technology. From his extensive contacts in the financial community, Cabral knew the person to call was Duane Kirkpatrick, head of international operations for Robertson Stephens in San Francisco, one of the leading investment banks in the world in financing for high-technology businesses. Kirkpatrick agreed to serve as an outside consultant to Pólo to assess Rio Grande do Sul's prospects for attracting investment from hightechnology companies.

After an extended visit to Rio Grande do Sul, Kirkpatrick came to the conclusion that high-technology investment would provide the state with high-wage jobs, in addition to linkages to the local economy. He also provided a number of suggestions about how Pólo and the state government of Rio Grande do Sul could attract such firms. Impressed, Pólo—in collaboration with Nelson Proença and Governor Britto—decided to focus future investment promotion efforts in this area.[29]

Rio Grande do Sul makes the short list: an exchange of visits

As part of the new strategy, in February 1998, José Cesar Martins and a number of representatives from Pólo flew to San Francisco to attend a symposium for high-technology industries sponsored by Robertson Stephens bank. By this time, Pólo, with the help of Kirkpatrick and its virtual agents at Banco Fator (Marcelo Cabral and Dennis Rodriques), had already identified a list of high-technology companies that it would like to attract to Rio Grande do Sul. One of these was Dell Computer Corporation.

During the conference, Marcelo Cabral came upon an article in *América Económica* magazine about Dell's interest in building a manufacturing plant in Brazil, and he showed it to Martins. Demonstrating just how quick and flexible Pólo could be, Martins and his staff immediately left the conference, went back to their hotel and put in a call to Dell. When they got through to Tom Armstrong, Dell's Vice President of Tax and Administration, Armstrong told him that the company's preliminary site selection team, reporting to Keith Maxwell, had already been to Brazil three times and was closing its short list of potential sites in Brazil. "You are going to lose a big opportunity," Armstrong said. Martins protested, "But we are fast!" Martins told Armstrong that he, his staff, and Nelson Proença (who was in New York at the time) could be at Dell's headquarters the next day. They packed up, left the hotel, and were on a plane to Texas that night.

At Dell headquarters, the group was to be received by some of Dell's senior executives, including Daryl Robertson, Vice President of Dell Latin America, Tom Armstrong, and Keith Maxwell. But before the meeting at which Proença and Martins would make their pitch to Dell, they were given a tour of Dell's facilities and manufacturing plant in Round Rock. During this tour, something fortuitous happened. One of the workers in the plant, a skilled technician, happened to be Brazilian. The group stopped briefly to speak with him in Portuguese.

"I'll tell you how to win the hearts of Dell management," he told José Cesar Martins. "Tell them that Pólo is like the Irish Development Authority."[30] He explained that Dell's executives had had an excellent experience working with that organization. The Irish Development Authority (IDA) was Ireland's investment promotion agency. Dell executives had returned from a site selection trip to Ireland raving about how professional and helpful the IDA had been. Dell's experience with the IDA was an important factor in its decision to build a plant in Ireland.

Significantly, although Pólo had not consciously modelled itself after the IDA, it had many of the same characteristics. Pólo was entirely private, but worked in close collaboration with the government. It also had a targeted investment promotion strategy: it selected specific industries, and then focused on attracting investment from specific companies in those industries. Similarly, IDA's targeted investment promotion strategy allowed it to research an industry and specific companies thoroughly to anticipate any questions that site selection teams might have and address questions, concerns, or potential problems in advance, before the team even raised them. This is what made the organization so effective.

In its effort to focus on high-technology companies, Pólo clearly was pursuing a strategy similar to IDA's. In the meeting with Dell's senior management, then, José Cesar Martins did emphasize that Pólo was like the IDA. He noticed that this comment definitely caught their attention. The Dell executives listened attentively to presentations from Proença and Martins, and asked a number of penetrating questions about Rio Grande do Sul's level of education, rules regarding unions, and infrastructure. The Dell executives told the visitors that members of the site selection team had already visited São Paulo, Paraná, and Minas Gerais, but would like to return to Brazil to visit Rio Grande do Sul.

The site selection team came to Rio Grande do Sul sooner than expected, only about a week after that first meeting. Nevertheless, with only a short advance notice of the visit, Pólo called upon all its speed and agility. Notified over the weekend that the Dell executives were arriving Monday, Martins immediately called his staff and explained that they would have to make some urgent preparations for the meeting: charts would have to be prepared, statistics ready; in short, everything that would be relevant to Dell's concerns. Martins also called Proença, who convinced the governor to cancel meetings that Monday in order to give a presentation to the visiting Dell team. Thinking ahead, Martins made sure to hold the Monday meeting with Dell in a hotel, rather than in Pólo's offices, in order to avoid unwanted press attention at this delicate stage of the negotiations process.

It helped Pólo's case considerably that Martins was able to use his contacts in the business community to arrange private interviews for the Dell team with important business leaders in the state. These included high-level executives from three local companies: Gerdau, a steel conglomerate; Ipiranga, a gasoline distribution firm; and Rede Brasil Sul de Comunicações (RBS), a media company. Also present was one U.S. multinational, Coca-Cola, with which everyone on Dell's team would be familiar. A businessman himself, Martins was sensitive to the concerns of business executives. He knew that the Dell team would want to talk privately with local business executives in order to gain a perspective that was independent of Pólo and the state government officials.

The Pólo officials also made sure, on the first night the Dell executives were in town, to take them to visit a very popular local microbrewery called Dado Bier. They knew that the ambience of this popular local restaurant and bar would make a favorable impression on the Dell executives, and it did. To the visitors from Dell, the obviously well-educated, high-energy young clientele at Dado Bier seemed very similar to the kind of crowd that frequented such places in Austin, Texas.[31] This seemed to be just another indication that Dell would be able to find the kinds of employees it needed in Rio Grande do Sul. In addition to executives, engineers, and technicians, Dell's new plant in Brazil (which would also become its headquarters there) would need a large staff of personable, articulate, and technically proficient employees to take orders and handle technical questions over the telephone.

All of Pólo's quick, highly focused preparations worked. After listening to the presentations, speaking privately with business executives already in the state, and touring greater Porto Alegre for possible manufacturing sites, the Dell team said that they were interested.[32] They would send more teams later to examine potential sites more carefully, to ask additional questions, and to negotiate financial incentives. The Dell executives made clear that they would continue to negotiate with other states, but that they had decided that Rio Grande do Sul was definitely one of the leading candidates. To that extent, then, Pólo had been successful. Rio Grande do Sul would now just have to win against the other competing states.

In the end, of course, this was what happened. Tom Armstrong and Charlene Coor, as well as others at Dell whose job it was to confirm the site selection team's initial findings, made more visits and continued negotiations. Ultimately, determined to win high-technology investment for the state, the Britto government offered Dell the best terms for its investment. Less than six months after beginning negotiations with Pólo and the state government, Maxwell recommended to Michael Dell that the company should build its manufacturing plant in Rio Grande do Sul.

ᵉ change in government

Michael Dell agreed with this recommendation, and the company's plans to build its plant finally appeared to be set. But then the time came for another round of gubernatorial elections in 1998. Unfortunately, Britto's challenger—Olivio Dutra, once again—did not approve of the deal that Britto had negotiated with Dell. A member of Brazil's socialist Partido dos Trabalhadores, the Workers' Party, Dutra was against the government's granting of benefits to foreign transnational corporations. One of the main charges he had raised against Britto in his last campaign for governor was that "excessive" concessions granted to foreign transnational corporations would have to stop.

Dutra had served as mayor of Porto Alegre, where both he and the PT had a reputation for honest and effective government. Moreover, the Workers' Party was popular in 1998 as Brazil's financial crisis deepened and the federal government attempted to solve it with higher interest rates and other austerity measures. Perhaps not too surprisingly, then, Dutra won the 1998 election.

Since during his campaign Dutra had talked so much about the excessive benefits given to TNCs, once he was in office he had to take action. During the first several weeks, he argued that the tax incentives granted to Dell, and also to Ford, which planned to build a multimillion dollar plant in the state and had been offered millions in incentives, would have to be renegotiated.[33]

Ford's attempts to negotiate with Dutra were futile. The new governor held fast to his position regarding the incentives by suspending the payment of loans the Britto government had promised the company.[34] Realizing that other states would offer the same incentives, and with minimal capital sunk into the project, Ford investigated its opportunities elsewhere. The state government of Bahia was quick to offer incentives identical to those the Britto administration had offered. Additionally, by locating its plant in Bahia, Ford would receive special incentives from the federal government for automobile manufacturers investing in the poorer northeastern states of Brazil.[35]

It helped Bahia's case considerably, of course, that the federal government was more than willing to intervene to make Bahia an attractive alternative to Rio Grande do Sul. Antonio Carlos Magalhães (ACM), President of the Brazilian Senate at the time, was an enormously influential politician from Bahia who was a key member of President Cardoso's governing coalition. It was ACM who pushed through the Congress a modification of the legislation on incentives for manufacturing automobiles in the northeast, so that Ford could still take advantage of it—even though the deadline for additional companies to do this had passed.[36] The federal government even approved additional incentives in order to make up for the extra costs Ford would face by putting its plant in Bahia rather than the more conveniently located Rio Grande do Sul. It was also significant that Brazil's national development bank, Banco Nacional de Desenvolvimento Económico e Social (BNDES), provided a low interest loan of over US$300 million to Ford, more than it had planned to give for Ford's investment in Rio Grande do Sul. Again, the justification was that the additional amount was needed to make up for the extra costs associated with locating the plant in Bahia.[37] Realizing that Ford was now likely to withdraw from its plan to invest in

Rio Grande do Sul, Dutra tried to negotiate with the company. But he was too late. Ford had already made its decision, and soon signed a contract with the Bahian state government.

The loss of Ford's investment was politically disastrous for Dutra. Residents of the town where the plant was to have been located protested.[38] The press lambasted the governor. And, of course, the political opposition had a field day lamenting the jobs that had been lost.

Nevertheless, Dutra had made his views very clear. It was at this point, by mid-March 1999, that Maxwell realized something had to be done.

Dell's options

Maxwell considered his options again:

1. *Dell could simply leave Brazil altogether.* After all, the country had just experienced a massive devaluation in January 1999. Dell had continued with its plans in the immediate aftermath of the devaluation, demonstrating its faith in Brazil's long-terms prospects. But the country clearly had a significant degree of economic volatility, and even a fair amount of political volatility, or at least policy uncertainty, as Governor Dutra's recent actions indicated.

2. *Dell could stay in Brazil but go to another state, such as Ford had done in Bahia.* Certainly, the other states on the list that the site selection team had considered offered some interesting possibilities. Bahia would not be an option for Dell, but Minas Gerais might be. Minas met Dell's basic selection criteria and had offered an incentives package that was very similar to what Dell had received in Rio Grande do Sul.

   Minas Gerais had other benefits also. It did not have the same level of partisan differences, at least with regard to attracting foreign direct investment, that Rio Grande do Sul seemed currently to be experiencing. INDI, the state government's investment promotion agency, had seemed interested in working with Dell and knowledgeable about Dell's needs, if not quite to the same extent that Pólo had been. Perhaps the impression that members of the site selection team had—that Minas Gerais was too oriented toward the mining and automobile industries—had been misleading. After all, that did not mean that the state could not also develop a niche in high-technology investment as well.

   Dell had not yet begun construction on the plant in Rio Grande do Sul. As of yet, it really had no sunk costs that would make it difficult to leave the state and go elsewhere. Going to Minas was definitely still a possibility.

3. *Dell could stay put and try to negotiate with the new governor.* Fernando Loureiro was a talented Brazilian executive whom Dell had already hired to serve as its new Corporate Affairs Director in Brazil. He proposed that Dell could attempt to negotiate with the governor by showing how keeping Dell in the state could help him, or at least would not be inconsistent with his own goals and agenda.

Loureiro's idea was that Dell executives could reason with the new governor by pointing out the harmony between the governor's objectives and Dell's. After all, Loureiro's argument went, Dell was a very different company from Ford. Unlike an automobile company, Dell did not manufacturesomething that damaged the environment; it manufactured computers. Computers provided people with access to the Internet. The Internet provided even people in poor slum areas access to information. This had a democratizing effect on society. Giving people everywhere access to information in this way could potentially create the conditions for a more just and egalitarian social order. Thus, Dell's goal to provide people with computers was in harmony with the governor's goal of working to create a more just and egalitarian society!

This last option seemed somewhat dubious to Maxwell. But, it was true that the governor had suffered a major political blow when Ford left. It would be very bad for him indeed if another major U.S. company decided to move to another state.

With such logic, perhaps the governor could be persuaded to let Dell keep all of its incentives. Loureiro had suggested this might be possible,

Appendix 1   Brazilian states

Appendix 2   Principal site options

	Rio Grande do Sul	Minas Gerais	São Paulo
General			
Population	10.2 Million	17.8 Million	37 Million
Area	281,749 Sq. KM	586,528 Sq. Km	1,522,000 Sq. Km
Demographic density	36.1 inhabitants / Sq. Km	30.5 inhabitants / Sq. Km	149.2 inhabitants / Sq. Km
Capital (population)	Porto Alegre (1.3 M)	Belo Horizonte (2.2M)	São Paulo (10.4M)
Economic Active population	53.5%	49.7%	47.6%
Life expectancy	71.7 years	70.4 years	70 years
Population Annual Growth	1.2%	1.4%	1.8%
Population distribution	Urban: 81.6%; Rural: 18.4%	Urban: 82%; Rural: 18%	Urban: 93.4%; Rural: 6.6%
Economic Indicators			
Total GDP	US$41.7 Billion	US$51.9 Billion	US$188.3 Billion
GDP per capita	US$ 4130	US$ 2928	US$ 5148
Commercial Balance	+ US$2.8 M	+ US$3.8 M	+ US$253 M
Principal Industries	Tobacco, Chemicals, Automobiles, Steel, Footwear, Foodstuffs	Metallurgy, General Engineering, Agribusiness, Minerals, Automobiles	Metallurgy, Automobiles, Foodstuffs, Engineering, Electronics
Infrastructure			
Homes with fixed telephone lines	67.9%	57.5%	77.9%
Paved roads	10,332 km	19,234 km	26,377 km
Incentives			
ICMS	75% reduction for 12 years	70% reduction for 10 years	N/A
Free land	no	Free land for plant site	N/A
Loan Agreements			
Amount	R$ 20 Million	R$ 20 Million	N/A
Grace period	5 year	4 year	N/A
Repayment period	10 year program	4 year program	N/A
Nature of Investment Agency	Pólo	INDI	Secretaria da Ciência e Tecnologia (SCT)
	Private, nonprofit agency	70% state-owned; 30% private	State institution

Source: Instituto Brasileiro de Geografia e Estatistica (IBGE)

provided that Dell offered to donate some computers to poor areas as a gesture of goodwill.

Should Dell take a chance on this last option or follow one of the others? Maxwell realized that there were risks either way. But he would be the one making the final recommendation to Michael Dell, and the decision would have to be made quickly.

Notes

1   The principal members of the initial team, in addition to Maxwell, included Daryl Robertson, Vice President, Dell Latin America; Tom Armstrong, Vice President, Tax and Administration; Kip Thompson, Vice President, Worldwide Facilities Management and Corporate Real Estate; and Charlene Coor, Director of International Tax.

2   Brazil's Partido dos Trabalhadores (PT), the Workers' Party, is a leftist political party with a socialist ideology.

3   "IDC Results Show Compaq Finished 1999 as Number One in Worldwide PC Market, but Dell Heads into Millennium Leading in the US," *PR Newswire*, January 24, 2000.

4   Talita Moreira, "Business Leaders Praise Responses to Incentives Dispute," *Gazeta Mercantil Invest News*, <http://lexis-nexis.com/universe>, January 11, 2000; Denise Neumann et al., "Guerra Fiscal Abala Finanças dos Estados," *Estado do São Paulo*, July 13, 1997, p. 31; and Maria Quadros, "Governors Fail to Find Consensus on Fiscal War," *Gazeta Mercantil Invest News*, <http://lexis-nexis.com/universe>, January 28, 2000.

5   Ricardo Caldeira, "Os Incentivos Fiscal Gera Desenvolvimento," *Gazeta Mercantil*, March 23, 1999, p. 2.

6   Interview with Ricardo Hinkelman, Former Technical Adviser, SEDAI, Porto Alegre, November 10, 1999.

7   Interview with Keith Maxwell, Senior Vice President, Dell Computer Corporation, Round Rock, Texas, March 20, 2000.

8   *Ibid.*

9   Interview with Jorge Funaro, Chief of Staff, Secretariat of Science, Technology and Economic Development, São Paulo, November 15, 1999.

10 Interview with Enrique Weber, President of CODIN, Rio de Janeiro, March 13, 2000.

11 Interviews with Fernando Sicuro, Technical Adviser of State Government of Paraná, and Clemente Simião, Coordinator, Secretariat of Industry, Commerce and Economic Development, State Government of Paraná, Curitiba, Parana, November 23, 1999.

12 Maxwell, March 20, 2000.

13 In fact, strictly speaking INDI did not have its own staff because all of INDI's personnel worked either for CEMIG, BDMG, or were outsourced from other agencies, and were technically on loan from these other institutions, Khoury Rolim Dias 2001, 2002.

14 Interview with Romulo Ronan Fontes, Manager of Technical and Economic Studies Department, INDI, Belo Horizonte, November 26, 1999.

15 INDI, <http:/shwww.indi.mg.gov 2001>, January 23, 2002. Clearly, INDI, an older, larger, more established institution with a wider range of investment promotion activities, did not have what Pólo was able to develop in a very short time: a specific focus on attracting high-technology industries.

16 Governo de Minas Gerais, Dell Proposal, Belo Horizonte, 1998.

17 Maxwell, March 20, 2000.

18 All computers were to be shipped by truck. This service was to be outsourced to local shipping companies.

19 Telephone interview with Keith Maxwell, August 4, 2003.

20 Guilherme Diefenthaeler, "O Dedo da Dell," *Amanha*, November, 1999, p. 39.

21 Of course, in order to qualify for a tax incentive, the federal government gave to the computer industry known as the Proceso Produtivo Básico (PPB), which included a

reduction of up to 50% of corporate income tax, companies such as Dell had to invest 5% of their total revenue in Brazil on research and development (R&D) within the country. At the time, at least 2% of this had to be invested in universities or other government-approved institutions; the rest could be invested inside the company. (Renato Bastos, "Computer Hardware and Peripherals," US Department of Commerce Industry Sector Analysis for Brazil, São Paulo, Brazil, 1998, p. 15.) As a result of these provisions, Dell would have to spend some money in Brazil on R&D in any case. The federal law, however, did not specify where in Brazil this expenditure on R&D would have to be made.

22   "Alvorada Instala Pólo Tecnológico Com A Dell," *Jornal do Comércio*, August 21, 1998, p. 8; and Paulo Ricardo Fontoura, "Empresa Receberá Mais de 25 Anos de Incentivos Fiscais," *Gazeta Mercantil* August 26, 1998, p. 4.

23   Interview with Telmo Magadan, former President of Pólo, Porto Alegre, December 17, 1999.

24   Pólo-RS, Agência de Desenvolvimento, <http://www.polors.com.br>, January 11, 2000.

25   "Portas Abertas Para Novos Investimentos," *Zero Hora*, December 30, 1998, p. 11.

26   Darcy Oliveira, "A Qualquer Custo," *Istoé*, April 14, 1997, pp. 34–6.

27   Interviews with Marcelo Cabral, Former Managing Director of Banco Fator, Porto Alegre, December 17, 1999 and José Cesar Martins, former president of Polo, Porto Alegre, November 11, 1999 and December 15, 1999.

28   Interview with Nelson Proença, Congressman, Chamber of Deputies, National Congress of Brazil, Brasília, December 5, 1999.

29   Interviews with José Cesar Martins, November 11, 1999 and December 15, 1999; and Nelson Proença, December 5, 1999.

30   Martins, November 11, 1999, and December 15, 1999.

31   Telephone Interview with Keith Maxwell, August 4, 2003.

32   Interviews with Miguelangelo Azário, Former Investment Analyst, Pólo, November 19, 1999, and November 1, 2001; Alex Martins, Former Director of Investments, Pólo, December 16, 1999, and Maxwell, March 20, 2000.

33   Rosane de Oliveira, "A Opção e Seu Risco," *Zero Hora*, March 22, 1999, p. 10.

34   Peter Fritsch, "Ford and GM Clash with Brazilian State—Dispute Over Incentives, Tax Breaks May Hurt Investment," *Wall Street Journal*, April 9, 1999, p. A11.

35   Nelson Silveira, "Ford Promove Festa Política na Bahia," *Jornal do Brasil*, June 29, 1999, p. 16.

36   Denise Madueño, "Governo Muda Lei Para Beneficiar Ford," *Folha de São Paulo*," June 30, 1999, p. 1.

37   Denise Chrispim Marin, "Receita e Ford Já Negociam Incentivos à Fábrica da BA," *Folha de São Paulo*, July 14, 1999, p. 1.

38   "Guiaba, De Luto, Grita 'Fica, Fica'; Prefeito Chora," *Folha de São Paulo*, April 30, 1999, p. 5.

Chapter 2

Kmart de México S.A. de C.V.[1] (Abridged)

IN FEBRUARY, 1993, THE recently appointed Chief Executive Officer (CEO) of Kmart de México, S.A. de C.V., sat behind his desk in the company's new head office located on Mexico City's famous Paseo de la Reforma, in the Zona Rosa district of the city. The past 11 months, since March, 1992, had been hectic but they had culminated in the signing of a joint-venture agreement between El Puerto de Liverpool, S.A. de C.V., and Kmart International Inc. of the United States. The companies had agreed to open a series of Super Kmart Centers in Mexico under the name Kmart. Understanding that the environment of business in Mexico was considerably different from that in the United States,

David Ager prepared this case under the supervision of Wendy Evans and Professor David Conklin solely to provide material for class discussion. The authors do not intend to illustrate either effective or ineffective handling of a managerial situation. The authors may have disguised certain names and other identifying information to protect confidentiality.

IVEY

Richard Ivey School of Business
The University of Western Ontario

Kmart de México's new CEO wondered if, and to what degree, the differences might impact the new retail enterprise. He realized that his first major decision would be whether the U.S. Super Kmart Center concept was transferable to Mexico or whether the concept would have to be tailored to suit the Mexican environment.

Kmart Corporation

By 1992, the Kmart Corporation was considered the number two operator of discount stores in the United States after rival Wal-Mart Stores Inc. Kmart Corporation operated 2,282 Kmart discount stores in the United States, 127 in Canada, 13 in the Czech Republic and Slovakia, and 13 in the islands of St. Thomas and St. Croix. The Kmart Corporation also operated more than 2,000 specialty stores in the United States under the names Waldenbooks, Builders Square, PayLess Drug Stores Northwest, OfficeMax, PACE Membership Warehouse, The Sports Authority, and Borders. Wal-Mart operated 1,880 Wal-Mart stores and 256 Sam's Club stores in the United States. In addition, it operated three Sam's Club stores in Mexico.

Kmart's net sales in 1992 were US$37.7 billion and its net income was US$941 million. This compared to Wal-Mart's 1992 net sales of US$55.483 billion and net income of US$1.995 billion. During 1992 sales per square foot at Kmart averaged US$184 compared to US$275 at Wal-Mart.

By 1992, Kmart Corporation was actively looking for a way to enter Mexico; Wal-Mart was already in Mexico and Kmart management thought that, with a population of 90 million, Mexico represented a growth economy and a market for U.S. products, particularly in the lower income consumer group.

El Puerto de Liverpool, S.A. de C.V.

El Puerto de Liverpool, S.A. de C.V., founded in 1847 in Mexico City was one of Mexico's oldest retail department store chains. Liverpool targeted upper income consumers. Its only direct competitor was Palacio de Hierro. The layout and merchandise mix of Liverpool could best be compared to that of Eaton's in Canada or Bloomingdale's in the United States.

The company also operated eight stores under the title of Fabricas de Francia. Similar in layout and merchandise mix to Liverpool stores, these locations were all outside of Mexico City. By 1993, Liverpool operated 18 stores throughout Mexico: nine El Puerto de Liverpool stores and eight Fabricas de Francia stores.

Total income for El Puerto de Liverpool, S.A. de C.V., in the year ended January, 1993, was N$[2]3.462 billion (approximately Cdn$1.562 billion, US$1.119 billion). This figure included revenue from the retail, real estate and financial operations of the company. Net profit for the same period was N$282.1 million (approximately Cdn$127.3 million, US$91.1 million).

In 1988, the management of El Puerto de Liverpool, S.A. de C.V., after a careful study of the Mexican retail industry, concluded that future corporate growth would have to come from sales to lower income groups. As well, new entrants to the Mexican retail industry such as Wal-Mart and Price Club had significantly altered the competitive environment within the industry. Because of these new entrants, and the threat of others such as Dillards and JCPenney, El Puerto de Liverpool management concluded that Liverpool did not have the skills, expertise, and competitive advantage to enter the discount, lower income segment of the retail market on its own. Yet this market segment was forecast to be the fastest growing segment in the coming years.

Mexico—employment

In 1993, the Mexican labour force was estimated at 26 million people, 30 per cent of the population. Although the labour-force participation rate appeared low, it was explained by the fact that approximately 38 per cent of the country's population was under the age of 15. As well, many Mexicans were employed in the informal economy.

Most labourers and store service personnel were poorly educated and, on average, had approximately five years of formal education. A major factor in the low level of education was the lack of accountability and parental participation in the education system, a problem which was exacerbated by the minimum school-leaving age of 12. As well, family economics were improved if children were sent out to work rather than sent to school. Economic improvement led many parents to question the benefits of education and to keep their children out of school illegally. As a result, although the labour pool was very large, it was also largely uneducated and unskilled. As a result, many employers found that delivering quality service was an enormous challenge.

The low average age of Mexican workers was viewed by many U.S. and Canadian corporations as a positive factor. They believed that younger people were more willing to learn and to implement new systems. In fact, productivity gains of approximately five per cent per year had been made in the manufacturing sector from 1989 to 1992.

Wages were controlled through pacts between government labour and employers' organizations. At the beginning of 1993, the minimum wage in Mexico was equivalent to US$3.94 a day or US$1,250 per year. Consequently,

> Mexican income distribution remained concentrated, with 10 per cent of the population controlling 38 per cent of the income. The poorest half of the population controlled a mere 18.7 per cent of the nation's income. Nearly half (49 per cent) of Mexico's economically active population earned less than two times the minimum wage, US$7.88 per day.[3]

While minimum wages were low compared to Canadian and U.S. rates, management salaries were not. For example, store buyers earned approximately US$40,000 per year while store managers were paid approximately US$120,000 per year. Unlike in Canada and the U.S., well educated, highly trained managers were not common in Mexico. Most belonged to the wealthy class, and demanded these salaries.

Although the country's closed economy had resulted in businesses that were less competitive, it had not rendered the country's people non-competitive. Many Mexicans, lacking the social safety structure of Canada and the United States, had opened their own small businesses as a means of survival. The entrepreneurial spirit was alive and well in Mexico, where it was estimated that over 70 per cent of all retail sales were made through small corner stores or street vendors.

Consumer craze

Liberalization of Mexican import policies in the late 1980s had given Mexican consumers access to U.S. consumer goods. The variety of products available to the general consumer had expanded significantly, and Mexicans flocked to retail outlets to buy U.S. products that they perceived to be of higher quality. Despite the long-standing resentment Mexicans felt toward the United States, many Mexicans were intrigued by their northern neighbours' culture, and many had been lured by the mystique of the U.S. advertisers. There appeared to be an attitude among many Mexicans that "if it is from the U.S., it must be better."

The Mexican retail environment

In 1992, the Mexican retail industry sales were estimated at US$75.3 billion. Of that amount, US$24 billion was spent at supermarkets and US$17.1 billion was spent in department stores. Of particular interest was the fact that almost US$34.2 billion was spent in non-store type venues such as street-side tiendas and open market stalls. Only 16 per cent of the Mexican population had a monthly income of over N$4,000 (US$1,300). The 84 per cent (75.6 million people) who earned less than US$1,300 a month spent an average of 60 per cent of their income on food. In aggregate, total Mexican food consumption accounted for approximately 38 per cent of income. Exhibit 3 provides a break-down of various expenditures for private consumption.

The decisions

Hiring

One of the first activities that faced Kmart de México's new CEO was to hire an executive team. Specifically, he needed a chief operating officer, a human resources manager, a chief financial officer, and a three-member buying team: one person for apparel, one person for non-apparel, non-food merchandise, and one person for food. He wondered whether these executives should be chosen from the Kmart U.S. operation or whether they should be recruited from Mexico.

Initially, Kmart de México would be required to bring store and department managers from the U.S. to Mexico, until such time as managers could be developed from the ranks of the Kmart de México employees. As such, the new CEO was unsure whether the managers hired from the United States should be U.S. managers of Mexican descent who had left Mexico to work in the United States or whether the managers should be U.S. citizens of non-Mexican background. He had heard that some Mexicans returning to Mexico brought with them an attitude of superiority. The returning Mexicans felt that because they had lived in the United States they were, for some reason, better than their fellow country people who had chosen to remain in Mexico. At the same time, their better understanding of the Mexican people and culture would give them a definite advantage in managing within the store environment.

The Super Kmart center shopping experience

The Super Kmart Center shopping experience was intended to represent an "event" in the life of the customer. Kmart management believed that customers were looking for a wide assortment of low price, high quality merchandise. Kmart executives believed that the Super Kmart Center satisfied these customer needs and, in addition, provided convenient one-stop shopping. The executives hoped that the supercenter would become the principal shopping venue for its customers and that ultimately supercenter customers would visit a Super Kmart Center two and three times a week to satisfy most of their shopping needs.

From the moment of entry into the Super Kmart Center through one of the two doorways, the customer was led into major center avenues that instantly communicated a different and unique shopping experience. Toward the front of the store were three large kiosks offering soup, salad, cookies, muffins, and cheeses. Toward the rear of the store was a food court with fresh meat, an entrée counter, fresh seafood, fresh produce, frozen foods, and dairy items. Each Super Kmart Center had an on-premise bakery, a meat-cutting and packaging department, and a pharmacy. All stores also offered dry cleaning, optical services, photograph processing services, a hair salon and banking. Throughout the store the customer was confronted with cross merchandising. For example, baby milk formula was put in the baby section, along with carriages, cribs and baby clothing. In this way, Kmart hoped to create a convenient and enjoyable shopping experience.

Associates

At a Super Kmart Center store in the United States, associates (employees) had the responsibility to create an environment that made a customer's shopping experience more appealing and customized. Associates were instructed to identify and to provide customer-defined values by getting closer to the mind set of the customer. To this end, store associates were encouraged to get involved with various local groups, to develop a better understanding of what types of products, brands, and themes interested the community. The associates were then expected to carry the customer message back into the store in order to match the in-store experience with the customer-defined values. For example, if the Super Kmart Center was located in a community in which sailing was popular, store associates were expected to ensure that the section of the sports equipment department devoted to sailing offered a wide assortment of sailing-related merchandise.

Super Kmart Centers, because of their enormous floor space, provided a plethora of opportunities for innovation and creativity. Each store associate was responsible for creating special events such as seasonal aisles and high profile aisles. As one consultant said, "Kmart is creating a new culture for the retail business."

By January, 1993, Kmart Corporation operated four Super Kmart Centers in the United States. The company planned to open 15 Super Kmart Centers in 1993 by remodeling existing stores, and intended to convert 400 to 450 of its stores to Super Kmart Centers between 1994 and the year 2000.

Corporate culture

Kmart's training programs emphasized three key elements: building teams, developing leadership, and motivating people. In the past, as the corporation transformed its culture from one in which direction came from the top to one in which associates were empowered to do whatever was needed to be done to support a market-driven, consumer-oriented store, it realized that these three elements represented the key to the transformation strategy.

Mexican tradition was one of hierarchical corporate structures in which senior managers took a paternalistic approach to management and problem solving. The top directed the middle and the bottom. Middle managers concentrated on implementing rather than planning, and employees remained silent about a manager's errors or omissions. Correcting or questioning a superior was considered rude. Similarly, accepting a superior's orders or suggestions without asking questions was a strong norm. In the case of a conflict, Mexicans referred to authority and hierarchy rather than to resolving the problem through consensus or on their own. Mexican employees were reluctant to assume responsibility because of their fear of punishment in the event of a mistake. As a result, it was very difficult to encourage decision-making at lower levels. As well, it was uncommon for employees to make suggestions about how a work situation might be improved.

Although empowerment was one of the underlying principles in Kmart's corporate strategy, Kmart de México's management team wondered whether they could overcome the cultural barriers that would resist a move in this direction. Specifically, they wondered in what way Mexicans would react to the new freedom of a Super Kmart Center and whether a top down approach to management might not be a more effective culture for the Mexican Super Kmart Centers.

Training

Kmart Corporation had developed a series of training courses and films to teach its employees about the various methods and procedures that were necessary to perform different tasks within the store. For example, in the United States, the cashiers' course required an individual to watch a film that demonstrated the different requirements of the cashier function. Employees were then required, on their own, to learn how to use the point-of-sale scanning system and the other equipment necessary for performing the cashier's function. Trainees were given a step by step check list that guided them through a series of exercises designed to facilitate the learning process. Similar programs had been developed for all operational positions within the store. The Kmart de México management team would have to decide whether the Kmart training programs, designed for U.S. trainees with at least a high school education would be effective for Mexicans, most of whom had only finished primary school. Furthermore, they wondered how Mexicans, who had traditionally been trained through "face to face" teaching, would adjust to video tapes and check lists.

Another issue of concern to the Kmart de México management team was the question of managers and manager training. In the United States, Kmart Corporation trained its managers to operate using the Franklin Time Management Process. Under this system, managers were required to record all store events on a daily basis, and to review the day's events with the intent of improving the way in which various situations were handled. The system represented a mechanical way of managing time and the new CEO wondered whether such a system would be effective in Mexico, where employees were used to a warmer, in touch with the people, management style.

The Kmart de México management team wondered what they should do about training. Should new methods, procedures and training courses be developed for Kmart de México, or were the materials and programs from the United States adequate? What problems might Kmart de México encounter in using the U.S. programs?

Mystery shoppers

Employee theft was a problem in Mexico. Employees devised elaborate schemes to skim money from employers or to pilfer merchandise. Women were believed to be more trustworthy than men, and single women more so than married women. Many stores had an unwritten policy that only women were to handle cash.

Mexico's long history of closed markets had rendered many retail operations less competitive than similar operations in the United States and Canada. In the past there had been enough customers to go around. As a result, Mexicans had become accustomed to delivering and receiving poor service. This complacency did not mean that store owners and management were not concerned about customer service, but rather that the level deemed acceptable was lower than that accepted in Canada, and significantly lower than that demanded in the United States.

A solution to theft and poor customer service was mystery shoppers. Most major retail chains used a private Mexican company that specialized in mystery shoppers. These people visited clients' establishments and evaluated employees according to a set of performance criteria. Generally, the mystery shopper was required to evaluate how quickly employees responded to customers, how well they discerned customers' needs, how adequately they demonstrated the benefit of the store's merchandise, and how quickly they closed a sale.

Kmart de México's management team would have to decide whether mystery shoppers were appropriate for Kmart de México. Experience had shown that the mystery shoppers provided quick and accurate feedback on employee performance. Further, what other mechanism existed to evaluate employee performance?

Store design

In designing the layout of the Super Kmart Center, Kmart de México and its parent companies wanted to maximize the productivity of the store format. It was necessary to weigh merchandise allocation against the available space in such a way that the store received the most for every dollar invested and from every square foot of space.

The merchandise mix of a typical Super Kmart Center in the United States was 40 per cent food and 60 per cent general merchandise. Specifically, the food area was divided into meat, fish, dairy products, vegetables and fruit, bread, packaged food, frozen food, and a restaurant. As well, the food area included household cleaning products, school supplies, party goods, and plastics. There were two main categories within the merchandise area: hard lines and soft lines. Hard lines included: records, plumbing and hardware, furniture, car accessories, lighting, sport equipment, toys, small electronics, and kitchen accessories (no appliances). Soft lines included: clothing for men, women, children and infants, as well as shoes, cosmetics, bedding and linens.

Food and customs

Food was a culturally complex issue in Mexico. A meeting centered around a delicious meal was still a very important aspect of Mexican life; many business people still spent two hours from 2:30 p.m. to 4:30 p.m. dining with associates or with their families, either at home or in restaurants.

Mexican consumers were reluctant to purchase frozen food because it lacked the preferred freshness. In general Mexicans believed that a significant amount of time had lapsed between when the food was picked or prepared and when it showed up in store freezers. Also, frozen and prepared foods tended to be more expensive than fresh foods. Recently, frozen foods had started to become more attractive to Mexicans because many were working longer hours and frozen food offered a quick and convenient means of preparing a meal, although they continued to prefer fresh food.

One study found that a woman's perception of her social role was extremely relevant to the way she shopped for food, especially when she was a mother. As a result, Mexicans insisted on fresh and natural food. A woman who worked outside of the home preferred to prepare her family's meals fresh. The purchase of ready-to-eat food and fast-food went against the image of being a good mother who looked after her children responsibly.

According to the study, of the top 16 per cent of Mexicans who had disposable income to indulge in ready-to-eat products, two groups emerged. In the first, the mother was likely to have given up her job to spend most of her time in the kitchen, or she had servants who did the cooking and shopping. Fresh foods were the preference, and very often daily trips for traditional ingredients were made to street markets.

In contrast to this conservative group, a second group existed. The consumers in this group were more likely to purchase ready-to-eat food, and did not hold strong traditional values concerning food. These people were generally younger, and were more likely to shop fewer times a week, but on average, purchased more food on each visit to the supermarket.

Sixty to 70 per cent of the Mexican population made daily purchases at small corner stores despite lower quality merchandise and higher prices. One of the reasons for this habit was that their low purchasing power precluded them from making large purchases that they believed were necessary if one was to enter a large Super Center. As well, many Mexicans did not own appliances. Hence, perishable foods could be stored for no more than two days. As a result, many Mexicans were accustomed to purchasing their food fresh, on a daily basis. The local butcher, fish shop, and baker were all phenomena that thrived in a retail environment where Mexicans insisted on watching the butcher carve their order from a particular side of meat; the same was true with luncheon meat and seafood.

The Kmart de México management team had several questions about the way in which they would organize the Super Kmart stores. In the United States, 40 per cent of the entire store was devoted to food. Would this be enough in Mexican Super Kmart Centers? What should they decide about prepared and frozen foods? Should frozen foods be included as part of the store's stock? Although the Super Kmart Center stores in the United States had a meat-cutting area, they did not permit customers to order their meat as they would in a butcher shop. Very often the first time the customer saw the meat was when it appeared in the display case. The management team also wondered: what department should be farthest from the door. How much floor space should be allocated to each department?

Merchandise distribution

Kmart USA insisted that all store shelves be fully stocked at all times. To comply with this policy without carrying too much inventory, the company had implemented a retail automation system that sped merchandise from 19 Kmart distribution centres to store shelves in less than 48 hours.

The first problem in Mexico was the absence of distribution facilities. Apart from Pepsico and Procter and Gamble, few firms had distribution facilities in Mexico because of the absence of a Mexican equivalent of the U.S. Interstate Highway System that was critical in assisting the flow of goods throughout the country. Roads deteriorated very quickly as one moved away from the large cities, from four lane highways, to two-lane roadways, to dirt roads full of pot holes. The poor roads made the transportation of products across Mexico a slow process. The system was slowed further because goods shipped by truck from Canada or the United States were required to be transferred at the U.S./Mexico border to Mexican trucks before they could be transported.

Kmart also ran an Electronic Data Interchange (EDI) system in its stores in the United States to monitor sales and stock levels. Such a system depended on suppliers affixing coded labels onto merchandise before it was shipped. This procedure was not done by Mexican suppliers because the labelling equipment was prohibitively expensive unless a manufacturer could obtain some sort of guarantee from the client about future purchases. As well, the system depended on reliable telephone lines to transfer information accurately to headquarters. In Mexico, although telephone service was improving, it was still expensive and inadequate, and long delays were often encountered in acquiring dedicated lines for computer communications and fax machines.

The Kmart de México management team needed to decide whether such an information system was necessary in Kmart de México stores. Furthermore, if they were to go to an EDI based system, they were unsure whether they should rely on the United States to produce their product or whether they should interact with Mexican suppliers and encourage them to make the investment in the required equipment by guaranteeing sales contracts.

Merchandise sourcing

The Kmart de México management team were concerned about where Kmart de México should source its merchandise. They had heard that Wal-Mart received 80 per cent of its hard and soft line merchandise from the United States, while the remainder came from Mexico. While the U.S. merchandise provided the advantage of price and quality, inadequate transportation would lengthen delivery times and force Kmart de México to keep larger inventories in their stores. Yet, Kmart had a policy of delivering quality, low priced merchandise. The Kmart de México management team wondered if customers would be prepared to compromise on these two elements when they saw that the merchandise was "hecho en Mexico" (made in Mexico). Maybe there was a way to make the merchandising mix (percentage U.S./percentage Mexican) work in Kmart de México's favour.

How should they proceed?

As the new CEO sat behind his desk he reflected on the decisions before his management team and him. How should they hire the executive team? Should they stay with the store layout provided by Kmart Corporation in the United States or should they design their own? How important was food in the overall format? Were the Kmart Corporation training programs adequate? What type of culture would they create in the store, hierarchical or flat? Would mystery shoppers be consistent with the store format? While the challenge appeared formidable, Kmart de México's new CEO was anxious to get started. He was determined that Super Kmart Centers in Mexico would make a noticeable impact on the Mexican retail environment.

Exhibit 1 Economic structure — Mexico

Economic Indicators	1979	1980	1981	1982	1983	1984	1985
GDP (billions of New Pesos)[a]	3.1	4.5	6.1	9.8	17.9	29.5	47.4
Real GDP growth (%)	9.2	8.3	7.9	−0.6	−4.2	3.6	2.6
Consumer price inflation (%)	18.2	26.4	27.9	58.9	101.8	65.5	57.7
Population (millions)	67.52	69.66	71.35	73.02	74.67	76.31	77.94
Exports (US$ billions)	8.982	15.570	19.646	21.214	21.819	24.407	22.112
Imports (US$ billions)	12.086	19.460	24.068	15.128	8.023	11.788	13.993
Current account (US$ billions)	−5.459	−10.750	−16.061	−6.307	5.403	4.194	1.130
Trade balance (US$ billions)	−2.830	−3.385	−3.846	6.795	13.762	12.941	8.451
Treasury Bill Rates (%)[b]	15.02	22.46	30.77	45.75	59.07	49.32	63.20
Exchange rate (New Pesos: US$)[c]	n/a	n/a	n/a	n/a	0.1503	0.1852	0.3102

Economic Indicators	1986	1987	1988	1989	1990	1991	1992
GDP (billions of New Pesos)[a]	79.2	193.3	390.5	507.6	686.4	865.1	1019.2
Real GDP growth (%)	−3.8	1.9	1.2	3.3	4.5	3.6	2.6
Consumer price inflation (%)	86.2	131.8	114.2	20.0	26.7	22.7	15.5
Population (millions)	79.57	81.20	82.84	84.49	86.15	87.84	89.54
Exports (US$ billions)	16.347	20.887	20.765	23.048	27.131	27.318	27.618
Imports (US$ billions)	11.997	12.731	19.591	24.438	29.969	38.124	48.160
Current account (US$ billions)	−1.673	3.968	−2.443	−3.958	−7.117	−14.896	−24.806
Trade balance (US$ billions)	4.599	8.433	1.668	−0.645	−4.433	−11.329	−20.667
Treasury Bill Rates (%)[b]	88.01	103.07	69.15	44.99	34.76	19.28	15.62
Exchange rate (New Pesos: US$)[c]	0.6374	1.3782	2.2731	2.4615	2.8126	3.0184	3.0949

a At market prices
b Period averages in per cent per annum
c Average for the year
Source: International Financial Statistics, International Monetary Fund

Exhibit 2 Breakdown of expenditures for private consumption Mexico—1992

Item	Total Consumption Expenditures (Percent)
Food, drink, tobacco	38.7
Clothes and shoes	7.7
Shelter and utilities	6.4
Furniture and household goods	8.8
Health care	3.3
Transportation and communication	14.0
Education	12.5
Other	8.6
Total	**100.0**

Source: Economist Intelligence Unit 1992/1993
Commercial Opportunities in Mexico City 1994

Exhibit 3 Kmart Mexico: vision, mission, values

Vision

Kmart will be the number one discount retailer in Mexico by the year 2000, that will provide for all Mexican people a unique shopping experience by making accessible to them the best merchandise assortment and quality at the low price they want.

Mission

To be the number one discount retailer for all Mexican people.

Values

1. Kmart Mexico operates honestly with our customers, employees, shareholders, suppliers, and community.
2. Kmart Mexico's people are our most important resource.
3. Kmart Mexico develops partnerships with its suppliers for price, quality, and marketing leadership through a "Partnership for Quality" program.
4. Kmart Mexico gives to its shareholders a positive return on their investment, for their guidance and their experience.
5. Kmart Mexico helps the community achieve the quality of life they are entitled to.

Source: Kmart Mexico, S.A. de C.V.

Notes

1. S.A. de C.V. in Mexico is the same as Limited or Incorporated in Canada.
2. N$ = New Peso. To help simplify foreign exchange transactions the Mexican government introduced a new peso on January 1, 1993. The new peso was worth 1,000 of the old pesos.
3. Russel, Joel, "Retailing by Numbers", Business Mexico (Editorial Abeja, S.A.: May 1994), p. 22.

Chapter 3

Unicord PLC

The Bumble Bee acquisition

LATE IN AUTUMN 1995, Dr. Juanjai Ajanant, special advisor to Unicord PLC's board, was contemplating strategies to rescue the company from significant financial difficulties. Headquartered in Bangkok, Unicord had gone from being a leading tuna processor and one of Thailand's most admired firms to a firm teetering on bankruptcy. Many believed that Unicord's woes stemmed, at least partly, from its acquisition of U.S.-based Bumble Bee Seafoods in 1991. While Dr. Juanjai deliberated how he could engineer a turnaround, he could not help wonder what had gone so wrong for Unicord, and what lessons other Thai companies could learn from the Unicord saga.

Unicord PLC

Established in 1978, Unicord operated a wide range of seafood-related activities that mostly involved the production and canning of seafood products. The

Dr. Hemant Merchant prepared this case with assistance from Nima Narchi solely to provide material for class discussion. The authors do not intend to illustrate either effective or ineffective handling of a managerial situation, and may have disguised certain names and other identifying information to protect confidentiality. However, all essential facts and relationships remain unchanged.

This case is based on library research, and was financially supported by the Social Science and Humanities Research Council of Canada. Permission to reproduce this case must be obtained in writing from the copyright holder. All requests for permission must be directed to: Dr. Hemant Merchant, Department of Management & International Business, Barry Kaye College of Business, Florida Atlantic University, E-mail: merchant@fau.edu.

company's business lines consisted of pet food, frozen shrimp, and canned tuna:

1.   Unicord manufactured and canned pet food for export markets worldwide;
2.   Unicord was a wholesale exporter of frozen shrimp which were sold under private labels to distributors who, in turn, supplied restaurants and institutional users;
3.   Unicord's main line of business involved the processing and canning of fresh tuna which were marketed worldwide under various brand names including Unicord's own.

Given the significance of tuna business to Unicord, this line was operated at the corporate level. In contrast, the pet food and shrimp businesses were operated by Unicord subsidiaries. These subsidiaries comprised: the Betargo Group, World Aquaculture Group, and Unicord Group. Betargo's domain included processing and distribution of pet food and animal feed products, whereas World Aquaculture's domain comprised shrimp farming. The domain of Unicord Group included shrimp farming as well as various operations that complemented the tuna canning business.

Unicord was born out of the belief of its founder and CEO, Mr. Dumri Konuntakiet (then only 27 years of age), that Thailand was strategically located for the development of tuna canning industry. At least three conditions supported Dumri's conviction: i) Thailand was geographically synonymous with prime tuna fishing grounds, ii) the Thai Board of Investment offered many fiscal incentives to support the tuna industry, and iii) skilled Thai workers commanded lower wages than those in other tuna processing countries. This configuration enabled Dumri to adequately "sell" his vision of establishing Thailand as a world center for tuna canning.

The global tuna industry

The tuna segment comprised a small portion of the worldwide seafood industry, but it had significant economic presence worldwide. The industry employed thousands of people, and was dominated by ten multinational firms with a market capitalization of multi-billion dollars. During the 1980s, these firms caught, processed, traded, or distributed more than 70% of all tuna and tuna products worldwide. They operated on every continent and at every level of the market: these firms dominated all transactions in harvesting, transshipping, and processing tuna for human consumption.

The global tuna industry consisted of tuna fishing as well as canning. In 1988, the global tuna catch was almost 625,000 tons. In the late 1980s, Thailand was the world's largest tuna exporter with a market share of over 60%. Its biggest export markets were North America (51%), Western Europe (27%) and Scandinavia (6%). The top ten importers of Thai canned tuna were: i) United States, ii) United Kingdom, iii) Canada, iv) West Germany, v) Malaysia, vi) Australia, vii) Netherlands, viii) Finland, ix) Japan, and x) Sweden. Worldwide,

United States was the largest importer of canned tuna. It imported 31% of the global tuna catch in 1990, more than 90% of it from South-east Asia, The top ten suppliers of canned tuna to the United States were: i) Thailand, ii) Philippines, iii) Indonesia, iv) Taiwan, v) Ecuador, vi) Singapore, vii) Malaysia, viii) Venezuela, ix) Japan, and x) Spain.

Tuna industry in Thailand

Thailand's rise to prominence in the global tuna industry was mainly due to its geographical location and the country's favorable economic climate during 1980s. Indeed, in late 1980s, Thailand was the world's leading seafood exporting country with tuna accounting for more than 70% of its canned seafood export. Thailand was located close to prime fishing grounds, and had very low labor costs of approximately $0.65 per hour. In contrast, the labor rate for an American firm's tuna processing plant located in American Samoa was about $2.85 per hour.

Given Thailand's cheap labor, the country became a hub for importing, processing, canning, and exporting to world markets. In fact, over 80% of all tuna processed in Thailand was imported. In 1990, Thailand had 22 tuna canning plants, of which three accounted for over 75% of the country's total tuna output: i) Unicord, ii) Thai Union Manufacturing Company, and iii) Ta Kong Food Industries. These firms competed fiercely for the tuna processing business in Thailand, and did all they could to achieve profitability in an industry that was driven by two main considerations:

1) Consistently obtaining a low-cost supply of tuna

Thai tuna processors usually purchased raw tuna from various suppliers in the region. This enabled the firms not only to hedge potential fluctuations in tuna catches but also to achieve operating efficiencies. Such diversification helped firms maintain negotiating power over suppliers and, importantly, safeguard against fluctuation of world currencies. For example, a stronger U.S. dollar would adversely affect the purchasing power of Thai tuna producers, and hamper their ability to compete in a "commodity" industry. In the late 1980s, the baht traded at a fixed rate of Baht 25 to a U.S. dollar.

2) Accessing major tuna markets worldwide

Competing profitably also meant that Thai firms had to successfully counter growing trade protectionism imposed by major tuna importing countries, including United States which had its own tuna processors. Barriers to competition existed in various forms: tariffs, import duties, and quotas as well as environmental and food safety standards. The tuna processors in Thailand perceived these barriers to be a significant competitive hurdle that needed to be overcome particularly in Europe and the United States.

Unicord goes shopping

Although Unicord was the world's largest tuna exporter, it was at the mercy of middlemen who bought tuna for resale to major brands, often at 20%–40% margins. Like other firms in the industry, Unicord relied on imports for production of canned tuna and sought long-term contracts to ensure uninterrupted supplies for its production lines. A steady supply of raw material was crucial to Unicord's expansion goals and for making it a global industry leader.

Unicord's strategy was to set up a network of factories on five continents that would give the company easy access to fresh tuna as well as major markets. At the strategy's core was a new tuna-handling process that reduced transportation costs and allowed Unicord to ship frozen tuna directly to American canneries. Doing so would help Unicord avoid high import duties imposed by United States on canned tuna, and more than offset higher American wage rates for canning tuna. Unicord believed it could successfully launch the process, given the firm's commitment to investment in modern technologies. Moreover, the process fit with the firm's cost-leadership strategy.

While Unicord size and prominence generally insulated it from supply-side fluctuations, these same factors also attracted regulatory attention. To circumvent undue notice in its export markets and to gain a foothold in these markets, particularly the United States, Unicord contemplated acquiring an American company, Bumble Bee Seafoods. Such an acquisition agreed with Unicord's global objectives, and appeared to be financially viable.

Bumble Bee Seafoods

Founded in 1899, Bumble Bee was the third largest American distributor of tuna after Star Kist and Chicken of the Sea respectively. Following its sale in 1988 for $242 million, Bumble Bee had been owned by the Pillsbury Company. In 1989, Pillsbury was acquired by Grand Metropolitan PLC of United Kingdom. Grand did not view Bumble Bee as a good fit with its core business and decided to sell it.

At that time, the global tuna industry had become increasingly competitive and had attracted regulatory attention from the United States. Part of this attention was due to the recent sale of Chicken of the Sea to an Indonesian firm, PT Mantrust, who had bought the company for $260 million from Ralston Purina. In part, the attention was fuelled by American firms who had lobbied the government to impose duties on imported tuna to protect United States-based tuna fleets that were dwindling due to a global industry restructuring.

Sensing an industry shakeout, H.J. Heinz's Star Kist offered to purchase Bumble Bee. The acquisition would reinforce Star Kist's leadership in the American tuna industry enabling it to better compete on a global scale. Despite this rationale, the American regulators disallowed Star Kist from buying Bumble Bee on grounds that the purchase would hinder free competition and violate U.S. antitrust laws. Such a ruling created a perfect opportunity for Unicord who had long wanted to enter the world's largest tuna market—a market that promised to become more protectionist.

Rationale for the acquisition

Obtaining access to tuna markets worldwide was an industry requirement for success. Since Unicord was selling tuna to United States solely as a foreign company, it was constantly at the mercy of U.S. trade regulations. An increase in American tariffs would render Unicord uncompetitive and lower sales. The current U.S. tariff on imported tuna was 6% if imports were below the specified benchmark, or 12% otherwise. Unicord anticipated a tariff increase because the American tariff were considerably lower in comparison with European tariff of 24%. Additionally, United States could impose non-tariff barriers which would also hurt Unicord. These non-tariff barriers included stringent health and safety standards.

Dumri reasoned that acquisition of Bumble Bee would insulate Unicord from the current American sentiment. Unicord would become a large employer within United States and, as such, be treated as an "American" company. Moreover, Unicord could now avoid American tariffs on canned tuna because Bumble Bee had canning operations in the States: Unicord would ship raw tuna directly to Bumble Bee's U.S. facilities to be canned there. It would circumvent tariffs and reduce transportation costs—effectively safeguarding against increases in product costs.

The Bumble Bee acquisition would also provide Unicord with opportunities for operational synergies. At least four such gains were possible. One, the purchase of Bumble Bee would help Unicord diversify and stabilize its supply of raw tuna. Two, Unicord would find a ready buyer for its white meat products. Three, Unicord would own Bumble Bee's distribution network that, moreover, could be used to push other Unicord products into the vast American market. Finally, Unicord would benefit from efficiencies arising from Bumble Bee's Puerto Rican manufacturing plants which enjoyed low tax and labor rates.

Strategically, Unicord would gain better access to its largest market, and secure a buyer for its tuna. Unicord would also be closer to its goal of owning facilities on all five continents. It would be less exposed to market fluctuations and could better secure its future. The Bumble Bee acquisition would make Unicord the world's biggest tuna canner, increasing the prestige of Unicord's owners and decision-makers, and even the Thai people.

The Bumble Bee acquisition

Although Pillsbury had many bidders for Bumble Bee, none except Unicord, the secondhighest bidder, seemed to be a serious contender (mostly because of American trade and/or antitrust laws). Unicord secured its bid for Bumble Bee for a total of $269 million plus $10 million in additional expenses. It contributed $35 million in equity to the highly leveraged deal that was advised by Chase Manhattan and Sutro banks. Bumble Bee had total assets of $150 million.

The acquisition was the largest ever carried out by a Thai company which had succeeded in buying an American firm twice its own size in the largest and most competitive tuna market in the world. The purchase underscored the economic prowess and confidence of Southeast Asian nations, and highlighted Thai governmental support for the purchase. Indeed, Chase had persuaded Bank of Thailand to approve the purchase notwithstanding its policy of tight control on foreign exchange leaving the country. The Bumble Bee acquisition was seen as a precursor to Thailand's emergence on the world stage. Unicord now was one of the country's largest companies. As its major shareholder and founding president, Dumri had become one of the most prominent businessmen in Thailand. This put him in the top echelons of the Thai society, and bestowed considerable power and prestige upon him. Dumri's rise coincided with Thailand's economic growth which was supported by a multitude of factors.

Thailand's economic growth

The success of Thailand's electoral process reform during the late 1980s had done much to restore local business confidence. In 1989, Thailand opened its economy to international investors. Shortly thereafter, following a bloodless coup, the Thai government took initiatives to embrace free market ideals and promote economic growth. As a result, the country's inflation had dropped from an eight-year high of more than 6% to 5.7%; it was expected to drop to 5% by the end of 1992. Such statistics and the persistence of government initiatives restored foreign investors' confidence in Thailand.

This outcome agreed with Thai government's policy of relying on foreign direct investment as an instrument of economic development, employment growth, and technology transfer. To sustain momentum, the government eased foreign investment restrictions and took steps to modernize and deregulate the country's financial sector. For example, Thai commercial banks were permitted to offer accounts in foreign currencies. These and other banking sector reforms contributed to a bullish sentiment on the Stock Exchange of Thailand. Indeed, many Thai companies considered acquisitions as a vehicle for growth. Even foreign acquisitions appeared to be commonplace since Thai businesses that generated profits elsewhere now could deposit these accruals abroad.

For its own part, the Thai Board of Investment took initiatives to promote the country's export sector. The Board assisted exporters import capital goods and raw materials that eventually would sustain export-based expansion and the country's economic growth. To this end, it was supported by reforms in the financial sector. Since tuna was considered to be a commodity without significant fluctuations in short-term worldwide demand, Thai financial institutions usually lent substantial funds to tuna processors. These funds were denominated in United States dollars. Collectively, the configuration of various recent Thai reforms were a boon to Thai exporters, including tuna processors. The euphoria of Thai exporters was in sharp contrast with that of tuna processors in the United States.

Tuna industry in United States

The American tuna industry was among the largest and most competitive industries in the world. It was also an industry with low profitability which depended crucially on producers' ability to sell high volumes. Consequently, market share accumulation was very important for American tuna processors for whom advertising was an unavoidable and large expense.

As profit margins decreased, many firms in the American tuna industry sold their fleets to foreign buyers. The industry moved towards nations with lower wage and environmental standards. The remaining American canneries moved out of the continental United States and expanded operations in Puerto Rico and American Samoa where they were received generous tax incentives and benefited from lower wages. The loss of thousands of industry jobs gave rise to protectionist sentiments in the United States. Indeed, the job losses occurred despite the industry's technology-based advantage in purse-seine fishing—a competitive gain that was being eroded as foreign fleets themselves invested in this state-of-the-art technology.

Purse-seine fishing

The purse-seine method was developed during the 1960s partly in response to the dumping of tuna in United States by Japanese fleets. Purse-seining relied on helicopters and high-speed boats to catch tuna. The technology-intensive nature of this method significantly increased productivity in comparison with traditional methods for catching tuna. The use of technology permitted fishermen to capitalize on the strong bond between tuna and dolphins who swam in close proximity to one another. It allowed fishermen to rely on dolphins to locate tuna.

Purse-seining used high-speed boats to herd tuna into a nylon net 600-feet deep and a mile long in circumference. The net was then drawn shut to prevent the tuna from escaping. Because of the bond between tuna and dolphins, the dolphins were also caught in the net. Although dolphins were able to jump over the net's cork lines, they usually did not. Instead, dolphins often were tangled in the net and drowned. While purse-seining yielded enormous catches of tuna (up to 250 tons per catch), the method was responsible for hundreds of thousands of dead dolphins. These systematic deaths sparked, what became known as, tuna–dolphin controversy.

The tuna–dolphin controversy[1]

The tuna–dolphin controversy has existed in United States as long as purse-seine fishing has existed. However, it had recently been brought to the forefront of American attention because of tuna processors' general disregard for dolphin killings and a rise in consumer activism. Various environmental groups challenged the efficacy of purse-seine fishing, and pressured industry incumbents as well as government over persistent dolphin killings.

As environmentalist groups gained strength and popularity, it became increasingly expensive for American tuna processors to operate profitably. The resistance by activist groups created crisis in the tuna industry whose actions now were deemed unacceptable by Americans. In contrast, the non-American processors did not face such obstacles.

In 1984, the U.S. Department of Commerce banned tuna imports from foreign fleets that did not have dolphin kill rates comparable to those of the U.S. fleets. However, as late as 1988, the Department had not produced any comparison methods. Frustrated by this (and earlier) failures, the environmentalists took other measures. They accused National Marine Fisheries Service (NMFS) of failing in its legal duty to protect mammals, and brought lawsuits in federal courts.

By 1988, the NMFS came under strong congressional pressure for delaying sanctions against foreign fleets that failed to reduce their dolphin kill rates. This pressure coincided with Marine Mammal Protection Act (MMPA) reauthorization hearings where Sam LaBudde, who worked as a cook in a Panamanian tuna boat, gave a very crucial testimony about the mass killing of dolphins. Apparently, LaBudde had shot a video of what he had witnessed.

The Earth Island Institute produced an 11-minute edited version of this video where ". . . where dolphins squealed in pain as they succumbed, in some cases being ground up alive by the gears of the [fishing] nets." This video was first aired in March 1988 to horrified American and West European audiences. According to the Institute, in 1989, foreign vessels were responsible for most of the dolphin kills in the Eastern Tropic Pacific, a tuna fishing region. The Institute's report implied American canners circumvented the issue of dolphin kills by purchasing tuna from foreign vessels.

By the late 1980s, the environmentalist groups had targeted large U.S. tuna processors as a means of protecting dolphins. These groups called for a boycott of three largest American tuna processors until they adopted dolphin-safe tuna fishing techniques. Star Kist, Chicken of the Sea, and Bumble Bee were all accused of buying tuna from fleets that did not use dolphin-safe fishing techniques. These firms collectively held almost 75% of the American tuna market. In 1990, in response to activist pressures, the three tuna processors began labeling their cans as dolphin-safe. The activist movement also seemed to be responsible for the Dolphin Protection Consumer Act that formalized various dolphin protection guidelines that had existed heretofore.

Unicord and the tuna–dolphin controversy

In April 1990, Heinz announced its Star Kist label was completely dolphin-safe. Chicken of the Sea and Bumble Bee followed suit. Bumble Bee bought several full page advertisements which asserted: "It is time to set the record straight, Bumble Bee is dolphin-safe." The advertisements further stated Bumble Bee supported legislation that protected dolphins and invited the environmental community to place an observer with its Thai parent, Unicord. The advertisements continued that if consumers wanted to protect dolphins, they should support responsible environmental groups, an obvious rejoinder to Earth Island Institute. The Institute counteracted that Bumble Bee was not transparent about its policies.

Having been so accused, Bumble Bee—unlike its competitors—conceded it needed six more months to implement a completely dolphin-safe policy. However, the company had started labeling their cans as dolphin-safe almost two months earlier, a fact that did not go unnoticed by the American media. In effect, Bumble Bee had deceived Americans for eight months and seemed to have jeopardized its own credibility.

Bumble Bee eventually admitted to lying, and pledged $500,000 to research institutes for studying how to catch tuna without killing dolphins. These killings had contributed to a drop in number of American fleets in the region. However, the decline had been replenished by Mexican and Venezuelan fleets who, too, were a potential threat to dolphins. In anticipation of continued dolphin killings, the environmental groups stepped up their pressure. By the end of 1990, the groups won an immediate embargo against all foreign fleets that could not prove reduced dolphin kills.

The tuna–dolphin controversy had both helped and damaged Unicord. On one hand, the controversy eliminated many small players in the U.S. tuna industry, effectively making Thailand the major world supplier of tuna. On the other hand, because of the controversy, Bumble Bee had attracted considerable negative publicity and incurred the wrath of U.S. consumers. At an industry level, the tuna–dolphin controversy not only had reduced profit margins but also fuelled a noticeable decline in tuna consumption in United States. These outcomes further intensified rivalry in a commodity industry.

Tuna price wars and thereafter

Not satisfied with Bumble Bee's position in world markets, Dumri saw industry turbulence as an opportunity to displace incumbents. Dumri's position was consistent with his goal of making Bumble Bee the leading distributor of canned tuna in the United States. Doing so would also move Unicord closer to its goal of accounting for 10% of Thailand's total exports. Unicord believed that the way to gain market share was to cut prices which it did aggressively.

The price-cutting strategy worked: Bumble Bee's U.S. market share grew from 17% in 1989 to 25.7% in 1992. Unicord's exports almost tripled from 987 million bahts to 2,890 million bahts in 1991. Cheered by its success, Unicord invested 189 million bahts to increase its (annual) Thai production capacity of processed tuna by 33%. The company was confident of further market share gains even though industry profitability remained low due to price wars involving powerful competitors. Unicord's belief appeared to be unjustified only a year later: 1992 appeared to be a turning point for Unicord and Bumble Bee.

In 1992, the U.S. per capita consumption of canned tuna continued to fall; it had dropped approximately 15% over the last three years. In a commodity industry, this was a significant drop. Bumble Bee lost $40 million on $400 million (1992 revenues). Between 1992 and 1993, Unicord's exports to United

States fell by 11%. Some industry observers believed that environmental actions against the tuna industry had affected consumption habits. Others suggested the industry was in a shakeout phase, and would stabilize itself. The fact remained that decreased consumption substantially increased competition. By mid-1993, Mantrust's Chicken of the Sea was in receivership. Both Star Kist and Bumble Bee were losing large sums of money which made their creditors nervous.

To protect their interests, Unicord's creditors demanded an end to price wars which had affected the company's ability to pay its debt (approximately $200 million in 1993). Bumble Bee complied with this requirement, and other competitors soon followed suit. Although tuna prices stabilized, and even increased, the companies themselves did not benefit from these developments. In anticipation of price wars, many brokers had bought canned tuna in bulk for redistribution. When tuna prices increased, only the brokers benefited because all profits were essentially redistributed from tuna canners to middlemen.

By 1993, it was clear to many that Unicord urgently needed to rethink its strategy, a need that was downplayed by Unicord management. One company official went so far as to claim that Unicord's problems were only of a financial, not competitive, nature. In May 1993, Unicord announced it would list Bumble Bee on the New York Stock Exchange within a year. It also went to the public with a profit forecast of $100 million (25% of 1992 revenues) despite a net loss of $40 million in 1992. This projection was in sharp contrast with the company's 1989 prospectus which projected a 1993 profit margin of no more than 9%. Clearly, Unicord was passing through a complicated phase.

The complications at Unicord headquarters were shortly intensified when the company's VP of Finance resigned in July 1993. The departure of Vichet Bunthuwong, who was also Dumri's close friend and right-hand man, took Unicord by surprise. Vichet was widely believed to be the only man who could talk openly to Dumri and keep his daring behavior in check. Almost a year later, the VP Finance position was unfilled. For Unicord's stakeholders, notably creditors, the existence of a crucial management void further obscured Unicord's future direction.

In mid-1994, Unicord was still negotiating with creditors to restructure its massive dollar-denominated debt that had become less serviceable because of a weakening baht-dollar exchange rate. The situation was very serious. Even Bumble Bee's asset sales could not end the troubles facing Unicord, and the company teetered on the verge of bankruptcy. Some analysts blamed Unicord's cost accounting method for the downfall, accusing the company of pricing tuna products lower than its production cost. Unicord's share price, once a healthy 150 bahts, now traded between 12 bahts and 15 bahts. Once an icon of Thailand's pride, Unicord now became the country's biggest embarrassment— one that was difficult to resolve because of Thai cultural norms.

One of these norms pertained to the strong sense of hierarchy in the Thai culture. Following its takeover by Unicord, Bumble Bee's top management sought autonomy from its parent on grounds of considerable familiarity with competitive environment in the large U.S. market. This predisposition was vetoed by Unicord where all decisions had to be ultimately approved by Dumri. Dumri's attempts to exercise such control on Bumble Bee were unsuccessful, however. Bumble Bee had changed owners three times in two years, and so had the tenacity to persist in its beliefs: Bumble Bee's senior management often did not comply with Dumri's directives. To illustrate, it did not carry out Dumri's instruction to shut down Bumble Bee's Puerto Rican operations and repatriate profits to Thailand. The cultural norms were no less forgiving at an institutional level either.

Despite Unicord's troubles, there was considerable government resistance to letting the company fail. Unicord's rise had brought Thailand to the forefront of economic prowess, and the country depended on Unicord's foreign exchange revenues to improve its foreign reserves. These reserves were crucial from a foreign-exchange standpoint in that they minimized currency fluctuations for the Thai baht. Such stability was vital for an economy that had grown at about 10% annually over the past few years. Domestically, Unicord employed many people: these individuals would lose employment if Unicord faltered. In a country where regime changes were commonplace, the current ruling government could not afford to risk voter preferences. Nor could it afford to alienate Dumri, a business magnate, with good relations in political circles. Indeed, lack of bankruptcy laws in Thailand made it even harder for the government to assist Unicord in any meaningful way.

Notwithstanding the configuration of conditions facing Unicord, or perhaps because of it, the Bangkok Bank insisted Unicord repay its $113 million debt by the end of 1995. As a result, the company's shares fell to a low of 5.80 bahts. These events collectively intensified the tremendous pressure on Dumri to chart Unicord's course out of troubled waters. On June 13, 1995, Dumri shot himself dead in his office. Following his suicide, Unicord fell into receivership, thus ending one of Thailand's greatest corporate success stories.

The decision

As Dr. Juanjai reflected on the events encountered by Unicord, he wondered about feasible ways to resuscitate the company. Although few options were still available, Dr. Juanjai first had to clearly establish what had gone so terribly wrong with Unicord in so short a time. A sophisticated grasp of events would be his only ally.

Note

1.   This section is based on Bonanno & Constance's (1996) book, *Caught in the Net: Environmentalism and the State.*

Chapter 4

Nora-Sakari
A proposed JV in Malaysia (Revised)

ON MONDAY, JULY 15, 2003 Zainal Hashim, vice-chairman of Nora Holdings Sdn Bhd[1] (Nora), arrived at his office about an hour earlier than usual. As he looked out the window at the city spreading below, he thought about the Friday evening reception which he had hosted at his home in Kuala Lumpur (KL), Malaysia, for a team of negotiators from Sakari Oy[2] (Sakari) of Finland. Nora was a leading supplier of telecommunications (telecom) equipment in Malaysia while Sakari, a Finnish conglomerate, was a leader in the manufacture of cellular phone sets and switching systems. The seven-member team from

R. Azimah Ainudden prepared this case under the supervision of Professor Paul Beamish solely to provide material for class discussion. The authors do not intend to illustrate either effective or ineffective handling of a managerial situation. The authors may have disguised certain names and other identifying information to protect confidentiality.

Richard Ivey School of Business
The University of Western Ontario

Sakari was in KL to negotiate with Nora the formation of a joint-venture (JV) between the two telecom companies.

This was the final negotiation which would determine whether a JV agreement would materialize. The negotiation had ended late Friday afternoon, having lasted for five consecutive days. The JV Company, if established, would be set up in Malaysia to manufacture and commission digital switching exchanges to meet the needs of the telecom industry in Malaysia and in neighbouring countries, particularly Indonesia and Thailand. While Nora would benefit from the JV in terms of technology transfer, the venture would pave the way for Sakari to acquire knowledge and gain access to the markets of South-east Asia.

The Nora management was impressed by the Finnish capability in using high technology to enable Finland, a small country of only five million people, to have a fast-growing economy. Most successful Finnish companies were in the high-tech industries. For example, Kone was one of the world's three largest manufacturers of lifts, Vaisala was the world's major supplier of meteorological equipment, and Sakari was one of the leading telecom companies in Europe. It would be an invaluable opportunity for Nora to learn from the Finnish experience and emulate their success for Malaysia.

The opportunity emerged two and half years earlier when Peter Mattsson, president of Sakari's Asian regional office in Singapore, approached Zainal[3] to explore the possibility of forming a cooperative venture between Nora and Sakari. Mattsson said:

> While growth in the mobile telecommunications network is expected to be about 40 per cent a year in Asia in the next five years, growth in fixed networks would not be as fast, but the projects are much larger. A typical mobile network project amounts to a maximum of €50 million, but fixed network projects can be estimated in hundreds of millions. In Malaysia and Thailand, such latter projects are currently approaching contract stage. Thus it is imperative that Sakari establish its presence in this region to capture a share in the fixed network market.

The large potential for telecom facilities was also evidenced in the low telephone penetration rates for most South-east Asian countries. For example, in 1999, telephone penetration rates (measured by the number of telephone lines per 100 people) for Indonesia, Thailand, Malaysia and the Philippines ranged from three to 20 lines per 100 people compared to the rates in developed countries such as Canada, Finland, Germany, United States and Sweden where the rates exceeded 55 telephone lines per 100 people.

The telecom industry in Malaysia

Telekom Malaysia Bhd (TMB), the national telecom company, was given the authority by the Malaysian government to develop the country's telecom infrastructure. With a paid-up capital of RM2.4 billion,[4] it was also given the mandate to provide telecom services that were on par with those available in developed countries.

TMB announced that it would be investing in the digitalization of its networks to pave the way for offering services based on the ISDN (integrated services digitalized network) standard, and investing in international fibre optic cable networks to meet the needs of increased telecom traffic between Malaysia and the rest of the world. TMB would also facilitate the installation of more cellular telephone networks in view of the increased demand for the use of mobile phones among the business community in KL and in major towns.

As the nation's largest telecom company, TMB's operations were regulated through a 20-year licence issued by the Ministry of Energy, Telecommunications and Posts. In line with the government's Vision 2020 program which targeted Malaysia to become a developed nation by the year 2020, there was a strong need for the upgrading of the telecom infrastructure in the rural areas. TMB estimated that it would spend more than RM1 billion each year on the installation of fixed networks, of which 25 per cent would be allocated for the expansion of rural telecom. The objective was to increase the telephone penetration rate to over 50 per cent by the year 2005.

Although TMB had become a large national telecom company, it lacked the expertise and technology to undertake massive infrastructure projects. In most cases, the local telecom companies would be invited to submit their bids for a particular contract. It was also common for these local companies to form partnerships with large multinational corporations (MNCs), mainly for technological support. For example, Pernas-NEC, a JV company between Pernas Holdings and NEC, was one of the companies that had been successful in securing large telecom contracts from the Malaysian authorities.

Nora's search for a JV partner

In October 2002, TMB called for tenders to bid on a five-year project worth RM2 billion for installing digital switching exchanges in various parts of the country. The project also involved replacing analog circuit switches with digital switches. Digital switches enhanced transmission capabilities of telephone lines, increasing capacity to approximately two million bits per second compared to the 9,600 bits per second on analog circuits.

Nora was interested in securing a share of the RM2 billion contract from TMB and more importantly, in acquiring the knowledge in switching technology from its partnership with a telecom MNC. During the initial stages, when Nora first began to consider potential partners in the bid for this contract, telecom MNCs such as Siemens, Alcatel, and Fujitsu seemed appropriate candidates. Nora had previously entered into a five-year technical assistance agreement with Siemens to manufacture telephone handsets.

Nora also had the experience of a long-term working relationship with Japanese partners which would prove valuable should a JV be formed with Fujitsu. Alcatel was another potential partner, but the main concern at Nora was that the technical standards used in the French technology were not compatible with the British standards already adopted in Malaysia. NEC and Ericsson were not considered, as they were already involved with other local competitors and were the current suppliers of digital switching exchanges to TMB. Their five-year contracts were due to expire soon.

Subsequent to Zainal's meeting with Mattsson, he decided to consider Sakari as a serious potential partner. He was briefed about Sakari's SK33, a digital switching system that was based on an open architecture, which enabled the use of standard components, standard software development tools, and standard software languages. Unlike the switching exchanges developed by NEC and Ericsson which required the purchase of components developed by the parent companies, the SK33 used components that were freely available in the open market. The system was also modular, and its software could be upgraded to provide new services and could interface easily with new equipment in the network. This was the most attractive feature of the SK33 as it would lead to the development of new switching systems.

Mattsson had also convinced Zainal and other Nora managers that although Sakari was a relatively small player in fixed networks, these networks were easily adaptable, and could cater to large exchanges in the urban areas as well as small ones for rural needs. Apparently Sakari's smaller size, compared to that of some of the other MNCs, was an added strength because Sakari was prepared to work out customized products according to Nora's needs. Large telecom companies were alleged to be less willing to provide custom-made products. Instead, they tended to offer standard products that, in some aspects, were not consistent with the needs of the customer.

Prior to the July meeting, at least 20 meetings had been held either in KL or in Helsinki to establish relationships between the two companies. It was estimated that each side had invested not less than RM3 million in promoting the relationship. Mattsson and Ilkka Junttila, Sakari's representative in KL, were the key people in bringing the two companies together. (See Exhibits 1 and 2 for brief background information on Malaysia and Finland respectively.)

Nora Holdings Sdn Bhd

The company

Nora was one of the leading companies in the telecom industry in Malaysia. It was established in 1975 with a paid-up capital of RM2 million. Last year, the company recorded a turnover of RM320 million. Nora Holdings consisted of 30 subsidiaries, including two public-listed companies: Multiphone Bhd, and Nora Telecommunications Bhd. Nora had 3,081 employees, of which 513 were categorized as managerial (including 244 engineers) and 2,568 as non-managerial (including 269 engineers and technicians).

The cable business

Since the inception of the company, Nora had secured two cable-laying projects. For the latter project worth RM500 million, Nora formed a JV with two Japanese companies, Sumitomo Electric Industries Ltd (held 10 per cent equity share) and Marubeni Corporation (held five per cent equity share). Japanese partners were chosen in view of the availability of a financial package that came together with the technological assistance needed by Nora. Nora also acquired a 63 per cent stake in a local cable-laying company, Selangor Cables Sdn Bhd.

The telephone business

Nora had become a household name in Malaysia as a telephone manufacturer. It started in 1980 when the company obtained a contract to supply telephone sets to the government-owned Telecom authority, TMB, which would distribute the sets to telephone subscribers on a rental basis. The contract, estimated at RM130 million, lasted for 15 years. In 1985 Nora secured licenses from Siemens and Nortel to manufacture telephone handsets and had subsequently developed Nora's own telephone sets—the N300S (single line), N300M (micro-computer controlled), and N300V (hands-free, voice-activated) models.

Upon expiry of the 15-year contract as a supplier of telephone sets to the TMB, Nora suffered a major setback when it lost a RM32 million contract to supply 600,000 N300S single line telephones. The contract was instead given to a Taiwanese manufacturer, Formula Electronics, which quoted a lower price of RM37 per handset compared to Nora's RM54. Subsequently, Nora was motivated to move towards the high end feature phone domestic market. The company sold about 3,000 sets of feature phones per month, capturing the high-end segment of the Malaysian market.

Nora had ventured into the export market with its feature phones, but industry observers predicted that Nora still had a long way to go as an exporter. The foreign markets were very competitive and many manufacturers already had well-established brands.

The payphone business

Nora's start-up in the payphone business had turned out to be one of the company's most profitable lines of business. Other than the cable-laying contract secured in 1980, Nora had a 15-year contract to install, operate and maintain payphones in the cities and major towns in Malaysia. In 1997, Nora started to manufacture card payphones under a license from GEC Plessey Telecommunications (GPT) of the United Kingdom. The agreement had also permitted Nora to sell the products to the neighbouring countries in South-east Asia as well as to eight other markets approved by GPT.

While the payphone revenues were estimated to be as high as RM60 million a year, a long-term and stable income stream for Nora, profit margins were only about 10 per cent because of the high investment and maintenance costs.

Other businesses

Nora was also the sole Malaysian distributor for Nortel's private automatic branch exchange (PABX) and NEC's mobile telephone sets. It was also an Apple computer distributor in Malaysia and Singapore. In addition, Nora was involved in: distributing radio-related equipment; supplying equipment to the broadcasting, meteorological, civil aviation, postal and power authorities; and manufacturing automotive parts (such as the suspension coil, springs, and piston) for the local automobile companies.

The management

When Nora was established, Osman Jaafar, founder and chairman of Nora Holdings, managed the company with his wife, Nora Asyikin Yusof, and seven employees. Osman was known as a conservative businessman who did not like to dabble in acquisitions and mergers to make quick capital gains. He was formerly an electrical engineer who was trained in the United Kingdom and had held several senior positions at the national Telecom Department in Malaysia.

Osman subsequently recruited Zainal Hashim to fill in the position of deputy managing director at Nora. Zainal held a master's degree in microwave communications from a British university and had several years of working experience as a production engineer at Pernas-NEC Sdn Bhd, a manufacturer of transmission equipment. Zainal was later promoted to the position of managing director and six years later, the vice-chairman.

Industry analysts observed that Nora's success was attributed to the complementary roles, trust, and mutual understanding between Osman and Zainal. While Osman "likes to fight for new business opportunities," Zainal preferred a low profile and concentrated on managing Nora's operations.

Industry observers also speculated that Osman, a former civil servant and an entrepreneur, was close to Malaysian politicians, notably the Prime Minister, while Zainal had been a close friend of the Finance Minister. Zainal disagreed with allegations that Nora had succeeded due to its close relationships with Malaysian politicians. However, he acknowledged that such perceptions in the industry had been beneficial to the company.

Osman and Zainal had an obsession for high-tech and made the development of research and development (R&D) skills and resources a priority in the company. About one per cent of Nora's earnings was ploughed back into R&D activities. Although this amount was considered small by international standards, Nora planned to increase it gradually to five to six per cent over the next two to three years. Zainal said:

> We believe in making improvements in small steps, similar to the Japanese *kaizen* principle. Over time, each small improvement could lead to a major creation. To be able to make improvements, we must learn from others. Thus we would borrow a technology from others, but eventually, we must be able to develop our own to sustain our

competitiveness in the industry. As a matter of fact, Sakari's SK33 system was developed based on a technology it obtained from Alcatel.

To further enhance R&D activities at Nora, Nora Research Sdn Bhd (NRSB), a wholly-owned subsidiary, was formed, and its R&D department was absorbed into this new company. NRSB operated as an independent research company undertaking R&D activities for Nora as well as private clients in related fields. The company facilitated R&D activities with other companies as well as government organizations, research institutions, and universities. NRSB, with its staff of 40 technicians/engineers, would charge a fixed fee for basic research and a royalty for its products sold by clients.

Zainal was also active in instilling and promoting Islamic values among the Malay employees at Nora. He explained:

> Islam is a way of life and there is no such thing as Islamic management. The Islamic values, which must be reflected in the daily life of Muslims, would influence their behaviours as employers and employees. Our Malay managers, however, were often influenced by their western counterparts, who tend to stress knowledge and mental capability and often forget the effectiveness of the softer side of management which emphasizes relationships, sincerity and consistency. I believe that one must always be sincere to be able to develop good working relationships.

Sakari Oy

Sakari was established in 1865 as a pulp and paper mill located about 200 kilometres northwest of Helsinki, the capital city of Finland. In the 1960s, Sakari started to expand into the rubber and cable industries when it merged with the Finnish Rubber Works and Finnish Cable Works. In 1973 Sakari's performance was badly affected by the oil crisis, as its businesses were largely energy-intensive.

However, in 1975, the company recovered when Aatos Olkkola took over as Sakari's president. He led Sakari into competitive businesses such as computers, consumer electronics, and cellular phones via a series of acquisitions, mergers and alliances. Companies involved in the acquisitions included: the consumer electronics division of Standard Elektrik Lorenz AG; the data systems division of L.M. Ericsson; Vantala, a Finnish manufacturer of colour televisions; and Luxury, a Swedish state-owned electronics and computer concern.

In 1979, a JV between Sakari and Vantala, Sakari-Vantala, was set up to develop and manufacture mobile telephones. Sakari-Vantala had captured about 14 per cent of the world's market share for mobile phones and held a 20 per cent market share in Europe for its mobile phone handsets. Outside Europe, a 50–50 JV was formed with Tandy Corporation which, to date, had made significant sales in the United States, Malaysia and Thailand.

Sakari first edged into the telecom market by selling switching systems licensed from France's Alcatel and by developing the software and systems to suit the needs of small Finnish phone companies. Sakari had avoided head-on competition with Siemens and Ericsson by not trying to enter the market for large telephone networks. Instead, Sakari had concentrated on developing dedicated telecom networks for large private users such as utility and railway companies. In Finland, Sakari held 40 per cent of the market for digital exchanges. Other competitors included Ericsson (34 per cent), Siemens (25 per cent), and Alcatel (one per cent).

Sakari was also a niche player in the global switching market. Its SK33 switches had sold well in countries such as Sri Lanka, United Arab Emirates, China and the Soviet Union. A derivative of the SK33 main exchange switch called the SK33XT was subsequently developed to be used in base stations for cellular networks and personal paging systems.

Sakari attributed its emphasis on R&D as its key success factor in the telecom industry. Strong in-house R&D in core competence areas enabled the company to develop technology platforms such as its SK33 system that were reliable, flexible, widely compatible and economical. About 17 per cent of its annual sales revenue was invested into R&D and product development units in Finland, United Kingdom and France. Sakari's current strategy was to emphasize global operations in production and R&D. It planned to set up R&D centres in leading markets, including South-east Asia.

Sakari was still a small company by international standards (see Exhibit 3 for a list of the world's major telecom equipment suppliers). It lacked a strong marketing capability and had to rely on JVs such as the one with Tandy Corporation to enter the world market, particularly the United States. In its efforts to develop market position quickly, Sakari had to accept lower margins for its products, and often the Sakari name was not revealed on the product. In recent years, Sakari decided to emerge from its hiding place as a manufacturer's manufacturer and began marketing under the Sakari name.

In 1989 Mikko Koskinen took over as president of Sakari. Koskinen announced that telecommunications, computers, and consumer electronics would be maintained as Sakari's core business, and that he would continue Olkkola's efforts in expanding the company overseas. He believed that every European company needed global horizons to be able to meet global competition for future survival. To do so, he envisaged the setting up of alliances of varying duration, each designed for specific purposes. He said, "Sakari has become an interesting partner with which to cooperate on an equal footing in the areas of R&D, manufacturing and marketing."

The recession in Finland which began in 1990 led Sakari's group sales to decline substantially from FIM22 billion⁵ in 1990 to FIM15 billion in 1991. The losses were attributed to two main factors: weak demand for Sakari's consumer electronic products, and trade with the Soviet Union which had come to almost a complete standstill. Consequently Sakari began divesting its less profitable companies within the basic industries (metal, rubber, and paper), as well as leaving the troubled European computer market with the sale of its computer subsidiary, Sakari Macro. The company's new strategy was to focus on three main areas: telecom systems and mobile phones in a global framework, consumer electronic products in Europe, and deliveries of cables and related technology. The company's divestment strategy led to a reduction of Sakari's employees from about 41,000 in 1989 to 29,000 in 1991. This series of major strategic moves was accompanied by major leadership succession. In June 1992, Koskinen retired as Sakari's President and was replaced by Visa Ketonen, formerly the President of Sakari Mobile Phones. Ketonen appointed Ossi Kuusisto as Sakari's vice-president.

After Ketonen took over control, the Finnish economy went through a rapid revival in 1993, followed by a new period of intense growth. Since the mid 1990s the Finnish growth had been bolstered by intense growth in telecommunications equipment manufacturing as a result of an exploding global telecommunications market. Sakari capitalized on this opportunity and played a major role in the Finnish telecommunications equipment manufacturing sector.

In 2001, Sakari was Finland's largest publicly-traded industrial company and derived the majority of its total sales from exports and overseas operations. Traditionally, the company's export sales were confined to other Scandinavian countries, Western Europe and the former Soviet Union. However, in recent years, the company made efforts and succeeded in globalizing and diversifying its operations to make the most of its high-tech capabilities. As a result, Sakari emerged as a more influential player in the international market and had gained international brand recognition. One of Sakari's strategies was to form JVs to enter new foreign markets.

The Nora-Sakari negotiation

Nora and Sakari had discussed the potential of forming a JV company in Malaysia for more than two years. Nora engineers were sent to Helsinki to assess the SK33 technology in terms of its compatibility with the Malaysian requirements, while Sakari managers travelled to KL mainly to assess both Nora's capability in manufacturing switching exchanges and the feasibility of gaining access to the Malaysian market.

In January 2003, Nora submitted its bid for TMB's RM2 billion contract to supply digital switching exchanges supporting four million telephone lines. Assuming the Nora-Sakari JV would materialize, Nora based its bid on supplying Sakari's digital switching technology. Nora competed with seven other companies short listed by TMB, all offering their partners' technology—Alcatel, Lucent, Fujitsu, Siemens, Ericsson, NEC, and Samsung. In early May, TMB announced five successful companies in the bid. They were companies using technology from Alcatel, Fujitsu, Ericsson, NEC, and Sakari. Each company was awarded one-fifth share of the RM2 billion contract and would be responsible for delivering 800,000 telephone lines over a period of five years. Industry observers were critical of TMB's decision to select Sakari and Alcatel. Sakari was perceived to be the least capable of supplying the necessary lines to meet TMB's requirements, as it was alleged to be a small company with little international exposure. Alcatel was criticized for having the potential of supplying an obsolete technology.

The May 21 meeting

Following the successful bid and ignoring the criticisms against Sakari, Nora and Sakari held a major meeting in Helsinki on May 21 to finalize the formation of the JV. Zainal led Nora's five-member negotiation team which comprised Nora's general manager for corporate planning division, an accountant, two engineers, and Marina Mohamed, a lawyer. One of the engineers was Salleh Lindstrom who was of Swedish origin, a Muslim and had worked for Nora for almost 10 years.

Sakari's eight-member team was led by Kuusisto, Sakari's vice-president. His team comprised Junttila, Hussein Ghazi, Aziz Majid, three engineers, and Julia Ruola (a lawyer). Ghazi was Sakari's senior manager who was of Egyptian origin and also a Muslim who had worked for Sakari for more than 20 years while Aziz, a Malay, had been Sakari's manager for more than 12 years.

The meeting went on for several days. The main issue raised at the meeting was Nora's capability in penetrating the South-east Asian market. Other issues included Sakari's concerns over the efficiency of Malaysian workers in the JV in manufacturing the product, maintaining product quality and ensuring prompt deliveries.

Commenting on the series of negotiations with Sakari, Zainal said that this was the most difficult negotiation he had ever experienced. Zainal was Nora's most experienced negotiator and had single-handedly represented Nora in several major negotiations for the past 10 years. In the negotiation with Sakari, Zainal admitted making the mistake of approaching the negotiation applying the approach he often used when negotiating with his counterparts from companies based in North America or the United Kingdom. He said:

> Negotiators from the United States tend to be very open and often state their positions early and definitively. They are highly verbal and usually prepare well-planned presentations. They also often engage in small talk and "joke around" with us at the end of a negotiation. In contrast, the Sakari negotiators tend to be very serious, reserved and "cold." They are also relatively less verbal and do not convey much through their facial expressions. As a result, it was difficult for us to determine whether they are really interested in the deal or not.

Zainal said that the negotiation on May 21 turned out to be particularly difficult when Sakari became interested in bidding a recently-announced tender for a major telecom contract in the United Kingdom. Internal politics within Sakari led to the formation of two opposing "camps." One "camp" held a strong belief that there would be very high growth in the Asia-Pacific region and that the JV company in Malaysia was seen as a hub to enter these markets. Although the Malaysian government had liberalized its equity ownership restrictions and allowed the formation of wholly-owned subsidiaries, JVs were still an efficient way to enter the Malaysian market for a company that lacked local knowledge. This group was represented mostly by Sakari's managers positioned in Asia and engineers who had made several trips to Malaysia, which usually included visits to Nora's facilities. They also had the support of Sakari's vice-president,

Kuusisto, who was involved in most of the meetings with Nora, particularly when Zainal was present. Kuusisto had also made efforts to be present at meetings held in KL. This group also argued that Nora had already obtained the contract in Malaysia whereas the chance of getting the U.K. contract was quite low in view of the intense competition prevailing in that market.

The "camp" not in favour of the Nora-Sakari JV believed that Sakari should focus its resources on entering the United Kingdom, which could be used as a hub to penetrate the European Union (EU) market. There was also the belief that Europe was closer to home, making management easier, and that problems arising from cultural differences would be minimized. This group was also particularly concerned that Nora had the potential of copying Sakari's technology and eventually becoming a strong regional competitor. Also, because the U.K. market was relatively "familiar" and Sakari has local knowledge, Sakari could set up a wholly-owned subsidiary instead of a JV company and consequently, avoid JV-related problems such as joint control, joint profits, and leakage of technology.

Zainal felt that the lack of full support from Sakari's management led to a difficult negotiation when new misgivings arose concerning Nora's capability to deliver its part of the deal. It was apparent that the group in favour of the Nora-Sakari JV was under pressure to further justify its proposal and provide counterarguments against the U.K. proposal. A Sakari manager explained, "We are tempted to pursue both proposals since each has its own strengths, but our current resources are very limited. Thus a choice has to made, and soon."

The July 8 meeting

Another meeting to negotiate the JV agreement was scheduled for July 8. Sakari's eight-member team arrived in KL on Sunday afternoon of July 7, and was met at the airport by the key Nora managers involved in the negotiation. Kuusisto did not accompany the Sakari team at this meeting.

The negotiation started early Monday morning at Nora's headquarters and continued for the next five days, with each day's meeting ending late in the evening. Members of the Nora team were the same members who had attended the May 21 meeting in Finland, except Zainal, who did not participate. The Sakari team was also represented by the same members in attendance at the previous meeting plus a new member, Solail Pekkarinen, Sakari's senior accountant. Unfortunately, on the third day of the negotiation, the Nora team requested that Sakari ask Pekkarinen to leave the negotiation. He was perceived as extremely arrogant and insensitive to the local culture, which tended to value modesty and diplomacy. Pekkarinen left for Helsinki the following morning.

Although Zainal had decided not to participate actively in the negotiations, he followed the process closely and was briefed by his negotiators regularly. Some of the issues which they complained were difficult to resolve had often led to heated arguments between the two negotiating teams. These included:

1. Equity ownership

In previous meetings both companies agreed to form the JV company with a paid-up capital of RM5 million. However, they disagreed on the equity share proposed by each side. Sakari proposed an equity split in the JV company of 49 per cent for Sakari and 51 per cent for Nora. Nora, on the other hand, proposed a 30 per cent Sakari and 70 per cent Nora split. Nora's proposal was based on the common practice in Malaysia as a result of historical foreign equity regulations set by the Malaysian government that allowed a maximum of 30 per cent foreign equity ownership unless the company would export a certain percentage of its products. Though these regulations were liberalized by the Malaysian government effective from July, 1998 and new regulations had replaced the old ones, the 30–70 foreign-Malaysian ownership divide was still commonly observed.

Equity ownership became a major issue as it was associated with control over the JV company. Sakari was concerned about its ability to control the accessibility of its technology to Nora and about decisions concerning the activities of the JV as a whole. The lack of control was perceived by Sakari as an obstacle to protecting its interests. Nora also had similar concerns about its ability to exert control over the JV because it was intended as a key part of Nora's long-term strategy to develop its own digital switching exchanges and related high-tech products.

2. Technology transfer

Sakari proposed to provide the JV company with the basic structure of the digital switch. The JV company would assemble the switching exchanges at the JV plant and subsequently install the exchanges in designated locations identified by TMB. By offering Nora only the basic structure of the switch, the core of Sakari's switching technology would still be well-protected.

On the other hand, Nora proposed that the basic structure of the switch be developed at the JV company in order to access the root of the switching technology. Based on Sakari's proposal, Nora felt that only the technical aspects in assembling and installing the exchanges would be obtained. This was perceived as another "screw-driver" form of technology transfer while the core of the technology associated with making the switches would still be unknown.

3. Royalty payment

Closely related to the issue of technology transfer was the payment of a royalty for the technology used in building the switches. Sakari proposed a royalty payment of five per cent of the JV gross sales while Nora proposed a payment of two per cent of net sales.

Nora considered the royalty rate of five per cent too high because it would affect Nora's financial situation as a whole. Financial simulations prepared by Nora's managers indicated that Nora's return on investment would be less than the desired 10 per cent if royalty rates exceeded three per cent of net sales. This was because Nora had already agreed to make large additional investments in support of the JV. Nora would invest in a building which would be rented to the JV company to accommodate an office and the switching plant. Nora would also invest in another plant which would supply the JV with surface mounted devices (SMD), one of the major components needed to build the switching exchanges.

An added argument raised by the Nora negotiators in support of a two per cent royalty was that Sakari would receive side benefits from the JV's access to Japanese technology used in the manufacture of the SMD components. Apparently the Japanese technology was more advanced than Sakari's present technology.

4. Expatriates' salaries and perks

To allay Sakari's concerns over Nora's level of efficiency, Nora suggested that Sakari provide the necessary training for the JV technical employees. Subsequently, Sakari had agreed to provide eight engineering experts for the JV company on two types of contracts, short-term and long-term. Experts employed on a short-term basis would be paid a daily rate of US$1260 plus travel/accommodation. The permanent experts would be paid a monthly salary of US$20,000. Three permanent experts would be attached to the JV company once it was established and the number would gradually be reduced to only one, after two years. Five experts would be available on a short-term basis to provide specific training needs for durations of not more than three months each year.

The Nora negotiation team was appalled at the exorbitant amount proposed by the Sakari negotiators. They were surprised that the Sakari team had not surveyed the industry rates, as the Japanese and other western negotiators would normally have done. Apparently Sakari had not taken into consideration the relatively low cost of living in Malaysia compared to Finland. In 2000, though the average monthly rent for a comfortable, unfurnished three-bedroom apartment was about the same (660 US$) in Helsinki and Kuala Lumpur, the cost of living was considerably lower in KL. The cost of living index (New York = 100) of basket of goods in major cities, excluding housing, for Malaysia was only 83.75, compared to 109.84 for Finland.[6]

In response to Sakari's proposal, Nora negotiators adopted an unusual "take-it or leave-it" stance. They deemed the following proposal reasonable in view of the comparisons made with other JVs which Nora had entered into with other foreign parties:

Permanent experts' monthly salary ranges to be paid by the JV company were as follows:

(1)   Senior expert (seven to 10 years experience)....... RM24,300–RM27,900
(2)   Expert (four to six years experience)................. RM22,500–RM25,200
(3)   Junior expert (two to three years experience)...... RM20,700–RM23,400
(4)   Any Malaysian income taxes payable would be added to the salaries.

(5)   A car for personal use.
(6)   Annual paid vacation of five weeks.
(7)   Return flight tickets to home country once a year for the whole family of married persons and twice a year for singles according to Sakari's general scheme.
(8)   Any expenses incurred during official travelling.

Temporary experts are persons invited by the JV company for various technical assistance tasks and would not be granted residence status. They would be paid the following fees:

(1)   Senior expert.. RM1,350 per working day
(2)   Expert.. RM1,170 per working day
(3)   The JV company would not reimburse the following:

- Flight tickets between Finland (or any other country) and Malaysia.
- Hotel or any other form of accommodation.
- Local transportation.

In defense of their proposed rates, Sakari's negotiators argued that the rates presented by Nora were too low. Sakari suggested that Nora's negotiators take into consideration the fact that Sakari would have to subsidize the difference between the experts' present salaries and the amount paid by the JV company. A large difference would require that large amounts of subsidy payments be made to the affected employees.

5. Arbitration

Another major issue discussed in the negotiation was related to arbitration. While both parties agreed to an arbitration process in the event of future disputes, they disagreed on the location for dispute resolution. Because Nora would be the majority stakeholder in the JV company, Nora insisted that any arbitration should take place in KL. Sakari, however, insisted on Helsinki, following the norm commonly practised by the company.

At the end of the five-day negotiation, many issues could not be resolved. While Nora could agree on certain matters after consulting Zainal, the Sakari team, representing a large private company, had to refer contentious items to the company board before it could make any decision that went beyond the limits authorized by the board.

The decision

Zainal sat down at his desk, read through the minutes of the negotiation thoroughly, and was disappointed that an agreement had not yet been reached. He was concerned about the commitment Nora had made to TMB when Nora was awarded the switching contract. Nora would be expected to fulfill the contract soon but had yet to find a partner to provide the switching technology. It was foreseeable that companies such as Siemens, Samsung and Lucent, which had failed in the bid, could still be potential partners. However, Zainal had also not rejected the possibility of a reconciliation with Sakari. He could start by contacting Kuusisto in Helsinki. But should he?

Exhibit 1 Malaysia: background information

Malaysia is centrally located in South-east Asia. It consists of Peninsular Malaysia, bordered by Thailand in the north and Singapore in the south, and the states of Sabah and Sarawak on the island of Borneo. Malaysia has a total land area of about 330,000 square kilometres, of which 80 per cent is covered with tropical rainforest. Malaysia has an equatorial climate with high humidity and high daily temperatures of about 26 degrees Celsius throughout the year.

In 2000, Malaysia's population was 22 million, of which approximately nine million made up the country's labour force. The population is relatively young, with 42 per cent between the ages of 15 and 39 and only seven per cent above the age of 55. A Malaysian family has an average of four children and extended families are common. Kuala Lumpur, the capital city of Malaysia, has approximately 1.5 million inhabitants.

The population is multiracial; the largest ethnic group is the Bumiputeras (the Malays and other indigenous groups such as the Ibans in Sarawak and Kadazans in Sabah), followed by the Chinese and Indians. Bahasa Malaysia is the national language but English is widely used in business circles. Other major languages spoken included various Chinese dialects and Tamil.

Islam is the official religion but other religions (mainly Christianity, Buddhism and Hinduism) are widely practised. Official holidays are allocated for the celebration of Eid, Christmas, Chinese New Year and Deepavali. All Malays are Muslims, followers of the Islamic faith.

During the period of British rule, secularism was introduced to the country, which led to the separation of the Islamic religion from daily life. In the late 1970s and 1980s, realizing the negative impact of secularism on the life of the Muslims, several groups of devout Muslims undertook efforts to reverse the process, emphasizing a dynamic and progressive approach to Islam. As a result, changes were introduced to meet the daily needs of Muslims. Islamic banking and insurance facilities were introduced and prayer rooms were provided in government offices, private companies, factories, and even in shopping complexes.

Malaysia is a parliamentary democracy under a constitutional monarchy. The Yang DiPertuan Agung (the king) is the supreme head, and appoints the head of the ruling political party to be the prime minister. In 2000 the Barisan Nasional, a coalition of several political parties representing various ethnic groups, was the ruling political party in Malaysia. Its predominance had contributed not only to the political stability and economic progress of the country in the last two decades, but also to the fast recovery from the 1997 Asian economic crisis.

The recession of the mid 1980s led to structural changes in the Malaysian economy which had been too dependent on primary commodities (rubber, tin, palm oil and timber) and had a very narrow export base. To promote the establishment of export-oriented industries, the government directed resources to the manufacturing sector, introduced

generous incentives and relaxed foreign equity restrictions. In the meantime, heavy investments were made to modernize the country's infrastructure. These moves led to rapid
economic growth in the late 1980s and early 1990s. The growth had been mostly driven by
exports, particularly of electronics.

The Malaysian economy was hard hit by the 1997 Asian economic crisis. However,
Malaysia was the fastest country to recover from the crisis after declining IMF assistance.
It achieved this by pegging its currency to the USD, restricting outflow of money from the
country, banning illegal overseas derivative trading of Malaysian securities and setting up
asset management companies to facilitate the orderly recovery of bad loans. The real GDP
growth rate in 1999 and 2000 were 5.4% and 8.6%, respectively (Table 1).

Table 1 Malaysian economic performance 1999 to 2002

Economic Indicator	1999	2000	2001	2002
GDP per capita (US$)	3,596	3,680	3,678	3,814
Real GDP growth rate	5.4%	8.6%	0.4%	4.2%
Consumer price inflation	2.8%	1.6%	1.4%	1.8%
Unemployment rate	3.0%	3.0%	3.7%	3.5%

Source: IMD. Various years. "The World Competitiveness Report."

Malaysia was heavily affected by the global economic downturn and the slump in the
IT sector in 2001 and 2002 due to its export-based economy. GDP in 2001 grew only
0.4% due to an 11% decrease in exports. A US$1.9 billion fiscal stimulus package helped
the country ward off the worst of the recession and the GDP growth rate rebounded to
4.2% in 2002 (Table 1). A relatively small foreign debt and adequate foreign exchange
reserves make a crisis similar to the 1997 one unlikely. Nevertheless, the economy remains
vulnerable to a more protracted slowdown in the US and Japan, top export destinations
and key sources of foreign investment.

In 2002, the manufacturing sector was the leading contributor to the economy,
accounting for about 30 per cent of gross national product (GDP). Malaysia's major
trading partners are United States, Singapore, Japan, China, Taiwan, Hong Kong and
Korea.

*Sources: Ernst & Young International. 1993. "Doing Business in Malaysia." Other online
sources.*

Exhibit 2 Finland: background information

Finland is situated in the north-east of Europe, sharing borders with Sweden, Norway
and the former Soviet Union. About 65 per cent of its area of 338,000 square kilometres is covered with forest, about 15 per cent lakes and about 10 per cent arable land.
Finland has a temperate climate with four distinct seasons. In Helsinki, the capital city,
July is the warmest month with average mid-day temperature of 21 degrees Celsius
and January is the coldest month with average mid-day temperature of −3 degrees
Celsius.

Finland is one of the most sparsely populated countries in Europe with a 2002
population of 5.2 million, 60 per cent of whom lived in the urban areas. Helsinki had a

population of about 560,000 in 2002. Finland has a well-educated work force of about 2.3 million. About half of the work force are engaged in providing services, 30 per cent in manufacturing and construction, and eight per cent in agricultural production. The small size of the population has led to scarce and expensive labour. Thus Finland had to compete by exploiting its lead in high-tech industries.

Finland's official languages are Finnish and Swedish, although only six per cent of the population speaks Swedish. English is the most widely spoken foreign language. About 87 per cent of the Finns are Lutherans and about one per cent Finnish Orthodox.

Finland has been an independent republic since 1917, having previously been ruled by Sweden and Russia. A President is elected to a six-year term, and a 200-member, single-chamber parliament is elected every four years.

In 1991, the country experienced a bad recession triggered by a sudden drop in exports due to the collapse of the Soviet Union. During 1991–1993, the total output suffered a 10% contraction and unemployment rate reached almost 20%. Finnish Markka experienced a steep devaluation in 1991–1992, which gave Finland cost competitiveness in international market.

With this cost competitiveness and the recovery of Western export markets the Finnish economy underwent a rapid revival in 1993, followed by a new period of healthy growth. Since the mid 1990s the Finnish growth has mainly been bolstered by intense growth in telecommunications equipment manufacturing. The Finnish economy peaked in the year 2000 with a real GDP growth rate of 5.6% (Table 2).

Table 2 Finnish economic performance 1999 to 2002

Economic Indicator	1999	2000	2001	2002
GDP per capita (US$)	24,430	23,430	23,295	25,303
Real GDP growth rate	3.7%	5.6%	0.4%	1.6%
Consumer price inflation	1.2%	3.3%	2.6%	1.6%
Unemployment	10.3%	9.6%	9.1%	9.1%

Source: IMD. Various years. "The World Competitiveness Report."

Finland was one of the 11 countries that joined the Economic and Monetary Union (EMU) on January 1, 1999. Finland has been experiencing a rapidly increasing integration with Western Europe. Membership in the EMU provide the Finnish economy with an array of benefits, such as lower and stable interest rates, elimination of foreign currency risk within the Euro area, reduction of transaction costs of business and travel, and so forth. This provided Finland with a credibility that it lacked before accession and the Finnish economy has become more predictable. This will have a long-term positive effect on many facets of the economy.

Finland's economic structure is based on private ownership and free enterprise. However, the production of alcoholic beverages and spirits is retained as a government monopoly. Finland's major trading partners are Sweden, Germany, the former Soviet Union and United Kingdom.

Finland's standard of living is among the highest in the world. The Finns have small families with one or two children per family. They have comfortable homes in the cities and one in every three families has countryside cottages near a lake where they retreat on weekends. Taxes are high, the social security system is efficient and poverty is virtually non-existent.

Until recently, the stable trading relationship with the former Soviet Union and other Scandinavian countries led to few interactions between the Finns and people in other parts of the world. The Finns are described as rather reserved, obstinate, and serious people. A Finn commented, "We do not engage easily in small talk with strangers. Furthermore, we have a strong love for nature and we have the tendency to be silent as we observe our surroundings. Unfortunately, others tend to view such behaviour as cold and serious." Visitors to Finland are often impressed by the efficient public transport system, the clean and beautiful city of Helsinki with orderly road networks, scenic parks and lakefronts, museums, cathedrals, and churches.

Sources: Ernst & Young International. 1993. "Doing Business in Finland." Other online sources.

Exhibit 3 Ten major telecommunication equipment vendors

Rank	Company	Country	1998 telecom equipment sales (US$ billions)
1	Lucent	USA	26.8
2	Ericsson	Sweden	21.5
3	Alcatel	France	20.9
4	Motorola	USA	20.5
5	Nortel	Canada	17.3
6	Siemens	Germany	16.8
7	Nokia	Finland	14.7
8	NEC	Japan	12.6
9	Cisco	USA	8.4
10	Hughes	USA	5.7

Source: International Telecommunication Union. 1999. Top 20 Telecommunication Equipment Vendors 1998. http://www.itu.int/ITU-D/ict/statistics/at_glance/Top2098.html.

Notes

1   Sdn Bhd is an abbreviation for Sendirian Berhad, which means private limited company in Malaysia.
2   Oy is an abbreviation for Osakeyhtiot, which means private limited company in Finland.
3   The first name is used because the Malay name does not carry a family name. The first and/or middle names belong to the individual and the last name is his/her father's name.
4   RM is Ringgit Malaysia, the Malaysian currency. As at December 31, 2002, US$1 = RM3.80.
5   FIM is Finnish Markka, the Finnish currency until January 1, 1999. Markka coins and notes were not withdrawn from circulation until January 1, 2002, when Finland fully converted to the Euro. As at December 31, 2000, US$1 = FIM6.31, and €1 = FIM5.95.
6   IMD & World Economic Forum. 2001. The World Competitiveness Report.

Chapter 5

Red Star China (A)

Discovering the essence of *Guanxi*

LATE IN SEPTEMBER 2002, Howard Zhao stood at the window of his 21st floor office in Pudong where he worked as the Senior Vice-President (Brokerage) at Red Star China Shipping Company. Though it was early in the morning, Howard's mind was agitated with thoughts about what, if anything, might have gone wrong in his attempt to build *guanxi* (connections) with Pan Weidong, Director of Logistics at Nanjing ZP Chemical Company (NCC), a Sino-German joint venture. In his mind, Howard replayed the events of past few months to understand what mistakes he may have made and, importantly, to find ways to rebuild guanxi with Pan.

For almost a year, Howard had been actively doing his best to fulfill the mandate to build guanxi with Pan—a charge Howard had received from Red Star's headquarters. Pan had recently been reassigned to one of NCC's smaller factories and it appeared he might have been demoted. It was said that the transfer was part of NCC's training program for the company's senior joint

Professor Neil Abramson and Professor Hemant Merchant prepared this case solely to provide material for class discussion. The authors do not intend to illustrate either effective or ineffective handling of a managerial situation, and may have disguised certain names and other identifying information to protect confidentiality. However, all essential facts remain unchanged.

Permission to reproduce this case must be obtained in writing from the copyright holder. All requests for permission must be directed to: Dr. Hemant Merchant, Department of Management & International Business, Barry Kaye College of Business, Florida Atlantic University, E-mail: merchant@fau.edu.

© Neil Abramson and Hemant Merchant / February 13, 2007

venture managers. Even so, it was highly unusual for a Chinese Communist Party member to be trained by first being transferred to a remote location.

The NCC joint venture would be the biggest producer of liquid chemical products in China, and was expected to become operational in 2005. Once operational, NCC would annually export 150,000 metric tons of liquid chemicals. Undoubtedly, NCC would require the services of a shipping company to handle its exports. Obtaining NCC's business would be very lucrative for Red Star China who intended to expand its business operations. Without NCC's business, the Red Star China office not only would not thrive but also severely jeopardize Red Star headquarters' China strategy. Howard was certain he would be in serious trouble with headquarters if he did not figure out how to success-fully rebuild guanxi with Pan.

Red Star and the shipping brokerage industry

The Red Star Group was one of Asia's largest shipbrokers. It was headquartered in Singapore and had offices in North America as well as Europe, and now China. With a team of 30 experienced brokers and 30 support personnel, Red Star provided shipping brokerage services for petroleum, chemicals, vegetable oils, and dry cargo. In 2001, Red Star had brokered 1.2 million metric tons of cargo. It had long-term business relationships with almost 1,000 ship owners and charters.[1]

Red Star China had been established in 1995. Located in Shanghai, Red Star China served as the gateway to Chinese chemical market for the entire Red Star network since Chinese chemicals were shipped worldwide. Red Star China specialized in spot chartering Chinese chemical products,[2] and maintained daily contact with approximately 200 ship owners and 150 charters. In 2000, 20% of Red Star Group's total tonnage had been booked by Red Star China. In March 2002, Red Star China expanded by opening a subsidiary in Nanjing. This was consistent with Red Star Group's long-term strategy. According to Red Star headquarters' general manager, Martin Zhu, Red Star intended to benefit as much as possible from China's booming economy.

Originally from Shandong province, Howard had been with Red Star China since it opened. Prior to that, Howard had been responsible for ship chartering at the Shanghai office of Sunway Chemical Company, an American chemical producer, where he had performed exceptionally well. In 1994, Red Star recruited Howard because of his performance and experience. After training for a year in Singapore, Howard was appointed as the manager of Red Star China's brokerage department.

As a manager, Howard was responsible for arranging water-based trans-portation for shippers (manufacturers) through shipping companies (ship owners and charters). He arranged contracts of affreightment (COA) with shippers.[3] After a COA was executed, Howard would notify the shipping companies, issue draft letters of indemnity and bills of lading, settle issues related to freight, demurrage[4] and claims, and provide supporting services required for vessel operations, ship arrivals and departures. For these services, Red Star China received a commission equal to 2.5% of the value of amount paid to the shipping companies. As Red Star China prospered, so did Howard who, by 2002, had three assistant brokers working for him. Over the years, Red Star China had become one of the largest liquid chemical products shipping service providers in China.

Many at the Red Star headquarters believed the Chinese subsidiary's success was largely due to Howard's ability to build guanxi. To a large extent, Red Star relied on an extensive network of government officials, ship owners, charters, port authority managers, and port agents that Howard had developed personal relationships with. It was Howard's comprehensive knowledge of ships, direct access to some of China's largest fleets, and good connections with local small and medium-sized ship owners that enabled Red Star China to provide first-class brokerage services.

Guanxi in China

Howard also believed the secret to his success was his ability to build guanxi. Guanxi, or personal connections, denoted a reciprocal flow of transactions and benefits between two parties (or within a network of relationships) over time. While many Western managers believed that guanxi was tantamount to corruption, because it involved offering and expecting gifts and favors, most Chinese believed that trust, shared goals, and mutual benefits were the essence of guanxi. In fact, very few Chinese interpreted guanxi as a questionable practice. Mutual trust and a personal relationship were developed based on long-term reliability. As a relationship became more durable, both parties developed *ganqing* (positive emotional) and personal feelings for each other. Once this occurred, the "gifts and favors" part of guanxi was just a symbolic exchange which further developed and signaled the ganqing feelings.

Guanxi was an important practice in China because the Chinese strongly preferred doing business through durable and trust-based relationships with individuals they regarded as insiders. The most durable relationships were with family members, who were always considered to be insiders. Next came relationships with long-time friends, such as school classmates. The least best relationships were "meat and potatoes" friendships established solely for business purposes—often over lunches and dinners—with people regarded as "outside" the circle of true friendship. Although the latter relationships were also secured with gifts and favors, the Chinese believed these relationships yielded only small and short-term obligations. To create successful business relationships, one needed to establish a durable "insider" friendship based on ganqing.

Howard's guanxi

Howard had his own definition of guanxi based on values he had accumulated while growing up in Shandong province where people were known to be especially hospitable, honest and candid with one another. Guanxi there was a process for transforming an outsider into an insider.

> Guanxi is an art. I heard many people say that guanxi was connection. However, I think connection touches only the surface part of guanxi. For me, it is not only connection. It is a special kind of relationship based on trust, reciprocity, common interests, and mutual obligations. The basic code of Confucianism—benevolence, righteousness, and fidelity—taught me how to act and deal in my relationship with others. Great attention is paid to people's morality according to the proverb "Learn to be a good man first, then learn how to do business."

Morality issues were of considerable significance to Howard who believed that the key to guanxi was building trust over time.

> If I'm not a man worthy of trust, I do not have the ability or willingness to repay my friends' favors anymore. Guanxi building is a long-term investment of time, money, and energy through social interactions such as gift-giving, voluntary favors, and banquets.

Over the years, Howard applied his principles to develop good guanxi with about 70 domestic ship owners and 35 charters. At Red Star China, Howard became known as "*hui zuo ren*," a person who is good at developing guanxi. Thus, in October, 2001, it was natural for Red Star headquarters to charge Howard with the task of building guanxi with NCC's logistics department to eventually obtain COAs for the shipment of NCC export production.

Nanjing ZP Chemical Company

In the Chinese proverb of the fox and the tiger, the fox receives no respect in the woods because of his lack of physical size and strength. No one takes the fox seriously but he is cunning and avoids traps. His solution is to make friends with a strong and respectable tiger. Then, the fox can walk through the jungle with his friend and enjoy the same fearful respect accorded the tiger. For Red Star China, NCC was a tiger and if it shared Red Star's vision and viewpoint, Red Star China would have the presence of a tiger.

Formed in 1998, NCC was a 50–50 joint venture between Germany's ZP Corporation and China United Chemical Company Limited, a state-owned petrochemical company based in Nanjing. Like many other multinational firms, the German company found it prudent to enter China's chemical market through joint ventures. The Chinese chemical market had grown at about 9% annually since mid-1990s, and was considered to be one of the fastest growing markets in China. In 2000, the total sales of petroleum and chemical products in China were US$ 172 billion. The value of China's international trade in the industry was another US$ 72 billion.

NCC was formed to build and operate a high-technology and integrated petrochemical site producing LDPE, toluene, and xylene. While most of NCC's output would be sold within China, about 150,000 metric tons would be shipped to international chemical markets after full production started in 2005. Meanwhile, German managers worked alongside their Chinese counterparts with the expectation that, by 2005, NCC would be primarily managed by local Chinese.

It was clear that NCC's chemical exports would have to be transported to international markets by bulk carrier ships. There was no pipeline planned and container ships were out of the question due to the liquid nature of the cargo. The only real transportation option was shipping brokerage because the chemicals (for export) would not be available for at least two or three years, and large bulk shipping companies could neither abandon existing customers nor commit themselves to build capacity for such an eventuality.

This attracted the attention of many logistics service providers. All approached NCC's logistics department knowing that a contract with NCC would guarantee them a strong position in Jiangsu province's liquid chemical transportation market. Of this multitude, only two companies had the size and international network to satisfy NCC's service and price requirements. One of these companies was Red Star China and the other was SSK Shipping Company Limited.

SSK Shipping was one of the world's largest and oldest independent ship brokering companies; it was the Red Star Group's strongest worldwide competitor. SSK was a London-based company with wholly-owned offices in 10 cities worldwide, including London, Jakarta, Singapore, and Hong Kong. Rumor had it that SSK planned to open an office in Shanghai to obtain NCC's business. Howard believed SSK's Hong Kong office had already established contact with NCC.

Other major brokerage companies could also set up subsidiaries in China but lacked much-needed credibility because it took as long as five years to build a reliable network of local shipping companies. Howard observed:

> The ship owners in China are not qualified enough to meet NCC's standards. Most cargo will need to be shipped by domestic shipping companies which are mainly small or medium-sized companies. It will be difficult to meet NCC's service and price requirements. NCC will be required to investigate the options. It will have to establish regular contacts with the major players to get fully prepared for full production in 2005. If it can't find a carrier at that time, NCC will be in trouble.

Brokering cargo space on ships was a "commodity" type business that favored large shipping firms. Because SSK was larger and had a more extensive worldwide network, Howard guessed SSK might be able to offer slightly better service and prices than could the Red Star Group. SSK might be especially aggressive if NCC was its key to entering Shanghai, and Jiangsu province. If Howard could successfully build guanxi with NCC, the relationship would differentiate Red Star's service. Howard observed:

> Its highly possible in a state-owned company that Chinese customers
> will pay more for reliable shipping. Also, if parties have good guanxi,

even though the shipping price is higher than somebody else, the guanxi partner will get the business.

If Red Star got NCC's business, it would ensure Red Star China's long-term success and perhaps block SSK out of Jiangsu, at least for some time. If Red Star did not get NCC's business, Red Star China's survival would depend largely on Howard's ability to retain his existing customers—much smaller than NCC—who, tempted by SSK's success with NCC, might switch to SSK. Success was also personally important to Howard. Everyone at Red Star thought of Howard as the master of guanxi. If he failed, he would lose face among his colleagues and likely also with his customers.

Building guanxi at NCC

It took Howard three long months of careful investigation to identify the one key person at NCC with whom he needed to build guanxi. This person was Pan Weidong, NCC's logistics director. Pan seemed to have the ultimate authority to determine who NCC would choose as its shipper. It seemed no other individuals, either inside or outside NCC, could direct NCC's business elsewhere. Three months was not too long to invest in making a correct decision. Building guanxi was a time-consuming and long-term investment of emotion, energy, and financial resources. One could not expect quick returns, and if one picked the wrong guanxi target, there would be no positive returns at all. Quoting a Chinese proverb, Howard said:

> You should use a long cord to catch a big fish. Otherwise it is highly possible that you will be treated as a "meat-and-potatoes" friend. Such a friendship can only be temporary. It is unreliable and shallow. They will not offer you precious support when you are in trouble.

To learn more about Pan, Howard visited a friend in the Nanjing municipal government to try to access Pan's personnel file since Pan worked for a state-owned company. In *The Art of War*, Sun Tzu had said that one needed to know both one's self and one's enemy to ensure victory. The great Communist leader Mao Zedong had said that business was war and that one had to have as much information as possible and think deeply before making every move. Howard's friend referred him to another friend in Beijing who used to work at the China United Chemical Company headquarters—NCC's Chinese joint venture parent.

Howard found out that Pan was born in 1955 in the city of Ningbo in Zhejiang province in southern China. This was important information because people from North and South China often viewed guanxi differently. Howard explained:

> With North Chinese, more attention will be given to the emotional attachment of guanxi. Generally speaking, North Chinese treasure friendship very much. If you have good guanxi with them, they will

give you the shirt off their back. South Chinese are more realistic and materialistic. As a result, mutual benefits or shared interests need to be emphasized. Favors should be tendered more frequently.

Pan was known to be an excellent Communist Party member. He had completed his Executive MBA degree at Shanghai Fudan University. Pan was married to a woman from Beijing, who had refused to give up her work in Beijing when Pan had moved to Nanjing to work at NCC. As a result, Pan traveled to Beijing every two weeks. The couple had one son who was planning to take the College Entrance Examination in 2003. One frustration for Howard was that he could not determine what hobbies Pan had. Howard said:

I like to collect information regarding friends' habits, hobbies, and their ways of working, and adjust my methods of getting along with them accordingly. I'd like to focus on my friends' hobbies in order to arouse their interests before conducting business with them.

Howard's first chance to meet Pan came in February 2002, at Pan's Executive MBA alumni reunion. One of Pan's classmates was the vice president of a Shanghai-based state-owned shipping company. He had also been doing business with Howard for three years and the two shared a guanxi relationship. He introduced Howard to Pan. Howard commented:

In my network, the guanxi with classmates, relatives, and fellow villagers is the core. My relationship with classmates is extremely important. It's the most stable and valuable intangible asset I have. Pure and real friendship was developed between classmates because we were young and did not have conflicts of interest when we were at university. Alumni association meetings are a good way for me to expand my guanxi network.

Howard hoped he could build a relationship with Pan based on classmate connections. This would already be one step higher than a "meat-and-potatoes" relationship. Howard and Pan exchanged business cards, and Howard told Pan he wanted to pursue an Executive MBA. Howard asked Pan for his advice. He told Pan he would be more than happy to go to Shanghai Fudan University if people like Pan had studied there. Pan seemed, however, uninterested in conversing with Howard and offered no advice.

It was difficult to know what Pan's real opinion was and his responses and reactions did not appear to be that positive to Howard. Pan only asked Howard how old he was and seemed surprised that a 30-year-old was the department manager in a foreign company. Howard's impression of Pan was that he spent his time quietly watching and studying people. Howard said:

It was difficult to tell if my endeavor was effective or not. Pan is composed and conservative. He is good at examining someone's words and observing their countenance. He's an excellent listener and much more cunning and conscious than I imagined. Confucius said that a true gentleman speaks slowly but acts quickly. Pan follows this proverb strictly.

To obtain more information about Pan, Howard directed Red Star China's manager in Nanjing to organize a dinner and karaoke party for Pan's subordinates. This gathering was a big personal success for Howard because it resulted in a chance meeting with one of Pan's subordinates, Mr. Zhang. Like Howard, Zhang was also from Shandong province.

Intimate personal relationships can be established quickly between individuals from Shandong if they meet outside their own hometowns. Over time, Howard bonded easily with Zhang through constant personal visits and entertainments. When Zhang's sister needed a job in Shanghai, Howard found her one through one of his guanxi contacts. When Zhang's mother had a heart attack, Howard got her into the best hospital in Shanghai and put up Zhang's father in Red Star's Shanghai dormitory. Howard could now keep close contact with an "insider" in Pan's department and would be able to obtain much more information about Pan and his preferences.

Zhang told Howard that Pan spent most of his time writing a thesis called *Chemical Logistics in China* and had written other articles on the same subject. Howard also found out that Pan had been invited to give a 30-minute presentation at a distribution logistics conference to be held in Shanghai in April. Howard prepared carefully for this event.

With Zhang's help, Howard gathered and studied all articles written by Pan. At the end of Pan's presentation, he asked several well-prepared questions. Pan was astonished at Howard's deep understanding of the subject, and provided him with detailed responses and recommended several references. In fact, Pan willingly agreed when Howard asked if he could come see Pan if he had any other questions. Subsequently, Howard visited Pan frequently to ask for assistance on logistics-related subjects. Howard always prepared well-designed questions beforehand. Howard said:

> I called him Teacher Pan and found him much more talkative on such occasions. I seldom spoke and pretended to be a good student and listener during these meetings. On one hand, what he said was meaningful and useful for my business. On the other hand, I was sure that Pan gained face when others appreciated his work.

Shortly after the April conference, Pan met with a car accident. The accident was not serious but Pan's doctor ordered him to rest at home for a week. Pan's wife came from Beijing to take care of him. Howard decided to meet Lin and arrange some entertainment or sightseeing for her. He hoped Pan would notice his friendly gesture and gain face. Howard followed the Chinese proverb that one must not only bow and scrape before a tiger, one must also seek every opportunity to ingratiate one's self with the tiger's relatives and friends. Howard asked Sina Du, his general manager at the Red Star Shanghai office, to accompany Lin. Sina invited Lin for a two-day shopping and relaxation trip in Shanghai in early-May after Pan had recovered. She also invited Pan but he declined due to work-related pressures.

For two days, Howard and Sina made themselves out to be the most warm-hearted hosts in the world. They booked Lin in a five-star hotel suite and rented a luxury Mercedes-Benz to show her around Shanghai. They all lunched and dined at top-notch restaurants or famous bars. Moreover, Howard and Sina offered to pay for Lin's shopping but she declined. During their excursions, Howard confirmed that Pan and Lin's son was studying for the College Entrance Exam, and discovered that Lin was afraid her son would not do well. After checking with Red Star's headquarters, Howard offered Red Star's help in getting Lin's son admitted into a Singaporean university. Lin said, "Howard, you are so nice! Pan should tell me beforehand that he has such a good friend like you in Shanghai." When Lin returned to Beijing, she sent gifts for Howard and Sina and invited them to visit Beijing.

A week later, Pan called Howard's cell phone to express his gratitude. Howard took it as a sign that Pan was touched by his friendship and understood the basic reciprocity principle of guanxi. "If you receive a favor, you need to repay it in the future but there is no need to repay it immediately," Howard said. In fact, it was a sign of greater trust and a stronger relationship when friends were willing to wait longer for a better return. Pan's gesture gave Howard much hope.

In a guanxi relationship, give-and-take is expected, and returns are balanced for both sides in the long term. What constitutes balance depends on the relative power and position of two parties. Each party is expected to give the best it can, but the "tiger"—by virtue of his stature—would be expected to give gifts greater than those a "fox" could offer. If the more powerful individual does not offer the greater gift, then s/he would be seen to lose face.

Howard wanted Pan to send NCC's business to Red Star China. This would keep other competitors like SSK away, and ensure Red Star's growth. At minimum, Howard hoped Pan would grant priority to Red Star China in the submission of quotations when NCC's output needed to be transported to international markets. In the meantime, Howard hoped Pan would signal his friendship for Howard by making frequent requests for market information and quotations. Howard said:

> In the beginning, [Pan] can only talk with me about the market, but gradually this increases intimacy with me and not with my competitors. This will be a sign that eventually the COA will come to me and not my competitors.

Howard wanted to give Pan a "big gift" to cement the relationship and to convey his own expectation of receiving a big favor from Pan. In guanxi, there were small gifts and big gifts. Small gifts represented friendship; what mattered was the emotional attachment these gifts symbolized—not their small worth. Small gifts created a sense of obligation far exceeding their monetary cost. On joyous occasions, such as festivals, Howard gave small gifts to his friends, and to the relatives and friends of those he hoped to influence. Howard had given small gifts to Pan and none had ever been returned. "Big" gifts were intended to seal a deal; they were given only to those with great influence. However, big gifts could be interpreted as bribes, and so were dangerous especially since the Chinese government had recently passed strict laws to prevent the spread of corruption. Many officials at Chinese state-owned enterprises had been jailed, and even severely punished, for accepting bribes. Howard noted:

> I have been considering preparing some big gifts for Pan. However, I finally gave it up. From my viewpoint, a big gift is a double-edged sword because the line between bribery and gift-giving is really difficult to distinguish. The big gift should be used wisely according to different situations and people.

On one hand, Pan was from southern China, suggesting that he would be more pragmatic, and be pleased to receive a big gift from Howard. On the other hand, Pan's wife was from Beijing where big gifts were especially dangerous. Pan was also an honored Communist Party member which indicated he must cherish his political reputation. Howard suspected that Pan would want to stay away from even the hint of a corruption scandal. Zhang supported this view saying, "I saw Pan refuse many people's personal visits on weekends. He once threw a bag out in the corridor when one guest tried to leave it in his room." Howard concluded his guanxi with Pan would definitely be jeopardized if he (Howard) was indelicate about giving Pan a big gift: "If I am not 100% sure about the result, I would rather forget it."

Howard observed Pan would only do favors for "qualified friends." These were people who not only enjoyed a good relationship with Pan but who were also capable of fulfilling a contract and handling mutual business properly. Howard repeatedly stressed Red Star's competitive advantage as one of the biggest chemical shipping brokers in China, arguing to Pan that Red Star could reduce NCC's shipping costs and expand NCC's business contacts worldwide.

To demonstrate Red Star's advantages, Howard arranged for David Zhou, a managing director at Red Star headquarters, to accompany him to visit Pan in June. David prepared a one-hour presentation about the history and core competencies of Red Star Group, and presented it to Pan's entire department. Clearly, Pan was impressed. He began contacting Howard for more information about the domestic and international liquid chemical markets, and freight-market trends. Pan also asked Howard to submit a quotation for regular spot ship chartering. Howard was excited by Pan's positive response and worked even harder to boost guanxi with Pan hoping to "strike while the iron is hot."

Terrible news

In end-September, Howard was shocked to learn that Pan was being reassigned to one of NCC's smaller factories in a small city outside Nanjing. It was claimed the reassignment was part of NCC's senior manager-training program to better qualify Chinese managers to run NCC by 2005. Howard doubted this claim. Since China's Cultural Revolution (during 1960s and 1970s), being sent to the countryside was considered to be a form of extreme punishment; very few individuals ever came back. Howard recalled his feelings:

I was so upset and surprised. The dilemma is what will happen next. If Pan won't come back after this program, then all my previous investments of time and money will be wasted. I have to start again from the very beginning with the new manager [who will replace Pan]. I need to decide whether or not to stay with Pan. If I continue building guanxi with Pan, my efforts will become worthless if he leaves NCC's logistics department.

Howard visited Pan in the small city where Pan had been reassigned, and tried to find out what had happened. It seemed to Howard that Pan was reluctant to talk about what had happened to him, and he didn't seem to want to say too much about his new assignment or status. Pan said, "Now I understand that what is out of sight is out of mind," joking that he was a dragon who went near the shallow water and got bullied by a fish. Howard terminated the meeting quickly after that. He simply didn't know what to say to pacify Pan. There was already a new German expatriate from ZP, Hans Hol, who had been appointed as Pan's replacement at NCC's logistics department.

Howard wondered what he should do. He could stick with Pan and hope for the best. If Howard kept building guanxi with Pan, and Pan recovered his position, then Pan would be very grateful for Howard's loyalty. Howard recalled a Chinese proverb, "Bad times help build good relationships," and was aware that Chinese use a crisis to test the true nature of guanxi. Howard remembered how foreign companies that had pulled out of China during the Tiananmen Square massacre (in 1989) had been unwelcome when they tried to come back later. Companies that had stayed in China had been rewarded later for their show of loyalty (to China) during a time of crisis.

Yet, to Howard, Pan had not sounded confident at all about his imminent return. If Pan did not come back to Nanjing within a couple of years, it could be too late for Red Star China. The point of guanxi was to invest time and energy in individuals whom one could most benefit from, either now or in the future. What advantage was there in developing guanxi with those from whom one could not benefit?

Business conditions changed quickly and unpredictably in China. The government could pass a new economic manifesto and suddenly change the entire basis of competition. The individual who ruled today could fall out of favor tomorrow, and someone else would be in charge. It was important to honor and maintain one's values, but it was also important to judiciously discriminate between standards that helped govern one's own life and standards one upheld hoping that others would like the person holding them. Sometimes one had to have the courage to do what one needed to do—without regard for what others might think. If Howard stuck with Pan and Pan was not rehabilitated quickly, then Pan would be pleased but Red Star China would lose NCC's business—and Howard would lose face with his colleagues who were counting on his abilities to acquire NCC's business. There was another proverb that the successful man played leapfrog. People and relationships that were of no further use were discarded. One always did one's best to leap to the top to gain endorsement from the established authorities and to ally one's self with the powerful and wise. It would be prudent to always leap towards an association with a tiger.

Howard wondered if he could switch his guanxi building efforts to Hans, who had replaced Pan as NCC's logistics director. Apparently, Hans was the new tiger of NCC's logistics department; he represented the German half of the joint venture. Howard could entertain Hans by taking him sightseeing, shopping and to meals. However, in Howard's experience, Germans were less likely than the Chinese to trade friendship for business. Hans probably thought "business was business," and would make decisions about NCC's choice of a brokerage firm based on the firm's service and price offering—and not on whether Hans was friends with Howard. Howard said:

> I find the whole prospect of building guanxi with Hans very confusing. I don't quite know what to do because my experience is in building guanxi with Chinese. Do the same things work with Germans or other foreigners?

Or, Howard could find another influential Chinese official in NCC and start building guanxi again. It had taken him a few months to identify Pan as the person to build guanxi with and his efforts had taken about a year. He still had two or three years left before NCC started producing chemicals for the export markets. If Howard could find a Chinese manager higher than Hans, perhaps that manager could influence Hans to do NCC's business with Red Star China. Certainly, this was the option Howard felt most confident about.

The decision

Standing in the window of his office looking down at Pudong and the Yangtze river, Howard worried that just when he was ready to walk through the forest with his friend, the tiger, he had to struggle all over again. Pudong was a shining symbol of China's economic transformation. Howard needed NCC's business as his own shining symbol to ensure that Red Star China would continue to be a part of the Chinese economic miracle. Howard's choices were limited. Each had its distinct merits and demerits. Howard had to decide what he needed to do.

Notes

1. Ship owners and charters would arrange their shipping schedules and routes to receive and deliver cargo arranged by brokers. Charters were companies that chartered ships from owners. Both were dependent on brokers because individual ships were unable to guarantee the comprehensive scheduling service requirements of shippers, and it was easier for shippers to arrange a schedule through a broker than deal with a host of individual ships.
2. Spot chartering involves arranging for cargo and ship space on the spot market.
3. A Contract of Affreightment (COA) was an agreement to book cargo space on vessels at specified times and prices.
4. Demurrage is the detention of a ship during loading or unloading beyond the scheduled time of departure, and the compensation to be paid as a result of the delay.

Chapter 6

Hero Honda Motors (India) Ltd.

Is it *Honda* that made it a *hero*?

Hero Honda Rides Splendor to Become World's No. 1

India has finally got a world leader in manufacturing with "no problem." Hero Honda Motors Ltd. (HHM) has attained the distinction of being the largest two-wheeler company in the world in volume terms. With a new factory on the anvil, it is gearing itself for Operation One Billion, targeting $1 billion revenues in 2002–03. "Next year, we will enter the (dollar) billionaire's club (in revenues). After Operation Million for volumes in 2001–02, our slogan for the next year is Operation One Billion," said Mr. Pawan Munjal, Director & CEO, HHM. The distinction of being the largest two-wheeler company in the world came in calendar 2001, with sales rocketing past the one million mark in the first nine months of the current fiscal year. This performance was in conjunction with Splendor, launched in 1995, becoming the world's largest-selling bike.

Business Standard, January 2002

THINGS COULD NOT HAVE possibly looked any better for Mr. Brijmohan Lal Munjal, the Chairman and Managing Director of Hero Honda

THUNDERBIRD
SCHOOL OF GLOBAL MANAGEMENT

Motors (HHM). Quarter after quarter, and year over year, HHM had continued to grow, delivering superb performance in India's two-wheeler marketplace. The company had come from nowhere to whiz past Bajaj Auto Ltd., the traditional leader of the pack in twowheelers. Mr. Munjal had not only earned the crowning title of heading the largest two-wheeler company in the world, but also the personal glory of having presided over one of the most successful joint ventures in the country. Having built a storied legacy, he could rest easy. Or could he?

The spectacular track record of the company was being threatened by predatory moves made by its Japanese partner, Honda Motor Company. The first dark clouds appeared on the horizon in August 1999. Honda Motor Company Ltd. (HMC), HHM's joint venture partner, announced that it would be setting up a 100% subsidiary, Honda Motorcycle & Scooter India (HMSI) to initially make scooters and later, motorcycles as well. HHM's stock plummeted by 30% on the day of the announcement. It was apparent that the investors were no longer optimistic about the company's ability to continue its sterling performance record, especially in the face of competition from Honda. Was this a portent of things to come? Adding another dimension to an arena already fraught with significant complexity, reports from the marketplace clearly showed increasing intensity of rivalry. Not only were domestic rivals getting better equipped to challenge HHM for supremacy, there were foreign interlopers as well who seemed determined on giving HHM a run for its money. It was definitely not a time to rest on past laurels.

The two-wheeler industry in India

History and background

India had the largest population of two-wheelers (around 41.6m vehicles) in the world.[1] They accounted for almost 70% of the country's automobile market in volume terms. India was the second largest manufacturer of two-wheelers in the world. Exhibit A provides comparative financial and operating statistics for the major two-wheeler manufacturers in India.

The birth of the Indian two-wheeler industry can be traced to the small beginnings that it made in the early 1950s when Automobile Products of India (API) started manufacturing scooters in the country. Although API initially dominated the scooter market with its *Lambrettas*, Bajaj Auto Ltd., a company that later became a legend in the global scooter industry, overtook it fairly quickly. Although a number of government and private enterprises also entered the scooter segment, almost all of them had disappeared from the market by the turn of the century. Baja Auto Ltd. stood the test of time perhaps due to its initial association with Piaggio of Italy (manufacturer of *Vespa*) that provided the technological know-how for the venture.

The *license raj* that existed prior to economic liberalization (1940s–1980s) in India did not allow foreign companies to enter the market, making it an ideal breeding ground for local players. Local players were subject to a very stringent capacity licensing process, and imports were tightly controlled. This regulatory

Exhibit A Comparative financial and operating statistics for the major two-wheeler manufacturers in India

	Kinetic Honda					Hero Honda				
	1990	1993	1996	1999	2001	1990	1993	1996	1999	2001
Sales (Gross)	132.1	157.7	315.2	321.1	423.1	149.8	301.5	632.7	1536.4	3177.2
Sales (Net)	110.4	126.8	257.6	264.9	350.8	149.3	300.3	630.8	1532.8	3171.2
Cost of goods sold	77.6	124.2	235.4	238.2	291.2	134.0	266.8	515.5	1240.9	2533.5
R&D expenditure	0.0	0.0	1.5	0.2	4.1	0.0	0.0	2.0	3.5	5.1
Advertising and sales expenditure	0.9	2.6	6.2	13.4	32.7	4.0	9.5	28.1	54.4	122.3
Capital expenditure	0.6	2.4	9.3	2.2	10.1	10.7	10.4	30.6	106.2	121.2
Imports (imported materials)	22.7	15.2	54.6	44.7	19.8	18.0	35.7	68.8	235.6	420.6
Imported materials (% of COGS)	0.3	0.1	0.2	0.2	0.1	0.1	0.1	0.1	0.2	0.2
Current assets	20.3	44.3	69.8	88.6	98.0	34.1	93.2	146.2	326.1	663.8
Current liabilities	15.4	24.1	55.6	63.1	72.7	57.1	59.3	145.6	308.7	460.1
PBDIT (operating profit)	10.7	5.6	11.5	16.4	34.6	12.4	32.4	59.7	220.4	459.6
Net income (PAT)	4.4	0.4	5.2	3.5	15.6	-0.2	16.7	26.8	120.1	250.1
Return on sales	0.0	0.0	0.0	0.0	0.0	0.0	0.1	0.0	0.1	0.1
Return on investment (ROI)	0.3	0.1	0.1	0.1	0.2	0.1	0.2	0.2	0.3	0.4
Return on average equity	1.0	0.0	0.1	0.1	0.3	0.0	0.4	0.3	0.5	0.5
Total debt	16.9	17.0	22.0	40.1	21.8	50.8	63.3	50.0	78.2	69.2
Net fixed assets	17.7	20.2	29.2	46.9	52.1	60.2	67.0	103.9	308.6	453.9
ROCE (% pre-tax)	40.3	16.0	27.3	23.3	45.7	46.8	34.7	55.5	122.3	78.6

Exhibit A — *continued*

	c1	c2	c3	c4	c5	c6	c7	c8	c9
Sales (Gross)									
Sales (Net)									
Cost of goods sold									
R&D expenditure									
Advertising and sales expenditure									
Capital expenditure									
Imports (imported materials)									
Imported materials (% of COGS)									
Current assets	47.1	150.9	160.3	322.3	315.1	350.1	871.3	1570.5	1547.4
Current liabilities	76.9	74.8	144.8	149.0	181.3	186.3	666.9	836.6	474.4
PBDIT (operating profit)	9.9	35.2	68.5	63.1	58.1	32.8	405.9	481.6	298.9
Net income (PAT)	-5.5	0.1	0.1	0.0	0.1	0.0	0.1	0.1	0.1
Return on sales	0.0	0.3	0.3	0.2	0.3	0.2	0.3	0.2	0.1
Return on investment (ROI)	0.1	0.5	0.4	0.2	0.2	0.1	0.3	0.2	0.1
Return on average equity	-0.4								
Total debt	36.5	33.5	142.4	225.2	159.6	164.4	197.2	351.2	527.3
Net fixed assets	54.1	97.6	187.5	436.1	301.4	291.9	559.7	921.8	1362.4
ROCE (% pre-tax)	64.3	86.8	61.2	29.8	51.4	38.4	46.8	31.1	14.2

maze created a seller's market, with customers often forced to wait 12 years just to buy a scooter from companies such as Bajaj. In 1980 Bajaj had a waiting list that was equal to about thirteen times its annual output, and by 1990 this list had doubled. Clearly, there was no incentive to implement proactive strategies to woo the customer. In a 1980 interview with a local magazine, Mr. Rahul Bajaj, the CEO of Bajaj Auto, observed, *"My marketing department? I don't require it. I have a dispatch department. I don't have to go from house to house to sell."* The motorcycle segment was no different; with only three manufacturers—Royal Enfield, Ideal Jawa, and Escorts—there was hardly any significant competition for the customer. While this segment was dominated by Enfield's 350cc *Bullet*, the only motorcycle with a four-stroke engine at the time, Jawa and Escorts also had a fair share of the middle and lower end of the market.

The winds of change began to take hold in the mid-'80s when the Indian government started permitting foreign companies to enter the Indian market through minority joint ventures. Under these relaxed regulations, the two-wheeler market witnessed a veritable boom with four Indo-Japanese joint ventures; namely, Hero Honda, TVS-Suzuki, Bajaj Kawasaki, and Kinetic Honda all lining up to target the Indian consumer market for motorcycles. The simultaneous entry of four players into this underserved market helped boost motorcycle revenues to stratospheric heights. For the first time, the market dynamics changed in favor of the Japanese players in both two-stroke and four-stroke vehicles, and the Indian manufacturers who had held sway for such an extended period of time were suddenly cornered. The entry of these new foreign companies transformed the very essence of competition from the supply side to the demand side. Confronted with a larger array of choices, the consumers were regaining their influence over the products that they bought. In keeping up with these higher customer expectations, the industry accelerated the launch of new models, and every company was trying to outdo the other in terms of styling, price, and fuel efficiency. The technological expertise that the foreign companies brought to the marketplace helped increase the overall quality and reliability of the products quite significantly. The old-guard companies soon found themselves under pressure to improve their offerings and bring their products on par with their global counterparts.

The Indian consumer

Two-wheelers had become the standard mode of transportation in many of India's large urban centers. Increasing urbanization, saturation of cities, and the lack of adequate roads helped to propel demand for two-wheelers. The two-wheeler was typically a prized possession in the average Indian household. It was normally used to transport both people and goods, substituting for a car that was prohibitively expensive. While a two-wheeler normally cost around Rs. 40,000 [1 U.S. $ = 49 Rupees (Rs.)], an entry-level car was priced around Rs. 300,000. Two-wheelers had long road lives, and were often used for even 15 years, passed down from one generation to the next. However, in global terms the market was far from mature. Industry watchers reported that India had a penetration rate of 10% as of the late 1990s (107 two-wheelers for every 1000 adults), far below the penetration rates of other developing countries. It was clear that the manufacturers had a lot of ground to cover.

There were indeed visible signs that the companies were gearing up to address this growing market. While the production and sales of motorcycles grew substantially (CAGR of 22% between 1996 and 2001), the performance of the other two segments of two-wheelers was poor. Scooter production grew by only 0.5%, while the production of mopeds fell by 29% during 2001–02.

The legend of Hero Honda

The Hero Group

The Munjals, owners of the Hero Group and promoters of HHM, had made a modest beginning as suppliers of bicycle components in the early '40s. Currently, the group's bicycle company, Hero Cycles, manufactured over 16,000 bicycles a day and had sold over 86 million bicycles in aggregate as of 2002. It had been acknowledged as the world's largest bicycle manufacturer in 1986 when it overtook the U.S. manufacturer, Huffy. Despite the lack of significant process automation, the company had been able to achieve among the highest levels of employee productivity and efficiency on a global basis. Although a publicly traded company, the family was extensively involved in day-to-day management of operations, as well as setting strategic direction.

Much of the company's strategy was anchored to the fundamental principle of providing products of superior value at reasonable prices to the consumer. This basic belief was reflected in the company's approach to product innovation, quality, and reliability. Over time, the group had nurtured an excellent network of dealers to serve India's expansive markets. This network was not just focused on the highdensity urban centers, but also encompassed rural outlying regions that typically did not attract the attention of large manufacturers. The company truly believed in its mission of bringing transportation to the masses.

Over the years, the Hero Group had entered multiple business areas, largely related to the transportation industry. The group evolved into a fairly integrated set of operations that spanned multiple areas of raw material processing, such as steel rolling, to the manufacture of subassemblies and components. Many of these ventures were owned and controlled by members of the Munjal family or operated by very close friends and associates. Thus, the company had seemingly established control over all facets of production and marketing. Exhibit B shows the portfolio of Hero Group businesses.

Honda Motor Company of Japan

Honda Motor Company had surprisingly similar origins like its counterpart in India. Founded in 1946 as the Honda Technical Institute by Mr. Soichiro Honda,

Exhibit B Portfolio of Hero Group businesses

Business			
Bicycles	**Hero Cycles Limited** Established in 1956 **Product:** Bicycles	**Hero Cycles Limited (Unit II)** Established in 1988 **Product:** Bicycles	**Gujarat Cycles Limited** Established in 1988 **Product:** Bicycles
Auto Two-Wheelers	**Hero Honda Motors Limited** Established in 1983 New Delhi **Product:** Motorcycles Collaborator: Honda Motor Co. Ltd., Japan	**Majestic Auto Limited** Established in 1978 **Products:** Mopeds and Fitness Equipment	**Hero Motors** (A division of Majestic Auto Limited) Established in 1988 **Product:** Mini-motorcycles **Collaborator:** Steyr Daimler Puch, Austria **Product:** Scooters **Collaborators:** Malguti, Italy
Bicycle and Auto Components	**Rockman Cycle Industries Limited** Established in 1960 **Products:** Automotive and Bicycle Chains; Steel and Aluminum Hubs	**Highway Cycle Industries Limited** Established in 1971 **Products:** Freewheels and Special Machine Tools	**Munjal Showa Limited** Established in 1985 **Product:** Shock Absorbers **Collaborator:** Showa Manufacturing Co., Japan
Castings and Steel	**Munjal Castings** Established in 1981 **Product:** Nonferrous Castings	**Sunbeam Castings** Established in 1987 **Product:** Nonferrous Castings	**Hero Cycles-Cold Rolling Division** Established in 1990 **Product:** Cold Rolled Steel Sheets and Coils
Services	**Hero Exports** Established in 1993 **Product:** International Trading Company dealing in Commodities and Engineering Items	**Hero Corporate Services** Established in 1995 **Product:** Corporate Services in Finance, HRD, IT, and Strategic Planning	**Munjal Sales Corporation** Established in 1975 **Product:** Sole Selling Agents of Bicycles and Bicycles Parts for India

the company produced its first bicycle engine a year later. There had been no looking back from that time on as the company grew to dominate the global automotive market, with over 100 plants in 33 countries selling 11 million product units as of 2002. The engine was the centerpiece of Honda's global expansion. It had parlayed this expertise into a wide range of products such as lawnmowers, generators, scooters, motorcycles, and cars.

Honda called its global strategy "glocalization" to signify its approach of building plants locally to meet local demand. Within this web of localized operations, the company had been able to leverage synergies in R&D and manufacturing by regionalizing its operations, consolidating local strategy at the regional level. It had worked quite well. The reach of wholly owned subsidiaries was augmented through astute management of select joint ventures, although not a preferred mode of entry for the company. In many cases, the company was motivated to enter into joint ventures either because of regulatory constraints or because of a desire to access local market knowledge that was not easily available.

Forging a partnership with Honda Motor Company

Given the impending liberalization of India's markets, HMC had come looking for suitors. Initial plans called for entry both into the two-wheeler market and the electric generator market. HMC identified a short list of Indian companies that it felt would make good partners. Topping the list in the two-wheeler category was Bajaj Auto, a company that traced its reputation to the storied history of Piaggio of Italy and the chic-yet-egalitarian brand of transportation it offered through its series of *Vespas*. When that first choice did not work out for HMC, it moved on to its second choice, the Firodia group, an automotive products conglomerate based in the prosperous western Indian state of Maharashtra. Kinetic Engineering Ltd. (KEL), the group's flagship company, manufactured the first mopeds in India. Hugely popular in the late '70s and early '80s, KEL had a 44% share of the Indian moped market and about 15% of the entire two-wheeler market. It seemed to hold much promise at the time, and thus attracted the attention of HMC. KEL and HMC entered into a 50/50 joint venture, Kinetic Honda Motors Ltd., with the express objective of launching a line of scooters in India. It was widely reported that KEL was offered a choice between scooters and motorcycles and chose scooters based on prevailing trends that favored scooters. Honda was already close to signing on another partner for its other venture in power products, and hence its bid for a motorcycle JV was all that was left in play.

HMC came to the Hero group as the last choice for its motorcycle venture. The market for motorcycles was not booming in any sense of the term in the early '80s. Many Indian consumers still believed that motorcycles were more accident prone and less safe for Indian roads. The market had been largely carved among three Indian firms with various levels of old imported technology. It was against this backdrop that the Hero group sought to throw its hat into the ring as a means of consolidating its position in the two-wheeler market. Since it had a flourishing bicycle business and a fairly strong moped business as well, the Munjals felt that entering into a joint venture with a company that enjoyed a worldwide reputation would help them achieve their goal of dominating the two-wheeler market in India. It was indeed a golden opportunity for Mr. Brijmohan Lal Munjal to achieve the distinction of *"beating Bajaj,"* a seldom-vocalized desire that he had harbored.

The deal is done

The negotiations between HMC and the Hero group had by all accounts gone quite smoothly. Although there had been some lingering resentment that HMC had come to Hero as a last resort, Mr. Brijmohan Lal Munjal had tried to maintain the enthusiasm amongst the members of the Munjal family, emphasizing the benefits of the alliance they were about to enter. The negotiations culminated in an agreement that was signed in June 1984 creating a joint venture firm called Hero Honda Motors Ltd.

Honda agreed to provide technical know-how to HHM and assist in setting up manufacturing facilities. This included providing the design specifications and responsibility for future R&D efforts relating to the product lines that the company would offer. For these services, HHM agreed to pay Honda a lump-sum fee of $500,000 and a 4% royalty on the net ex-factory sale price of the product. Both partners held 26% of the equity with another 26% sold to the public and the rest held by financial institutions. HHM became a public company listed on the Bombay Stock Exchange (BSE).[2]

A 13-member board was formed to oversee the governance of the company. Honda had four key appointees including the Joint Managing Director, a particularly powerful position in Indian companies. The Hero group was represented by four family members and appointed the chairman of the company. Honda brought in its staff of technical experts to run the engineering and quality support functions. Hero brought in local talent to manage all other functions including marketing, finance, and HR. A seven-member top management team drawn almost exclusively from local ranks took charge of the daily operations of the venture. Both partners agreed to review the terms and relevance of the agreement in 1994 when the current joint venture arrangement would lapse. Time was short, and it was clear that HHM would have to act very quickly to build a foothold in the motorcycle business.

Rubber hits the road

The manufacturing plant which was established in Dharuhera in the state of Haryana started manufacturing the CD–100 model motorcycle in 1985. The CD–100 was powered by India's first four-stroke engine, the unique selling point that put Hero Honda in the driver's seat in the marketplace. Soon, the CD–100 set the standards for fuel efficiency, pollution control, and quality. Perhaps the most appealing characteristic of the CD–100 was its fuel efficiency (approximately 80 km/litre), an attribute highly valued by the Indian consumer. As the CD–100 was the only one with a four-stroke engine at the time, it became a runaway success. Interestingly, it was Mr. Munjal who persuaded HMC to launch the 100cc vehicle instead of the 70cc version that HMC had originally planned to offer. Given his long experience with the manufacture of bicycles and mopeds, he really understood the intricacies of the Indian marketplace very well. *"Our bicycle and moped manufacturing background gave us insights into the customer psyche that the running cost of the vehicle had to be low,"* he recalled in a press interview focusing on the rationale behind the CD–100. The organization had since spearheaded many "firsts" for the auto sector in India, being the first two-wheeler manufacturer to implement an ERP across the functions, and the first to implement initiatives such as six-sigma.

Under the stewardship of Mr. Munjal, HHM had grown consistently, earning the title of the world's largest motorcycle manufacturer after having churned out 1.3 million vehicles in 2001. Its motorcycle volumes nearly quadrupled during the period 1997–2001, a feat unparalleled in the Indian two-wheeler industry. While the motorcycle market grew at an average 21.74% per annum between 1997 and 2001, Hero Honda averaged a growth rate of 35.46% a year. In 2001–02, it again doubled volumes from 0.76 million in 1999–2000 to 1.3 million. However, there were several significant bumps on the road along the way.

The CD–100 had captivated the Indian consumer when it was first launched, but the uniqueness soon wore off. Exhibit C illustrates some of the product offerings from HHM. Competitors such as TVS-Suzuki and Bajaj-Kawasaki were introducing feature-rich models that were vying for the attention of customers. Many of these vehicles boasted comparable fuel efficiency and some were priced much lower than the CD–100. However, Mr. Munjal was boxed in by the relationship with HMC. His dependence on Honda for all product innovation inputs hobbled HHM's ability to respond to emerging changes in the market. Honda had decided to consolidate all its R&D activities worldwide in three countries, and India was not one of them. Therefore, Hero Honda was forced to wait its turn before getting any changes vetted by Honda's R&D. New product designs did not materialize as fast as the market demands dictated. It was quite difficult to sustain customer interest when all HHM could do was to release newer models that were only variations of the CD–100 platform. This was particularly costly for the company, since it did not have any new products, when competitors were releasing new products to ride the boom in demand from 1993 to 1996, when industry sales grew at a cumulative average rate of 31% per year.

HHM managed to dampen some of the negative impact of these years through astute marketing and by leveraging its knowledge of customers and markets. It had built an expansive network of dealers who were extremely loyal to the company. Much of this network was culled from Hero Group's bicycle operations. The company instituted modern programs and incentives to motivate its dealer network. The best dealers were chosen to visit the Japanese operations of Honda each year. They formed an extended family and HHM was perceived as being very supportive of its dealers. As of 2000, the company had close to 400 dealers across the country. It was this well-penetrated dealer network that allowed the firm to actively market its products in rural India, a

Exhibit C Some offerings from the Hero Honda stable

significant departure from other firms that concentrated solely on the urban market. The challenge of rural marketing would have been quite difficult without intimate knowledge of the dramatic differences, not only between the urban and rural consumer, but also the various shades of gray that differentiated rural consumers in one region from another.

The dealers were strongly supported through major advertising campaigns. HHM retained the best advertising agencies to execute its campaigns. Its *"fill it, shut it, forget it"* campaign promoting the maintenance-free nature of its motorcycles was a major hit with the Indian public. These campaigns also leveraged the Honda name to maximum advantage. Capitalizing on Honda's reputation for the quality of its engines, HHM ran advertisements that proclaimed, *"It is the Honda that makes it a Hero."* Exhibit D provides an illustration from this advertising campaign.

Hero Honda was among the first manufacturers to understand the impact of product differentiation and market segmentation on sales revenues. While

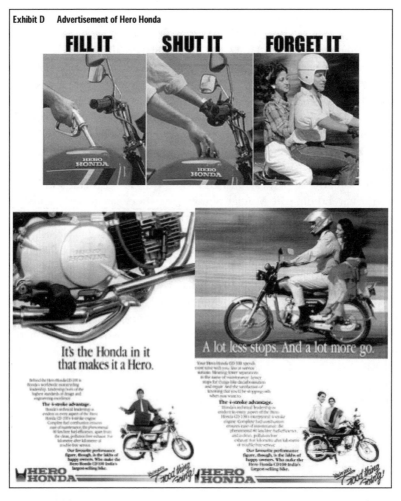

Exhibit D   Advertisement of Hero Honda

Exhibit D Advertisement of Hero Honda

the differentiated positioning brought price premiums, the customer got a much more fuel-efficient and reliable product in exchange. The mantra of fuel economy formed the core of all HHM's product launches. On a single platform (CD–100 series), it devised three models catering to different market segments. The CD–100 bike was an excellent pick for the rural and semi-urban customer for whom cost was critical consideration. The CD–100 SS was a basic model for the urban market. *Splendor* catered to the middle-class, office-going segment. Since all these products came from a single platform, product development costs were spread over higher volumes, and after-sales service quality was maintained, thereby reducing costs and increasing margins.

The influence of the Hero group was quite visible in the way the supply chain was organized at HHM. The company had built an extensive network of primary and secondary suppliers for components and subassemblies. Since the Indian government had stipulated that the joint venture must indigenize production within a fairly short period of time, developing the supplier network was deemed crucial. By 1996, over 95% of the motorcycle was manufactured from locally procured parts, a rate of localization that even Honda at times thought would be difficult to achieve. However, the Munjals realized that it was not only in the interests of the Indian government to indigenize but also in their own interests, since they would otherwise be held hostage to the rupee–yen exchange rate which had historically been unfavorable to Indian firms relying on imported components. The Munjal family had set up a range of firms to supply components, not just to HHM, but also to other buyers. These operations ranged from the manufacture of shock absorbers and wheel rims, to aluminum castings and plastic products. Munjal family interests ran seven of its crucial supplier firms. HMC had also helped established some of these ventures, and HHM had a controlling shareholding in Munjal Showa, for shock absorbers, and Sunbeam Castings and Munjal Castings, both of which supplied castings.

Honda did not seem to be concerned about the rate at which foreign sources were replaced with Indian suppliers. However, HHM shareholders had expressed some concerns. The preferred provider network of suppliers was filled with either Hero family companies or firms that were run by promoters who were closely aligned with Munjal family interests, and this posed a potential conflict of interest. Since HHM was a publicly traded company, it was felt that the profitability impact of outsourcing to allied firms would affect shareholder returns. The flip side of this sourcing approach was the reliability of the network and its ability to respond quickly to environmental change. There was very little inventory in process or waste due to supply chain bottlenecks, which resulted in better margins. Of course, this also ensured that many among the Munjal family were gainfully engaged.

Renegotiating the venture in 1994

As 1994 rolled around, the sentiments amongst the Munjal family were mixed but largely negative. Some felt that while Hero had ploughed a lot into making HHM a success, HMC had not contributed as much. There was a lack of new product innovation and much uncertainty surrounded the negotiations at that time. Even routine design changes were taking too long, and HMC's R&D engineers did not appear cooperative on this count at all. The impending negotiations paralyzed HHM, and it had to sit on the sidelines while its competitors roared past. Archrival Bajaj had introduced a new four-stroke engine for its motorcycle line and usurped the lead that HHM had carefully nurtured. In the meantime, HMC had negotiated new ventures with other Indian partners for manufacturing automobiles and power equipment. Mr. Munjal would have liked very much to have been part of the automobile venture, but did not allow this disappointment to color the relationship.

Perhaps in protecting its own destiny, Hero had been evaluating alternative product lines and market approaches right from 1986. It entered into a collaboration agreement with Steyr Daimler Puch, an Austrian subsidiary of Daimler A.G., to manufacture motorcycles in the 50cc–65cc range. This business was organized under the Hero Motors banner and targeted both Indian and foreign markets. Hero Motors was successful in exporting completely knocked-down (CKD) kits for assembly in Spain, Iran, Mauritius, Vietnam, Bangladesh, and Egypt. Bolstered by these initial successes, Hero Motors even entered into discussions with BMW of Germany to manufacture 650cc bikes. Although these talks eventually fizzled out, they could hardly have inspired any trust or confidence at Honda headquarters.

It was 1995 by the time the joint venture agreement was renegotiated and extended until 2004. HHM was able to negotiate far more attractive terms from HMC with respect to royalties. They were able to persuade HMC to accept a paltry Rs. 200 per vehicle in 1995. Licenses to manufacture future models were dealt with on a case-by-case basis using a mix of lump sum payments and royalties. By 1999, the proportion of royalty payments to sales revenues had declined considerably from a high of 4% at founding to about 0.5%. Honda displayed new willingness to share its R&D and product suites in a more timely fashion. Subsequent to the 1995 contract renewal, Honda licensed HHM to manufacture *Street*, a model that was based on Honda's recent global hit called the *Dream*, which had sold over 25 million worldwide. In addition to the reduced royalties and fast-track transfer of technology, HMC agreed to increase the extent of components and subassemblies purchased from Hero's supplier network.

With the emergence of significant competition from similarly positioned offerings from Bajaj and TVS-Suzuki, Hero Honda had become more aggressive in terms of its marketing with new product launches and market segmentation. The company had announced new product launches (two every year) to continue this effort. This phenomenal rate of new product introductions was, of course, solely dependent on HMC's continuing its R&D support, since HHM had not explored setting up R&D facilities in India. HHM had also undertaken significant expansion of its distribution network.

The going was good for HHM, and the financial results followed. The company had reported flawless quarter-on-quarter growth for 18 consecutive quarters between 1997 and 2001. Hero Honda's quarterly sales during the period grew 303.28% and its net profit jumped from Rs. 16.28 crore[3] to Rs. 98.34 crore. HHM hardly required any incremental working capital over the seven-year period following the renegotiation. In fact, its working capital was lower in 2001 than in 1994 by Rs. 1160m, despite sales having grown by approximately 7X during this period. Return on average capital employed (ROACE) at 65% was among the highest in the country. Hero Honda was among the few Indian companies that enjoyed the distinction of generating a positive economic spread for an extended period of time. Between 1995 and 2001, the economic spread (difference between WACC and ROIC) expanded from 16.5% to 65.4%. This performance had not been lost on the investors who helped the share rise among the ranks of established blue chips. Exhibit E charts the performance of HHM shares. However, just as things appeared to be set for a smooth sailing, storm clouds appeared.

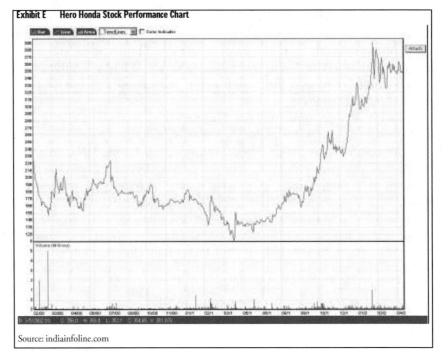

Exhibit E   Hero Honda stock performance chart
Source: indiainfoline.com

Storm clouds and silver linings

Competition began to intensify in the late '90s as many of the foreign joint ventures in the Indian motorcycle industry reached maturity. Players such as Kawasaki and Yamaha were helping their local companies mount a credible assault on Hero Honda. Closer to home, HHM partner HMC was forced to dissolve Kinetic Honda Ltd., the venture it set up with Kinetic Engineering to manufacture scooters. This left a void in HMC's product suite in India and it was poised to enter the scooter market on its own. Both of these developments were cause for significant alarm.

The competition revs up

The competitors for HHM were Kawasaki-Bajaj, TVS-Suzuki, and Yamaha Motors, a familiar bevy of powerhouses from Japan. Table 1 shows the key competitors by two-wheeler category in the Indian marketplace. Refer to Exhibit F for recent sales and production figures for these players in the two-wheeler market.

Table 1

Subsegment	Major Players
Motorcycles	Hero Honda, Bajaj Auto, Yamaha Motors Escorts, TVS-Suzuki, Eicher
Scooters	Bajaj Auto, LML, Kinetic Motor Co., Maharastra Scooters, TVS-Suzuki
Mopeds	TVS-Suzuki, Kinetic Engineering, Majestic Auto, Bajaj Auto

Exhibit F Comparative sales and production figures for two-wheeler manufacturers

Two-Wheelers (April 2001 to February 2002)

	Production		Sales	
	Number	% Change	Number	% Change
Motorcycles	2,666,456	33.7	2,650,822	36.4
Hero Honda	1,288,933	37.7	1,289,838	38.3
Bajaj Auto	654,051	29.2	649,920	32.9
TVS Motor Co.	399,151	20.0	395,494	22.8
Yamaha Motor	212,954	29.6	210,568	40.0
LML	40,380	15.6	42,115	44.6
Kinetic Engg	48,992		40,937	
Eicher	21,995	10.6	21,950	11.7
Scooters	808,185	0.5	808,768	−1.6
Bajaj Auto	347,997	10.0	347,785	7.0
TVS Motor Co.	136,070	2.3	135,432	1.8
LML	119,163	−24.6	121,857	−23.3
Kinetic Motor Co.	103,253	−7.8	103,292	−10.7
Mah Scooters	54,532	−35.9	53,601	−39.8
Honda Motorcycle	47,170		46,801	
Mopeds	454,680	−29.2	451,784	−28.8
TVS Motor Co.	246,317	−28.6	247,136	−27.6
Kinetic Engg	96,606	−31.8	91,467	−32.5
Majestic Auto	75,997	−23.7	77,014	−24.3
Bajaj Auto	35,760	−36.4	36,167	−35.2

Bajaj Auto

Bajaj Auto Limited was one of India's largest two- and three-wheeler (three-wheelers, also known as auto-rickshaws, are unique to the South Asian region) manufacturer. The Bajaj group came into existence in 1945 and got a start by importing scooters and three-wheelers from Italy for sale in India. In 1960, it struck a technical know-how agreement with Piaggio of Italy, and the company became a public corporation the same year. Scooter production commenced in 1961 and three-wheeler production was followed in 1962. The Piaggio collaboration expired in 1991. Since then, the company's scooters and three-wheelers were sold under the brand name of Bajaj. As of 2001, Bajaj had become a market leader in scooters with annual production in excess of 1.34 million units. It offered products in all segments such as mopeds, scooters, motorcycles, and three-wheelers.

Subsequent to the opening up of the two-wheeler sector to foreign technology and equity participation in the mid '80s, Bajaj Auto entered into a technical collaboration agreement with Kawasaki of Japan. It started production of Kawasaki 100cc motorcycles in 1986. Bajaj became a key manufacturing base for Kawasaki and accounted for 60% of the latter's global sales. The company had chalked out a strategy for co-existence with Kawasaki, wherein Bajaj would concentrate on developing products in the price range of Rs 30,000–60,000 and Kawasaki would offer a wider choice of products priced from Rs 35,000 up to Rs 250,000. Though the company planned to introduce some high-tech motorcycles from the Kawasaki range, it was fighting an uphill battle trying to shed its image of a "screwdriver" company (assembler as opposed to manufacturer) by developing its own range of motorcycles.

TVS-Suzuki

A leading producer of automotive components, the TVS group was formed as a transport company in 1911. Originally incorporated in 1982 as Indian Motorcycles Pvt. Ltd. to produce motorcycles in collaboration with Suzuki, Japan, the company later went public under the banner Ind-Suzuki Motorcycles Limited, which was later renamed TVS-Suzuki Limited. The perfect blend between the best design engineers and the latest technology made TVS-Suzuki one of the leading two-wheeler manufacturersin the country.

However, the relationship between Suzuki and TVS was far from amicable. A divorce was on the cards for nearly a decade. In August 2001, TVS bought out the 25.97% stake of the Japanese partner in August 2001, increasing its equity holding to 32%. The parting also meant that Suzuki would not be allowed to enter India for a 30-month period. The decision to buy out Suzuki was prompted by the fact that the partners felt it was in their own long-term interests to pursue their own interests separately rather than through the joint venture.

The TVS Group wanted to promote the TVS brand, grow their revenues, and develop products indigenously. Further, they wanted to export TVS-made vehicles to the rest of the world, a proposition Suzuki Motors opposed. From Suzuki's point of view, its contribution to the joint venture was shrinking. With the exception of the two-stroke Suzuki Max 100R, an evolution of the original Ind-Suzuki, none of the company's fast-selling two-wheelers had a major Suzuki contribution. TVS-Suzuki's bread-and-butter product, the moped, was fully Indian. The hugely successful *TVS Scooty* was also a non-Suzuki product. It was only in two-stroke motorbikes that TVS-Suzuki had to rely on the Japanese parent. However, with the decline of two-stroke motorcycles in India, and with the recent launch of the all-Indian *TVS Victor*, it was clear that the Indian partner could do without the Japanese collaborator.

As per the terms of the joint venture agreement, there was to be a 30-month licensing arrangement, during which time the joint venture would continue to pay royalty to Suzuki. After this period, TVS was free to sell the four licensed vehicles (*Samurai, Max 100, Max 100R,* and *Fiero*) as TVS vehicles. As it turned out, TVS had localized production ahead of schedule and voted to terminate the agreement before the 30-month period could lapse.

Escorts-Yamaha (EYML)

EYML was a joint venture between Escorts Ltd., the flagship company of the Escorts Group, and the global giant, Yamaha Motors Co. Ltd. of Japan. Ever since signing the first technical assistance agreement between the two companies in 1985, Yamaha Motor Company Limited (YMC) and Escorts Limited had built a cooperative relationship dedicated to the manufacture and sales of Yamaha-brand motorcycles. In November 1995, the two companies established the joint venture company, Escorts Yamaha Motors Limited, based on a 50–50 capital investment. In June 2000, that investment ratio was changed to 74% for YMC and 26% for Escorts Limited, and YMC assumed managerial control of the company with the name being changed to Yamaha Motors Escorts Limited (YMEL). It then undertook numerous measures to build the company's motorcycle manufacturing and marketing operations. In June 2001, an agreement was reached between YMC and Escorts Ltd. under which YMC acquired the remaining 26% of the stock held by Escorts. The stated aims of this move to make YMEL a 100% YMC subsidiary were to increase the overall speed of managerial and business decisions, to improve product development capabilities and production efficiency, while also strengthening the marketing organization.

Kinetic Honda Ltd.

Kinetic Engineering Ltd. (KEL), one of the leading manufacturers and exporters of two- wheelers for over 20 years, came into existence in 1970. It manufactured scooters, motorcycles, and mopeds that were all well known for their fuel economy and quality. KEL was the beneficiary of Honda's advances when the Japanese company first came to India shopping for partners. They set up a 50–50 joint venture called Kinetic Honda Ltd. (KHL) to manufacture and market scooters. Unfortunately, the terms of the agreement specified that KHL could not enter the motorcycle business. KHL seemed to be doing an excellent job in cornering the market and was within striking distance of a leadership spot in the race for market share. When the two-wheeler business began to boom in the early 1990s, Honda wanted to take charge, an idea that was welcomed by the Indian partner. KEL felt that such a move might motivate Honda to bring in new products more quickly to India. Strangely, Honda began to lose interest in the venture and decided to turn off the spigot, putting the brakes on R&D spending, which was a paltry 0.31% of sales when Indian competitors were spending 1.5%. It also decelerated its advertising spending significantly when the competition was blitzing the consumer with new campaigns. All these actions hurt the sustainability of the company, and soon the personal relationship started to sour and culminated in a KEL buyout of Honda's interests. This effectively released Honda to pursue its own agenda in the scooters segment.

Other challengers

In addition to domestic competition, another competitive threat took shape in the form of cheap Chinese imports when import restrictions were lifted in 2001. A relatively unknown company named Monto Motors in Alwar (Rajasthan[4]) was the first to import Semi-Knocked-Down (SKD) kits from one of the top motorcycle manufacturers in China. A 72cc motorbike from China cost the customer Rs. 27,000 on road, a 125cc would cost Rs. 33,000, and a 250cc motorbike would cost Rs. 36,000. The Indian models seemed frightfully expensive in comparison. In early 2002, a moped cost around Rs. 22,000, a 100cc motorbike cost around Rs. 45,000, and a 125cc motorcycle cost around Rs. 50,000. The domestic two-wheeler industry was bound to feel the pinch, especially in the mid and lower price segments of the motorcycle, scooter, and moped segments.

The other shoe drops

HMC, having extricated itself from the KHL venture, announced plans to set up a new company, Honda Motor Scooters India Ltd., for the sole purpose of manufacturing scooters for the Indian market. At that time, it also announced that it intended to enter the motorcycle market in 2004, ominously the very year when the HHM joint venture agreement would come up for its next revalidation. This announcement shocked the top brass at Hero Group. Mr. Munjal put on a brave face and announced that Honda had made its plans public only after Hero signed off on its plans. This led to further speculation as to why Mr. Munjal would give his blessings to a venture that would place the destiny of HHM in peril.

HMSI was indeed a troubling development for the Munjal family and the shareholders of HHM. However, Mr. Munjal was looking for the silver lining in what was apparently a huge storm cloud brewing. He announced that HHM had negotiated three key concessions from Honda. First, Honda agreed to delay entry into the motorcycles segment until 2004. It also agreed to form a four-person committee with two members from HHM to examine any new motorcycles that it would release post-2004. Lastly, it offered an opportunity to HHM to share in the equity as a minority holder in HMSI. These assurances were followed by a visit by Mr. Yoshino, the CEO of Honda from Japan, for the launch of Honda's first scooter in India. At the launch ceremony, he addressed the simmering problems that were perceived by HHM and its investors. He observed, "*By 2003 the two companies will together be selling 25% of the world's projected seven million market for two-wheelers.*"[5] The President and CEO of HMSI, Mr. Takiguchi painted a similar scenario in his interview with a leading news magazine. He said, "*The discussion in 2004 will not be on whether to continue with the joint venture. We will sit and discuss about the products which both the companies—Hero Honda and HMSI—should build on.*"[6] However, in the same breath, he also observed, "*Our strategy will be to offer motorcycles which keep up with the overall market trend in the post–2004 scenario.*"[7] It was anybody's guess what that statement truly meant.

Honda was already bolstering its dealership network and had plans to set up over a 100 dealerships by the end of 2002. It was also spending Rs. 1 billion to set up a manufacturing plant that would double HMSI's existing capacity.[8] Given the rate of growth of scooters that was in the 4% range, it was difficult to imagine how Honda would be able to use the capacity effectively without stepping onto HHM's turf. Mr. Munjal seemed to be reassured about the situation, however. After Mr. Yoshino's visit, he proclaimed, "*His visit has made a lot of difference to the outlook at Hero Honda.*"[9]

Are there road hazards ahead?

Mr. Munjal sifted through the various options he had in front of him. While the investors were sated with the flurry of announcements and reassurances for now, what would the future hold for HHM? How should the company arm itself for the post-2004 marketplace? How would the competitors, especially the Japanese companies, respond to the uncertainties that faced HHM? What if HMSI, despite all its assurances, saw the potential marketplace in 2004 and decides to push HHM to the periphery and engineer a frontal assault on the motorcycle business? Would HMC go back to its old ways of withholding R&D now that it had plans to make motorcycles in India post-2004? The joint venture had been in existence for a very long period of time by international standards. Perhaps its time had come. Would HHM have to be dismantled in the same way its competitors in India had been? These were troubling questions, but nevertheless very critical ones. Charting the future strategy of HHM would undoubtedly require clear answers to all these questions. These were indeed the best of times and the worst of times for HHM.

Bibliography

http://www.herohonda.com/web/index.htm
www.yamaha-motor.co.jp
http://www.indiainfoline.com
www.securities.com
http://www.expressindia.com/ie/daily/19980823/23550444.html
http://www.businessworldindia.com/archive/7Jan99/corpo3(1420).html
Transcript of interview with Ms. Sulajja Firodia Motwani, Joint Managing Director of Kinetic Engineering, February 22, 2002
Business World, January 28, 2002
Report on TVS Motor Company Limited—ICICI Securities, January 18, 2002

Business Line, Sunday, Sept 30, 2001
Business Line (International Edition), Tuesday, June 19, 2001
Reports on Hero Honda Motors Limited:
HSBC, March 28, 2002
HSBC, September 21, 2001
Merrill Lynch, June 20, 2001
CSFB (Hong Kong), July 6, 2000
Probity, December 16, 1998
Dresdner Kleinwort Benson Research, May 8, 1998
Morgan Stanley, May 31, 1996
Reports on Automotive Sector in India
LKP Shares & Securities Limited, February 2002
Scope Marketing, September 2001

Notes

1   Two-wheelers include all motorized vehicles using a two-wheel chassis (e.g., motorcycles, scooters, and mopeds).
2   Bombay Stock Exchange is one of the two biggest stock exchanges in India. http://www.bseindia.com
3   1 Crore = 10 million
4   Rajasthan is one of the states in West India.
5   *Business Standard*, Entrepreneur of the Year issue, 2001.
6   Hindu, *Businessline*, June 19, 2001.
7   Ibid.
8   moneycentral.com, July 25, 2002.
9   *Business Standard*, Entrepreneur of the Year issue, 2001.

Chapter 7

Strategic crossroads at Matáv

Hungary's telecommunications powerhouse

Introduction

IN SEPTEMBER 2004, FOUR months after Hungary had joined the European Union, the strategy group at Matáv—Hungary's largest communications company—was working on the mid-term strategic plan.

Since being privatized from the state in 1993, the company had seen several changes in its strategy, structure and culture. Nearly 15 years later, the company was a fully integrated telecommunications company involved in a broad range

Jordan Mitchell prepared this case under the supervision of Professor Paul Rouse solely to provide material for class discussion. The authors do not intend to illustrate either effective or ineffective handling of a managerial situation. The authors may have disguised certain names and other identifying information to protect confidentiality.

IVEY

Richard Ivey School of Business
The University of Western Ontario

of services including fixed line telephony, mobile communications, Internet services, data transmission and outsourcing.

In 2000, Matáv's management had convinced its parent, Deutsche Telekom, to allow Matáv to expand internationally by buying up the majority share of Makedonski Telekomunikacci (MakTel), Macedonia's state-run telecommunications company. By September 2004, the acquisition of MakTel was considered to be a success. Matáv's management believed that international expansion was necessary to realize dynamic growth as its domestic fixed line business was declining. As well, Hungary's mobile market was highly competitive and saturated, with 80 per cent of the country having a mobile phone. While there were opportunities to grow the Hungarian Internet and broadband market, Matáv was looking to the Balkans and specifically the small country of Montenegro for its second international acquisition.

Matáv had a strong financial position with positive cash flow and had taken steps to reduce its net debt ratio to 31.6 per cent from 46.6 per cent two years earlier. Matáv's strategy group, led by 32-year-old András Balogh, felt that Matáv was at a strategic crossroads with three main options: expansion in Hungary, regional expansion or focusing on organic growth in existing product lines. Balogh and his team had to consider all the lines of business in developing a strategy for the next three years. In forming the plan, Balogh had to consider the role of Matáv within Deutsche Telekom and whether Matáv's resources and organization were suitable for a healthy future. Balogh commented:

> It's about the making the right strategic choices in a declining industry. When you look at the market and you look at our performance, everything seems OK. So why change? It's when you see the dark times are coming—you have to decide what you want to do to protect against it.

History of Matáv

In 1989, the government of Hungary separated Magyar Posta (Hungarian Post) into three divisions: postal, broadcasting and telecommunications. For four years, the government operated the telecommunications arm as Matáv (short form for Magyar Távközlési Rt.), and in 1993, they initiated the first round of privatization permitting the consortium MagyarCom, a joint venture between Deutsche Telekom and Ameritech International, to purchase 30 per cent of the company for US$875 million. In the two subsequent privatization rounds, the government sold off the entire company (save one golden voting share), with MagyarCom retaining controlling interest and shares being traded on the Budapest and New York Stock Exchange. Later, Deutsche Telekom took over majority ownership with 59.5 per cent interest in Matáv. The privatization was the biggest in Central Europe, and Matáv was the first company from Eastern Europe to list in the United States.

In making the transition, Matáv changed its focus from an inefficient government agency behemoth to an efficient customer-oriented organization. As of

1990, the company had a waiting list of 600,000 people for fixed telephone lines; some waiting 10 to 12 years for a phone line. Klára Armuth, director of the business portfolio management branch recalled the early days:

> We wanted to learn the best in class in Europe. Everyone was pretty enthusiastic, and people wanted to do things in new ways. The government said, "We cannot give you any resources." So, that made it clear that it would go through privatization. [The challenge was] to build the infrastructure. And, we had two main choices. We could go with the "island" or the "overlay" strategy. The island was build everything and the overlay, which was the one we eventually chose, was first build it as a backbone and work step by step. By 1997, we no longer had a waiting list.

János Szitás, a director in the strategic planning department who had joined Hungarian Post in 1965, talked about how Matáv changed:

> In early 1990, I saw the problem—lack of money. The government was inviting different investments. But Hungarian Post was not too attractive. However, the Telecom was very attractive to foreign investors. There are a lot of differences compared with today. Before privatization, we did not deal with the customer. We did not deal with the organization. Now we try to match the organization to the customer. We had terrible network quality. We put fibre-optic cables in the local network, and the quality improved immediately. The other important factor was the experience of the new owners, Deutsche Telekom and Ameritech. They gave us experience from the customer side and technical expertise. There were 30 to 40 expats that came from Germany to help with the network development and network reconstruction. [The company's culture changed to] customer orientation.

With 80 per cent of the country's fixed line telephone system, Matáv practically had a monopoly in Hungary; however, there were four other incumbents such as the Hungarian Telephone and Cable Company (HTCC) as well as Monortel, Emitel and Invitel, who operated fixed lines in the remaining 20 per cent of the country. In 2001, the Hungarian government introduced a new telecommunications act, which allowed for greater competition and for other companies to resell time on fixed lines.

The government had also been involved in a decision to increase competition in the cable TV market by blocking Matáv's attempt to gain more market share. Klára Armuth recalled the government's involvement in the cable TV decision:

> In 2001, the government saw that the cable market was being dominated by us, and they don't like it when any company starts owning too much. In 2001, the government made the amendment, and they wanted to promote other competition. It was binding this to ownership, and there was a limit to the amendment to 2004. So, as of the

1st of January in 2004, we're able to compete in cable. Really this
move by the government only helped one company, which was UPC.
Everyone knew that. The other companies couldn't really grow. But
UPC became big.

New competition came in the form of several well-established international
powerhouses such as KPN Telecom who had a majority holding in Pantel, a fixed
line and Internet and cable operator; TeleNor from Norway who established the
mobile operator Pannon GSM; and, British leader Vodafone who entered into
the growing Hungarian mobile market as well. In fact, Matáv lost its first
important government contract to Pantel to deliver information technology (IT)
services to Hungarian Post (the same organization from which Matáv had been
born) in late 1999, emphasizing that old government ties did not translate to
winning contracts.

With a relatively short history of being a publicly traded company themselves, executives of Matáv took the opportunity to make their first foray into an
international market in 2000. Matáv became the majority shareholders in a
consortium that bought 51 per cent of Macedonia's state-run enterprise—
MakTel. The remaining 49 per cent was controlled by the Macedonian government. Exhibit 1 shows Matav's key operating statistics.

Matáv's majority shareholder: Deutsche Telekom

With €55.9 billion in revenues and €3.4 billion in operating income, Deutsche
Telekom headquartered in Bonn, Germany, was one of Europe's largest tele-
communication companies. The company, which was 36 per cent owned by the
German government, was involved in the entire gamut of telecommunications
services including fixed-line services, mobile telephony through its subsidiary
T-Mobile, Internet services and a whole range of other communications
services. Exhibit 2 displays Deutsche Telekom's financials and Exhibit 3 shows
Matáv's financials.

Deutsche Telekom had been actively involved in the transformation of
Eastern and Central Europe by purchasing three fully integrated telecommunications companies, which included Slovakia Telecom, Croatia Telecom and Matáv
in Hungary. One article from a telcom industry magazine discussed the role of
Eastern European telecos in Deutsche Tekekom's portfolio:

> In the 1990s, many operators, including Deutsche Telekom, Vodafone
> Group PLC and France Telecom SA, established a presence in the
> region, but it was never a strategic focus. The investments were made
> for a simple reason: They were inexpensive and Western incumbents
> had more cash than they knew what to do with. But as Western
> markets become increasingly competitive and saturated, Deutsche
> Telekom, Europe's largest operator by revenue, and its peers are
> taking a second look at the East. Overall, however, its holdings form
> more of a hodgepodge than a tight network, something management

is intent on changing. At a shareholders meeting in May [of 2004], Chief Executive Kai-Uwe Ricke said he was going to put a "special focus" on Eastern Europe.[1]

Matáv products and services

Matáv has four lines of businesses: business services, residential services, Internet and mobile. Exhibit 4 shows Matav's revenue by division and Exhibit 5 shows a selection of advertisements for each of their key services.

In business services, Matáv has 61 per cent market share supplying a full range of communications including leased lines, network integration, Internet Protocol (IP) products, system integration, info communication solutions and IT and telecommunications outsourcing. The company had introduced six specific packages for solutions developed for security, shared Internet, customer relations, remote access purposes and software for the convergence of telecommunications and IT in the hotel and commercial sectors. The company's outsourcing was mostly focused on the operation of one subsidiary called Rába Szolgáltatóház, which it bought in 2003 to service the automotive part maker Rába Automotive Holdings.

In its residential services business line, Matáv had 81 per cent of the market with 2.9 million fixed lines of which 18.3 per cent is digital (ISDN). The company had introduced what it believed to be innovative pricing with 1.4 million customers using fixed tariff packages. These tariff packages allow free local calls during certain times[2] as well as a program that allowed half the monthly subscription fee to be applied to local or long distance phone calls. Under its residential services, Matáv also launched an Open Internet service in 2003, which permitted users to log on to the Internet paying for the cost of a local phone call per minute.

Matáv's Internet division was called Axelero and had nearly 300,000 subscribers with 44 per cent of the Hungarian market. Axelero was an Internet Service Provider (ISP) that served residential, business and online content markets. The division had realized superb growth in the last three years, growing at an annual average of over 40 per cent. The company set up one the country's leading portals called "origo.hu," which boasted 10 million page impressions per day.

Matáv's mobile business had been under the name Westel until it was changed to T-Mobile, a name consistent with Deutsche Telekom's mobile service in Germany and other countries. T-Mobile Hungary, owned by Matáv, had 47 per cent market share with 3.8 million customers, which represented a 10 per cent increase over the prior year. The company's mobile division had won a number of awards, being heralded for its consistent performance of revenue growth, return on investment, after-tax profits as well as a place for university graduates to seek employment.

Strategy

"We are an integrated telco and Deutsche Telekom wants us to remain as one because that is suitable for a small country like Hungary," explained András Balogh. By being the country's sole integrated telecommunications company, Matáv was involved in all the major telecommunications and communications sectors in the country. While this provided synergies across divisions, it also produced difficult strategic choices. In 2001, the company made the decision to restructure into four business areas to provide focus and dedicated management teams for business services, residential services, Internet and mobile. Péter Koncz, a senior project manager in the group planning division who had joined Matáv during the restructuring, expressed his view: "There may have been another alternative, which was to put fixed line and Internet together. It may not be best to separate them."

Matáv paints its strategy with the backdrop of the overall worldwide telecom industry classifying time periods into four main times: "euphoria" (1998–2000); "disappointment" (2001–2002); "retrenchment" (2003–2004); and, "sustainable growth" (2005 and beyond). The strategy group of Matáv believed that they were in the "retrenchment" period with the key initiatives being the competitive response to the core customer base, consolidating financial performance, maximizing productivity, building on available and existing growth opportunities like broadband and preparing for future growth opportunities.

The company used several measures to evaluate its progress along its strategy with key measurements being revenue growth, EBITDA and Economic Value Added (EVA). Balogh assessed the measures for the appropriateness of the telecom industry:

> With the traditional fixed line business the margins are quite good. But the margins are dropping and the costs of the teleco aren't dropping. One of the key measures we use in the telecommunications business is the EBITDA because there is such a large fixed cost base. EVA is a bit difficult. You may have some assets that are in the ground for over 100 years. So, we use EBITDA and that's about 35 per cent. It's a better and more important measure for us than even net income.

Business units

Within each business unit, the company focused on other measures, which gauged the relative performance against the industry. For example, the key measurement in the fixed line business was the number of fixed telephone lines per fixed-line full-time telephone employee. Matáv's measurement lagged behind other European best-in-class integrated telecom companies (who averaged 500 fixed lines per fixed line employee) with a measure of 353 fixed lines per fixed line employee. The other key measures in the fixed line business were the number of minutes per month at about 220 minutes and the fixed line ARPU (average revenue per user) at 30 euros per month. One of the key trends that Matáv's planning group recognized was the continuing fixed-mobile substitution. Péter Koncz commented:

> One challenge is the customers: the fixed mobile substitution as well as the corporate customers. Teleco experts talk about corporate customers wanting to rationalize what they spend on communications. Plus, all the new entrants are fighting on price.

In the mobile business, key measurements were ARPU and minutes of usage. Approximately 80 per cent of the users purchased prepaid minutes while the remaining mobile users had a contract with an operator. Klára Armuth talked about the challenges in competing in the mobile sector:

> With putting in the bid for UMTS (third generation mobile infrastructure) licence, there is no sound business case. But, we also know that if we don't do it, it could be dangerous in the future. So, we bid, licence, and we don't necessarily see the market being ready yet for the technology. We looked at the scenarios if we can win and if we can't win the licence and, looking 10 years down the road, it's a lot worse if we can't win the licence. But, at what price, we don't know. Vodafone and Pannon GSM are also bidding. But the real problem is if there's a new entrant. There are currently three operators. If they give a licence to a fourth, that's not something we would like to see. I don't see a lot of reason for it or why they would. In Hungary, we have about 80 per cent penetration, so there is not a lot of room for that many new subscribers.

In the Internet area, the key measurements were the number of subscribers and ARPU. While Matáv had realized growth of over 40 per cent in the past two years, many Hungarians did not have computers at home. Éva Somorjai, Matáv's human resource director, explained:

> The main issue is that people can't afford computers. The government has a program that subsidizes computers, so you can get one for about €400 to €500. But the average salary is around €370 per month. Matáv pays more than that. But, for the majority of people, you save for one year to get a computer and at the end of the time, the government will give you €120 towards it. But, you still need to save the money in the first place. [To compare to monthly rent,] a small flat [apartment] would be around €250 on the outside of town. A decent flat would cost about €350, but that's not a house. And the savings they have is from their gross salary . . . so buying a computer is not necessarily a high priority.

An investment analyst from JP Morgan saw Matáv's largest opportunity to reside in broadband subscriptions:

We estimate that Hungary's current broadband penetration is extremely low at only two per cent of population, though slightly higher than the one per cent in Poland and the Czech Republic. We estimate that as prices of PCs and ADSL come down, broadband subscriptions will accelerate. Moreover, we estimate that initiatives taken by the Hungarian government will also stimulate broadband growth. For example, the government offers tax incentives for purchases of PC and ADSL subscriptions. We are projecting that Hungary can reach a broadband penetration of nine per cent by 2010, and we estimate that ADSL revenues can go from four per cent today to making up 12 per cent of fixed revenue by 2010.[3]

Competition

Matáv faced increasing competition in all its business sectors, either through established companies or new entrants. Exhibit 6 shows a list of the competitors in each segment and their relative positioning.

In the fixed line business, Matáv faced off against four other companies including HTCC with eight per cent, Monortel with six per cent, Invitel with three per cent and Emitel with three per cent. Matáv had recently purchased the holdings of Emitel.

In the mobile segment, Matáv controlled 47 per cent of the market fought against Pannon GSM with 37 per cent (owned by TeleNor from Norway) and the British giant, Vodafone with 16 per cent. András Balogh assessed the mobile competitive field:

> There's a great deal of competition between fixed and mobile services now. Vodafone entered the market late, which is why they have such a low percentage. It's usual that they are the first or second in all the markets they are in. But, in order to get new subscribers, they are targeting younger people. They also started a price war. It led to a situation where the mobile premium is extremely low. And, Pannon GSM was not differentiating themselves, so they decided to become the lowest cost operator. There's a negative price spiral and more or less saturation in the market. There's promise of the third generation of mobiles and what that will do.

Péter Koncz commented on Matáv's approach to price wars in the mobile arena: "T-Mobile is very clear that we will follow them in the price war. So, we are saying, 'Look guys, we don't agree with what you're doing, but we will match your prices.' In one and a half years, they have halved the cost of having a mobile." Koncz went on to assess the key competitive actions at a macro level:

> For me the biggest threats are those that are getting more active in the corporate segment like Tele2 or Monortel. In Internet, Pantel owned by KPN from Holland is doing quite well. Pantel is getting really

active in the corporate segment—HTCC is taking over Pantel however. And, this gives them the business. They can be active now in corporate and residential. And, in mobile, the most important is Vodafone. But also you have Tele2 from Sweden, who are resellers. They get the time from Matáv and resell through pre-sales. I also think UPC from Holland, owned by UGC is very important with cable TV—they offer Internet and they're in a test phase, also using their cable for voice transmissions. So there would be no need to use the fixed line. Since they are in Internet, they can offer this.

The Macedonian experience: MakTel

After winning the bid to buy the controlling interest of MakTel through a consortium called Stonebridge (which was owned by Matáv and two other minority partners) in early 2001, Matáv executives had their work cut out for them. Matáv had done extensive due diligence before the purchase. There were 10 key criteria that Matáv considered, which included: country risk, market size, market growth, no conflict with Deutsche Telekom, attractiveness of the business model, restructuring potential, revenue, market share, regulatory risk and EBITDA non-dilution. Matáv saw a good regulatory environment with four-year exclusivity on local, long distance and international services in the fixed line business as well as permission to rebalance[4] the pricing on fixed lines. Matáv also saw a good strategic opportunity as penetration in all of the key segments was low—25 per cent of the country had fixed telephone lines, five per cent had mobiles and under one per cent had Internet.

Some of the key tasks were to install key account management, rebalance the pricing of the fixed line business and work to compete more aggressively in the mobile segment as the competition on the mobile market had been continuously intensifying since the Greek mobile operator, Cosmofon, entered the market as a second player in 2003.

The consortium of which Matáv was a majority shareholder had purchased 51 per cent of MakTel for €343 million and had made capital expenditure investments of over €100 million since 2001. The company had instilled a market-oriented doctrine and had trained local staff. It successfully transferred its knowledge of a financial control system, professional regulatory management and tariff packages to rebalance fixed line fees. MakTel's revenues had grown from €201 million in 2000 to €277 million in 2003, with EBITDA moving from €82 million to €157 million in the same period. MakTel increased the number of fixed lines by 21 per cent from 2000 to 2003 and mobile subscribers were five times higher in 2003 than in 2000. MakTel was the biggest employer in Macedonia and accounted for eight per cent of the country's GDP and five per cent of the country's tax revenues. Exhibit 7 shows MakTel's performance.

Éva Somorjai reflected on the main issues of purchasing MakTel:

The language was an issue—also a lack of experience in management—they were about 15 to 20 years behind us in infrastructure. So that meant that we had an investment in capital expenditures and, at the beginning, it was impossible to lay off people. After four years, we have a changed workforce; we have to train them. We also had to start the mobile business there and a complete reform of the fixed line business. We had to train and show them best practices.

With over 36 per cent unemployment, the country of Macedonia presents several challenges. Tamás Morvai, director of business development and mergers and acquisitions, talked about MakTel's business as well as the country's challenges:

In the mobile arena in Macedonia, MakTel hasn't really reached saturation yet. They've been seeing growth of 20 to 30 per cent per year and that's what they know. They know very little about being in a situation of saturation. In my opinion, I do not see there being great growth necessarily with 3G. I see it remaining mostly voice. On top of these industry challenges, there's the country. For instance, right after Matav made the investment, there was a small civil war. Last year the president of Macedonia died. I actually went to the funeral and, since his death, there have been three different presidents. The country is pretty stagnant as far as GDP growth. MakTel is also the country's largest employer. There's not been a lot of foreign investment, and it's not really growing. So we're definitely pioneers there in the way we operate.

Klára Armuth talked about MakTel:

MakTel was a possibility to show Deutsche Telekom that we were capable. Deutsche Telekom is a huge company and, like many other big companies, they want to be global. And they see the Balkans as an opportunity. However, they don't want to be there directly. They accept that Matáv will work in that region. Obviously if they wanted, they could do it. They're a huge company with many resources. But it's more efficient to go through Matáv. Realistically, the salaries of Hungarians are much less than Germans. I think, as well, we may understand the area better.

Other international expansion: Montenegro and the Balkans

"We're searching. We've made our intent in Montenegro public, so I expect that in 2005, we could make a foreign acquisition. We're also looking at the southeastern regions of Europe such as Bulgaria, Romania and Serbia," stated Elek Straub, Matáv's chairman and chief executive officer (CEO).

Matáv's management was keen to expand through the Balkan region. The second expansion target was the government's sale of Montenegro Telecom (TCG). Montenegro was a country of 800,000 people situated to the west of

Serbia. Exhibit 8 shows a map and key social and economic data of the region and Exhibit 9 shows key facts about Montenegro Telecom. Éva Somorjai gave her view of why the expansion had not happened sooner, "Our owners wanted to see the results of MakTel. Now, they have seen some of the results, they are allowing us to go forward with Montenegro, because they see we have developed a local expertise."

András Balogh explained why the company was targeting Montenegro as its second international acquisition:

> There is a clear reason we're bidding for Montenegro, which is because it is for sale. It's worth acquiring. It's very small and it's the only fixed line operator. There's one other mobile competitor who has 58 to 60 per cent of the market and Telecom Montenegro has about 40 per cent of the market. So, one of the first tasks will be to reposition the mobile business. Then, there's the issue of price rebalancing. The local calls are very cheap. The government subsidized local calls and of course, international and long distance calls are much more expensive. Operators lost money on local calls. But on other calls the prices are so much higher than costs. Ultimately, customers aren't going to be happy, because it means higher prices on local calls.

Balogh explained how the Macedonian experience helped Matáv's understanding of the region:

> At MakTel, we encountered a similar thing where we were cutting costs and restructuring the company. It's difficult cutting people in large companies in small countries. Especially in ex-Communist countries. Governments don't like that. Matáv has had a lot of experience in how to deal with governments. On one hand, governments like in Macedonia want to be capitalists but expect to generate profits while lowering prices for the people. We had experience rebalancing the prices and with trade unions, and also with headcount reduction and setting up an employee centre. We know how to make decisions in the Balkans. We're assessing all the countries, but as of yet, we don't have any immediate plans. But Montenegro is a good step to get into the Balkans . . . and there are geographic boundaries—we don't know about Georgia, Azerbaijan or Kazakhstan. But the Balkans are different. First of all, they're geographically close. There are good flight connections. The countries are relatively small. And the financial plan for buying a company is not an impossibility.

Prospects for future growth

The strategy group wanted to propose a strategy to grow. Péter Koncz talked about the rationale for growth,

One of the hot and pressing issues is expansion. If you look at our share price, it's really stagnant. And, from a fundamental side, it is good, it is cost effective, but the one thing that is missing from the company is dynamic growth. I'm glad that Deutsche Telekom is looking at the composition of growth, and not looking at us just as a financial investment. They treat us like a Central/Eastern European hub.

Balogh talked about his view of what the strategy should be:

There are really three pillars to the strategy, which are: organic growth, synergies and international expansion. The organic growth means that we will do everything that we do today but better than today. So, in fixed, we're offering new, mainly flat rate packages so we can slow the decline and still be profitable. You have one wire that goes into almost every house, and whether you have a call or not, it's pretty much the same. Not, entirely, but almost. So that allows us to have a flat rate. We're also bundling the fixed services with Internet and broadband. For the mobile business, organic growth means managing the price competition with prices on the new services such as the capability with WAP, GPRS and SMS. They're newer and newer products and people can download games, music, ring tones and attachments. The idea with the organic plan is that in both fixed and mobile, we will cut costs and cut the procurement costs—and share the network costs.

Tamás Morvai shared his idea of how Matáv might look in the future:

I can still see a lot of the revenues coming from Hungary, but we would probably have operations in four to five countries. Take a country like Bulgaria—it's quite possible that we'll look for a way to grow there, but not in the typical way. Not necessarily as a mobile operator but perhaps as an ISP or systems integration or an alternative telephone operator. We really want to leverage the knowledge of the international operations. And we're doing that to some extent right now. We moved into Macedonia in 2001, and we'd probably take some of the Macedonian staff into Montenegro. We are not a very international company right now, and we need to become a lot more international. I'm not saying it would necessarily make sense to have people from all over. It would be people who understand the region.

Balogh went on to explain the need to continue to expand internationally:

It is a must for Matáv. Mostly because there is limiting growth opportunity at home. In the fixed line business we are losing lines to mobile lines. It's not as bad as a place like Slovakia that has lost 25 per cent in one year, which translates to about 300,000 lines. Hungary has 3.5 million fixed lines and eight million mobiles. And with mobile services we see them slowing down. We've reached a saturation point. We don't necessarily see dynamic growth. We do see big growth and we are pushing ADSL and broadband services. We expect about 200,000 broadband subscribers by the end of 2004. And we'll likely have about 500,000 by 2006—that's an aspirational target. However, in the fixed telephone business, we're losing customers because of mobile substitution, and people aren't bothering with getting fixed lines.

Conclusion

Balogh and the rest of his team knew they must provide leadership on the strategic business plan for the overall company. While Matáv had been successful with its international expansion into Macedonia, the future was uncertain. Fixed line subscriptions were deteriorating, the ARPU of both fixed lines and mobiles was falling, and Matáv was facing intense competitive pressure in all segments of its business. The direction from Deutsche Telekom was clear—Matáv was to remain an integrated telecom company. However, a strategic crossroads lay in front of Matáv's management team. In the complex and dynamic world of telecommunications, what strategic direction should Matáv's strategy group recommend?

Exhibit 1 Hungary and Matáv's fixed line coverage

	2002	2003	Change %
Number of fixed lines			
residential	2,055,338	2,012,672	−2.1%
business	282,406	261,642	−7.4%
public	33,316	28,799	−13.6%
Number of ISDN channels ("B")	511,326	527,728	3.2%
Total fixed lines (Matáv)	2,882,386	2,830,841	−1.8%
Number of fixed lines incl. ISDN, Emitel	79,460	78,638	−1.0%
Number of fixed lines incl. ISDN, MakTel	594,213	619,236	4.2%
Network ditialization with ISDN	87.1%	89.9%	
Fixed line penetration (Matáv service area, per 100 inhabitants)	38.4	37.7	
Number of Group employees	16,114	14,710	−8.7%
Number of fixed line employees	9,153	8,071	−11.8%
Number of fixed lines per employee	315	351	11.4%
Total mobile customers, T-Mobile	3,426,133	3,766,274	9.9%
Number of mobile customers, MakTel	366,348	523,664	42.9%
Mobile penetration (Hungary, per 100 inhabitants)	67.8	78.5	
Number of internet subscribers	149,962	210,680	40.5%
Number of internet subscribers, MakTel	34,222	49,040	43.3%
Number of cable television customers	338,625	362,366	7.0%
Number of managed leased lines	12,716	11,480	−9.7%
Domestic traffic ('000 minutes)	8,820,201	7,958,292	−9.8%
International outgoing traffic ('000 minutes)	150,999	138,485	−8.3%
Domestic traffic, Emitel ('000 minutes)	179,670	152,614	−15.1%

Exhibit 1—*continued*

	2002	*2003*	*Change %*
International outgoing traffic, Emitel ('000 minutes)	2,545	2,253	−11.5%
MOU (minutes of Usage per User/Month) T-Mobile	118	114	−3.4%
ARPU (Average Traffic Revenue per User/Month) T-Mobile	5,732	5,261	−8.2%

Source: Matáv Annual Report, Front fold-out, December 31, 2003.

The growth of fixed and mobile lines

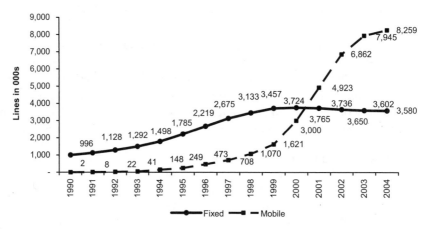

Key fixed-line measures: September 2004

Total fixed lines	3,569,031	Total including Emitel, Hungarotel, Matáv, Monortel and Invitel
Penetration of total population	35.3%	Out of 10,102,000 people
% of fixed lines with ISDN	16.6%	
% of total population waiting	0.3%	
Average duration of phone call	2.93 mins	
% of total households with fixed line	71.1%	Out of 3,822,200 households

Fixed line segment

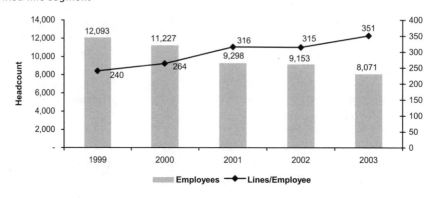

Key mobile measures: September 2004

Overall market	8,379,824
Active	7,774,466
Penetration	83.0%
Monthly increase	0.76%
Year-on-year increase	10.68%

Mobile market in Hungary

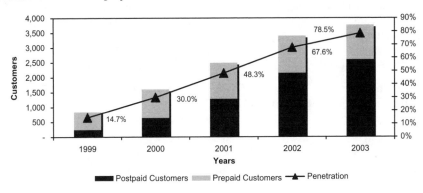

Revenue composition

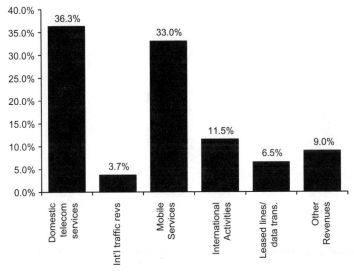

Source: Company files.

Exhibit 2 Deutsche Telekom's financials (in € millions except where noted)

	Dec 03	Dec 02	Dec 01
Income Statement			
Revenue	55,907.3	53,790.4	48,599.6
Cost of Goods Sold	21,064.8	28,581.7	25,781.8
Gross Profit	34,842.5	25,208.7	22,817.8
Gross Profit Margin	62.3%	46.9%	47.0%
SG&A Expense	18,503.6	13,505.3	12,186.6
Depreciation & Amortization	12,900.1	36,949.3	15,311.9
Operating Income	3,438.9	(25,245.9)	(4,680.7)
Income Before Taxes	1,400.1	(26,837.0)	(2,517.0)
Income Taxes	(225.4)	(2,487.8)	812.7
Net Income After Taxes	1,625.5	(24,349.3)	(3,329.7)
Total Net Income	1,254.3	(24,633.5)	(3,475.3)
Diluted EPS from Total Net Income ($)	0.30	(5.87)	(0.94)
Dividends per Share	–	0.31	0.63
Balance Sheet			
Assets			
Cash	9,137.9	1,908.8	2,885.0
Net Receivables	5,769.1	8,197.8	10,430.3
Inventories	1,433.5	1,558.7	1,680.6
Other Current Assets	3,338.5	1,884.9	2,138.9
Total Current Assets	19,680.6	13,549.2	17,135.9
Net Fixed Assets	47,326.1	54,056.6	59,060.4
Other Noncurrent Assets	49,215.9	58,451.2	89,354.7
Total Assets	**116,222.6**	**126,057.9**	**165,550.9**
Liabilities and Shareholders' Equity			
Accounts Payable	4,148.4	3,813.7	4,820.7
Short-Term Debt	13,117.5	9,894.8	13,432.7
Other Current Liabilities	5,086.6	4,977.5	5,890.7
Total Current Liabilities	22,352.6	18,685.9	24,144.0
Long-Term Debt	55,479.6	53,267.7	54,001.5
Other Noncurrent Liabilities	3,618.0	16,971.8	15,325.5
Total Liabilities	**86,427.7**	**94,570.6**	**104,190.3**
Preferred Stock Equity	0.0	0.0	0.0
Common Stock Equity	29,794.9	31,487.3	61,360.6
Total Equity	29,794.9	31,487.3	61,360.6
Shares Outstanding (millions)	4,195.1	4,195.1	4,197.8
Cash Flow Statement			
Net Operating Cash Flow	14,333.6	12,486.6	12,006.0
Net Investing Cash Flow	(2,075.4)	(10,058.9)	(5,397.4)
Net Financing Cash Flow	(5,232.3)	(3,441.7)	(4,839.9)
Net Change in Cash	6,982.8	(1,028.3)	1,742.7
Depreciation & Amortization	12,900.1	36,949.3	15,311.9
Capital Expenditures	(5,468.9)	(13,213.4)	(15,635.9)
Cash Dividends Paid	(92.4)	(1,585.4)	(1,916.5)

Source: Deutsche Telekom Corporate Capsule, www.hoovers.com, accessed November 19, 2004.

Exhibit 3 Matáv's financials (in € millions, except per share)

	Euros 2002	Euros 2003	Hun Forints 2002	Hun Forints 2003
F/X Rate—HUF to Euros (average)	243.0	253.4		
Revenues	**2,431**	**2,396**	**590,585**	**607,252**
Employee-related expenses	(367)	(347)	(89,264)	(87,920)
Payments to other network operators	(334)	(333)	(81,078)	(84,449)
Cost of telecommunication equipment sales	(164)	(161)	(39,744)	(40,811)
Other operating expenses	(558)	(567)	(135,518)	(143,674)
Total Operating Expenses excl. depreciation	(1,422)	(1,408)	(345,604)	(356,854)
EBITDA	**1,008**	**988**	**244,981**	**250,398**
Depreciation and Amortization	(505)	(506)	(122,741)	(128,334)
Operating Profit	503	482	122,240	122,064
Net interest and other chartges	(115)	(158)	(27,919)	(40,002)
Share of associates' results before income tax	3	4	691	963
Profit Before Income Tax	391	328	95,012	83,025
Income tax expense	(55)	(54)	(13,245)	(13,685)
Profit after income tax	337	274	81,767	69,340
Minority Interest	(56)	(47)	(13,639)	(11,865)
Net Income	**280**	**227**	**68,128**	**57,475**
Basic earnings per share	0.27	0.22	65.66	55.38
Diluted Earnnings per share	0.27	0.22	65.66	55.38

Exhibit 3—*continued*

	Euros 2002	Euros 2003	Hun Forints 2002	Hun Forints 2003
F/X Rate—HUF to Euros (year-end)	235.9	262.2		
Assets				
Cash and cash equivalents	38	84	8,851	22,132
Financial instruments held for trading	2	2	447	494
Trade and other receivables	377	362	88,921	94,909
Inventories	55	38	13,063	9,997
Assets held for disposal	10	14	2,285	3,612
Total Current Assets	481	500	113,567	131,144
Property, plant and equipment	2,735	2,368	645,087	620,990
Intangible assets	1,251	1,103	295,199	289,234
Other non-current assets	100	67	23,598	17,469
Total non-current assets	4,086	3,538	963,884	927,693
Total Assets	**4,567**	**4,038**	**1,077,451**	**1,058,837**
Liabilities and Shareholders' Equity				
Loans and other borrowings—third party	278	253	65,569	66,292
Loans from related parties	690	483	162,771	126,644
Trade and other payables	432	387	101,857	101,373
Other current liabilities	76	33	17,865	8,557
Total Current Liabilities	1,475	1,155	348,062	302,866
Loans and other borrowings—third party	305	182	71,992	47,669
Loans from related parties	312	281	73,675	73,675
Other non-current liabilities	35	16	8,142	4,243
Total non-current liabilities	652	479	153,809	125,587
Minority Interests	252	268	59,436	70,274

Shareholders' Equity

Common stock	442	398	104,281	104,281
Additional paid in capital	116	104	27,382	27,382
Treasury stock	(19)	(15)	(4,488)	(3,842)
Cumulative translation adjustment	(18)	3	(4,348)	825
Retained earnings	1,667	1,646	393,317	431,464
Total Shareholders' Equity	2,188	2,136	516,144	560,110
Total Liabilities and Shareholders' Equity	**4,567**	**4,038**	**1,077,451**	**1,058,837**
Net Cash Flows from Operating Activities	844	756	199,043	198,116
Net Cash Flows from Investing Activities	(508)	(361)	(119,941)	(94,701)
Net Cash Flows from Financing Activities	(339)	(351)	(80,054)	(92,035)
Change in Cash and Cash Equivalents	(5)	51	(1,266)	13,281
Cash and Cash equivalents, beginning of year	43	34	10,117	8,851
Cash and cash equivalents, end of year	38	84	8,851	22,132

Source: Matáv Annual Report, pp.40–43, December 31, 2003.

Exhibit 4 Financial information by division (in € millions)

	Euros 2002	Euros 2003	Hun Forints 2002	Hun Forints
F/X Rate—HUF to Euros (average)	243.0	253.4		
Revenues				
Total revenue of fixed line segment	1,384.1	1,280.7	336,306	324,552
Fixed line revenue from other segments	(47.8)	(46.8)	(11,620)	(11,870)
Fixed line revenue from external customers	1,336.3	1,233.8	324,686	312,682
Total revenue of mobile segment	957.4	1,002.8	232,612	254,141
Mobile revenue from other segments	(140.1)	(115.8)	(34,043)	(29,335)
Mobile revenue from external customers	817.3	887.1	198,569	224,806
Total revenue of international segment	278.1	276.3	67,562	70,014
International revenue from other segments	(1.0)	(1.0)	(232)	(250)
International revenue from external customers	277.1	275.3	67,330	69,764
Total revenue of the Group	2,430.7	2,396.2	590,585	607,252
Depreciation and amortization				
Fixed line	315.5	283.6	76,664	71,862
Mobile	145.8	157.4	35,423	39,895
International	43.8	65.4	10,654	16,577
Total	505.2	506.4	122,741	128,334
Operating profit				
Fixed line	179.7	174.0	43,664	44,096
Mobile	215.6	217.1	52,390	55,030
International	107.8	90.5	26,186	22,938
Total	503.1	481.7	122,240	122,064

F/X Rate—HUF to Euros (year-end)	235.9	262.2		
Assets				
Fixed line	2,390.5	1,976.5	563,917	518,308
Mobile	1,532.6	1,374.5	361,535	360,423
International	669.3	699.1	157,894	183,336
Inter-segment elmination	(63.5)	(39.2)	(14,979)	(10,269)
Total segment assets	4,528.9	4,011.0	1,068,367	1,051,798
Unallocated assets	38.5	26.8	9,084	7,039
Total assets	4,567.4	4,037.8	1,077,451	1,058,837
Capital expenditures on tangible and intangible assets				
Fixed line	208.8	151.2	49,245	39,662
Mobile	176.1	141.6	41,532	37,131
International	81.4	53.4	19,211	13,995
Total	466.2	346.2	109,988	90,788
Liabilities				
Fixed line	373.3	274.2	88,073	71,907
Mobile	171.7	164.8	40,503	43,218
International	46.8	26.9	11,046	7,043
Inter-segment elmination	(63.5)	(39.2)	(14,979)	(10,269)
Total segment liabilities	528.4	426.7	124,643	111,899
Unallocated liabilities	1,599.1	1,207.2	377,228	316,554
Total liabilities	2,127.5	1,633.9	501,871	428,453

Source: Matáv Annual Report, p.54, December 31, 2003.

Exhibit 5   Product line advertising

Matáv fixed line and ADSL Internet ads

Matáv's T-Mobile ads

Axelero Internet ads

Source: Company files.

Exhibit 6 Competitors in Hungary

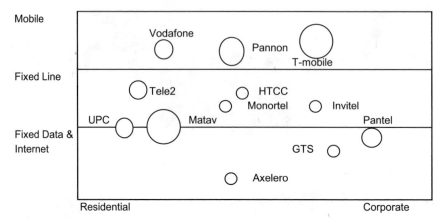

Source: Company files.

Key Numbers	MATÁV	Equant	HTTC	KPN	Industry	Market
Annual Sales (euros million)	2,502.1	2,348.5	47.5	12,923.2		
Employees	16,114	9,547	600	32,736		
Profitability						
Net Profit Margin	9.5%	−13.0%	38.3%	21.2%	4.1%	6.2%
Return on Equity	10.3%	0.0%	40.2%	38.1%	10.3%	12.4%
Return on Assets	5.4%	−14.9%	13.5%	11.3%	3.0%	2.1%
Return on Invested Capital	8.4%	−28.5%	17.1%	16.7%	5.2%	6.1%
Valuation						
Price/Sales Ratio	1.50	0.51	2.32	1.31	0.96	1.30
Price/Earnings Ratio	15.81	−	6.12	6.21	32.20	22.50
Operations						
Days of Sales Outstanding	56.32	90.68	34.31	37.18	50.46	49.71
Financial						
Current Ratio	0.43	1.26	1.04	0.98	0.97	1.43
Quick Ratio	0.40	0.80	0.80	0.80	0.70	1.00
Leverage Ratio	1.89	1.92	2.97	3.37	3.46	5.85
Total Debt/Equity	0.56	0.09	1.76	1.29	1.26	1.29
Interest Coverage	2.80	−	3.70	3.70	2.30	2.90
Growth						
36-Month Revenue Growth	0.0%	12.9%	10.3%	9.3%	15.9%	6.5%
36-Month Net Income Growth	4.3%	0.0%	25.3%	0.0%	0.0%	41.6%
36-Month EPS Growth	98.8%	0.0%	26.3%	0.0%	0.0%	40.1%
36-Month Dividend Growth	38.3%	0.0%	0.0%	0.0%	−20.7%	4.9%

Source: Matáv Corporate Capsule, www.hoovers.com, accessed November 19, 2004.

Exhibit 7 Performance measures: Maktel in Macedonia (in € millions)

	2000		2001		2002		2003
Revenue	201	22.0%	246	13.0%	278	−0.4%	277
EBITDA	82	71.0%	140	8.0%	151	4.0%	157
Net Income	47	83.0%	86.1	17.0%	101	−1.0%	88
EBITDA Margin	41.0%	40.0%	57.0%	−5.0%	55.0%	4.0%	56.0%

MakTel customer base

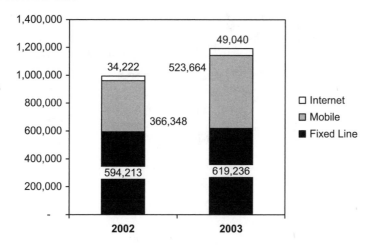

Penetration in Macedonia

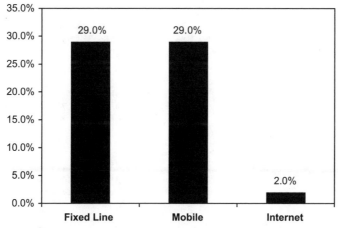

Source: Company files.

Exhibit 8 Map of the Balkan region

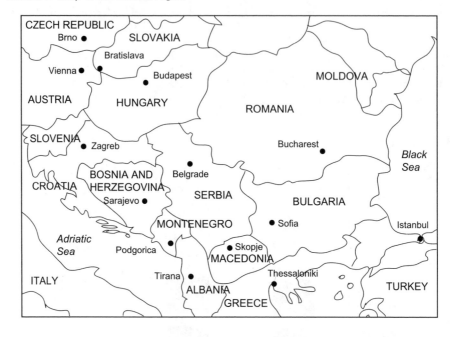

Country data (in US$)

	Hungary	Macedonia	Serbia & Montenegro	Bulgaria	Romania
Population	10,032,375	2,071,210	10,825,900	7,517,973	22,355,551
Age Structure					
0–14 years old	16.0%	21.5%	18.3%	14.4%	16.2%
15–64 years old	69.0%	67.8%	66.8%	68.5%	69.4%
+65 years old	15.0%	10.7%	14.9%	17.1%	14.4%
Median age	38.4	32.8	36.6	40.5	36.1
Population Growth %	−0.25%	0.39%	0.30%	−0.92%	−0.11%
GDP (billions $)	139.8	13.8	23.9	57.1	155.0
GDP Growth Rate	2.9%	2.8%	1.5%	4.3%	4.9%
GDP/capita ($)	13,900	6,700	2,200	7,600	7,000
GDP by sector					
Agriculture	3.3%	11.3%	15.2%	11.4%	13.1%
Industry	32.5%	32.1%	28.2%	30.0%	38.1%
Services	64.2%	56.6%	56.5%	58.6%	48.8%
Inflation	4.7%	1.2%	11.2%	2.3%	15.3%
Unemployment	5.9%	36.7%	34.5%	14.3%	7.2%
Public Debt as % of GDP	57.0%	30.2%	123.2%	48.0%	25.5%

Source: CIA World Fact Book, www.cia.gov, accessed January 20, 2005.

Exhibit 8 (continued) Potential target companies in Balkans

Name of Company	Country
Mobitel	Bulgaria
Mobtel	Serbia
Orange	Romania
BTC	Bulgaria
Tel Srbja	Serbia

EBITDA % of potential targets

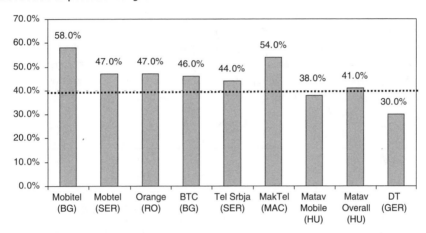

Revenue growth %—2001/2002

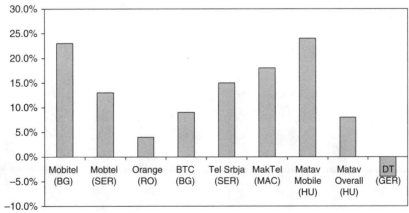

Source: Company files.

Exhibit 9 Facts about Montenegro Telecom

Telecom Montenegro is the leading operator in telecommunication field on the territory of Montenegro. It was registered as a separate legal entity on 31 December 1998. Telecom Montenegro was created from the separation of the state owned PTT Montenegro, which provided postal, telegraphic, and telecommunication services. Telecom Montenegro is the legal successor of the PTT Montenegro in all areas of telecommunication activity. Telecom Montenegro's activities include maintaining and exploitation of the telecommunication system on the territory of the Republic, development of telecommunication technologies and providing services to end users. Through high quality services Telecom Montenegro intends to satisfy needs of the users, business partners and investors.

Ownership structure: 51 per cent Government of Montenegro, 49 per cent private investment funds and private capital.

Telecommunication Market: The principal service providers in the Montenegrin telecommunication market are Telecom Montenegro, fixed line operator; ProMonte, the first GSM mobile service provider; and Monet, the second GSM mobile service provider. On 27 December 2000, the Government of Montenegro passed a new telecommunications law in order to provide a clear regulatory framework for Montenegro's telecommunications sector. In accordance with the Telecommunication Law, The Telecommunication agency was established in March 2001 as an independent regulatory agency for the telecommunication sector. The Agency is responsible for promoting competition and access to networks, issuing licenses to operators and regulating tariffs in accordance with the Law.

Montenegro Telecom	2000	2001	2002
Residential	160,767	167,454	169,699
Business	16,833	18,379	20,166
Total number of lines	177,600	185,833	189,865
Percent of Digitalization	80.0%	87.0%	92.5%
Number of Employees	1,289	1,298	1,348
Number of Subscribers	27.0%	28.0%	28.8%

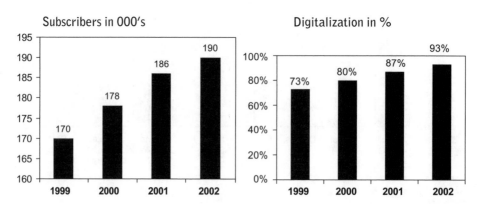

Source: Agency of Montenegro for Economic Restructuring and Foreign Investments, www.agencijacg.org/ostalo/profil_telekom_eng.pdf, accessed January 20, 2005.

Notes

1. "Deutsche Telekom looks east for deals," *Total Telecom*, August 11, 2004.
2. It is common in Europe that telecommunication companies would charge for local phone calls.
3. "Matav: Initiating Coverage," *JP Morgan Analyst Report*, September 22, 2004, p.1.
4. Rebalancing involves the restructuring of tariff rates taking into account the overall portfolio of services such as fixed-line local, fixed-line long distance and mobile telephony and the costs associated with each service.
5. Balazs Koranyi, "Interview—Hungary's Matáv seeks Balkan Acquisition," *Reuters News*, September 27, 2004.

Chapter 8

Managing Pibrex Russia (A)

New crisis, old grievances

ELENA MICHAILOVA WAS EXHAUSTED after a long day at the office. It was late in the evening and she still had much work left to do. In less than two weeks time (December 22, 1998), she would meet with Pibrex Russia's steering committee to discuss the fate of Russian operations, including recommendations for restructuring. The steering committee consisted of three senior managers from Pibrex Region Europe North (PREN), the division to which Russia belonged. PREN was formed following the Russian financial crisis of August 1998 to develop strategy for the region and to assist Pibrex Russia in the difficult post-crisis challenges it faced. Michailova was preparing a list of

Rachel Doern and Carl F. Fey prepared this case solely to provide material for class discussion. The authors do not intend to illustrate either effective or ineffective handling of a managerial situation. The authors may have disguised certain names and other identifying information to protect confidentiality.

Richard Ivey School of Business
The University of Western Ontario

recommendations for which she knew she would have to be conservative. Given the current unstable situation in Russia, Michailova believed that once again the steering committee would ultimately focus on survival—that is, on increasing profits and reducing costs. However, in light of the company's deteriorating operational situation, this time the task would prove challenging.

Just a few short months earlier, Michailova had been the managing director of the Pibrex sales office in St. Petersburg, Pibrex AO. However, in late August 1998, she had been reassigned to Pibrex KZ, Pibrex's largest Russian subsidiary located just outside Moscow in the suburb of Khemki, to perform a financial audit of the entire Pibrex Russian operation.

On August 17, 1998, the central bank of Russia suspended payments on short-term loans (GKOs), resulting in a sharp devaluation of the ruble and the corresponding inability of many Russian banks to repay all clients who wanted their money in cash. These events resulted in a crisis state unseen since the fall of the Soviet Union in 1991. In the wake of the crisis, foreign investors scrambled to withdraw their holdings.

Pibrex, a European leader in the production and development of polymers used in adhesives, resins and moulded products within the plastics industry, had three subsidiaries in Russia at this time. Following the crisis, Pibrex, too, proceeded to respond quickly to hedge operations against devastating exchange rate losses and defaults by supply chain players and customers. Within a matter of hours, a decision was made by Pibrex to apply anti-crisis management—the goal was simply survival. Pibrex Russia had been integrated into the company's complex global matrix organization. However, after the crisis in Russia a different structure was required such that decisions could be taken rapidly and control over Pibrex's Russian subsidiaries centralized, in this challenging time. It was, therefore, decided by Pibrex AB, the parent company in Sweden, that forming the above-mentioned steering committee was the best solution to fulfil these needs. The steering committee was tasked with finding a way that Pibrex could survive in Russia and at least break even in the near future. The steering committee was viewed as the key mechanism for formulating strategy in Russia.

Michailova's financial knowledge and experience in St. Petersburg had earned her the responsibility of auditing all three Pibrex Russia subsidiaries as the new financial controller for Pibrex in Russia. Michailova was requested to begin with Pibrex KZ, Pibrex's largest polymer manufacturing facility in the country. For reasons unclear to the steering committee, the plant had been producing financial losses since 1997 and was, therefore, considered extremely vulnerable following the crisis. Michailova was consequently sent in by the steering committee to help identify the problem(s) and to recommend solution(s).

Russian plastics industry structure

Plastics consist of bonded chains of polymers or plastic resins, derived from building blocks called hydrocarbons found in petroleum or natural gas. Production within the chemical industry in Russia, the larger industry structure to which plastics belonged, accounted for 28 per cent of the country's gross national product (GNP) in 1998.[1] Approximately 6,082 chemical companies operated within Russia at this time. By the end of the second quarter of 1998, 1,591,000 tons of plastic were produced in the country, an increase of two per cent from 1997. Production in 1997 was divided between several areas or resins, the most popular being polyethylene (35 per cent), polyvinyl chloride (17 per cent), polypropylene (seven per cent), and polystyrene (three per cent).[2] These divisions in turn supported a number of domestic industries including packaging, construction, equipment, furniture, and consumer goods.

Background

Based in Gothenburg, Sweden, Pibrex AB, which began operations in the early 1900s, is one of the world's largest developers of petrochemical-based polymers, specializing in the production and distribution of formulated adhesives and engineering/commercial resins. (Adhesive materials are used widely to bond and shape products, while resins, which come in various forms, including powders, flakes, and/or liquids, are commonly used as coating agents for machines, or as compounds in structural moulds, among other things.) These divisions combined, served a number of industrial markets including product assembly, automotive and transport, packaging, and building/construction. Over the years, Pibrex became well known for its commitment to research and development, its sophisticated manufacturing processes, safety standards, and its commitment to quality and customer service.

The first substantial growth phase of the global plastics industry did not take place until the Second World War, coinciding with military production. In the 1960s, the industry enjoyed another dramatic increase due to the proliferation of key commodity and engineering resins. Led by technical progress and international expansion, Pibrex established two companies in Russia in 1910 (one in Kaliningrad and one in Moscow). Operations were short-lived, however, once the Russian Revolution of 1917 brought in a Communist government and everything was nationalized. When the companies were seized, Pibrex had little choice but to export products to the Russian market via the company's Finnish operations.

Pibrex did not officially attempt to establish an operating presence within the country again until 1992, after the fall of the Soviet Union. Although sources indicated Pibrex was reluctant to re-enter the market at all, the company could not ignore the potential for earnings in Russia. Russia was both a world-leading supplier of raw materials and producer of military goods, and, thus, the opportunities for Pibrex were enormous. A number of research institutes dedicated to polymer development were established in Russia over the 1940s and 1950s. However, post-war polymer production was limited to a couple of old soviet plants. In addition, none of Pibrex's western competitors had a strong foothold in Russia yet. Finally, the entire country was in need of structural renovations that required plastic mouldings and other polymer-based products. Thus, when the plant in Kaliningrad was privatized, Pibrex was presented with the attractive opportunity of reclaiming some of its earlier investments.

For these reasons, in 1992, Pibrex decided to enter Russia in several regions quickly. The Kaliningrad plant (renamed Pibrex KAZ) was registered as an open joint stock company (meaning shares were open to the public—held by employees, private investors and the state), and Pibrex succeeded in reacquiring full stock ownership by the end of 1994. A second manufacturing facility was acquired in Khemki (renamed Pibrex KZ) to cover market opportunities in Moscow and the Moscow region. The plant in Khemki, originally named Khemki Zavod (KZ), was constructed in the mid-1940s by the state to supply plastic mouldings, in addition to the company's traditional polymer products, to varying industries in Moscow and the surrounding area.

The suburb of Khemki, located 20 kilometres from the nation's capital, was small and tight-knit, home to more than 300,000 people. The plant, which employed primarily local residents, had close ties to the community as one of its largest employers. (By 1994, it employed more than 500 people.) The privatization agreement between Pibrex and the state committed the company to invest US$15 million in operations, retrain staff, and refrain from laying off any employees (with a few exceptions) over an initial three-year period. These stipulations meant Pibrex enjoyed minimal operational control of their Russian subsidiaries until 1997.

Also, in 1994, Pibrex opened a sales office in St. Petersburg (Pibrex AO) and head office in Moscow (Pibrex Russia). Pibrex hired and trained its own staff to work in these offices. The new recruits were young, educated and enthusiastic. Michailova, having joined Pibrex AO, in 1995, as the manager of marketing and sales, recalled a spirit within the company that could be explained only by shared goals and strategies. An experienced team of expatriates was selected to manage the head office in Moscow and to oversee operations across the country. Pibrex expected that the Moscow head office would soon be the headquarters for a large empire of subsidiaries all across Russia. The opportunities seemed overwhelming. However, Pibrex's dreams for Russia were short-sighted due to several organizational obstacles and the realization that a slower expansion pace in Russia was needed until the country's economic situation stabilized. Organizational obstacles included:

- Pibrex Russia was never legally registered as the Russian mother company.
- The Russian subsidiaries were opened at different dates and, therefore, registered as independent entities.
- The distance between subsidiaries was substantial and led to taxation restraints.

Russian law required each of the four Pibrex subsidiaries to maintain separate bank accounts and to pay local taxes. This meant, instead of consolidating quarterly figures and reports, figures were presented separately to avoid double taxation. Because the subsidiaries operated independently, the role of Pibrex Russia was never firmly established. This, in turn, affected the relationship between Pibrex and the acquired subsidiaries. Although Pibrex Russia's management worked together, with directors of the three subsidiaries, in setting budgets and approving all costing decisions and strategies before sending them to Sweden, it also created unnecessary bureaucracy. The following scenario described a typical request for new computers by Pibrex KZ in 1995 (see Exhibit 1):

> A request for new computers was made to the department head of the subsidiary, the manager of customer services and information technology. The department head, in turn, made the proposal to the managing director. If the request was not approved by the director, the department head took the request to the next level, that being the representative mirror department within head offices in Moscow (Pibrex Russia), the director of customer services and information technology. Then the request was forwarded to the president, who, if he approved, told the plant director to buy the computers.

By 1997, obligations to the state had been fulfilled and Pibrex substantially scaled back continued investments. (All investments in Russia from this point forward appeared short-term to protect the company from further losses.) While having a separate headquarters in Moscow might have made sense had Pibrex's ambitious expansion plans to include a network of subsidiaries all across Russia been achieved, with only three subsidiaries, it seemed more logical to locate headquarter's staff (which included all Pibrex expatriates in Russia) at nearby Pibrex KZ. Thus, Pibrex closed the head office in Moscow and, after moving its staff to the plant in Khemki (a move most local and foreign employees alike approved), proceeded to lay off 50 per cent of the subsidiary's production workers over the next two years. (The names Pibrex KZ and Pibrex Russia were thereafter used interchangeably to describe the plant in Khemki.) Following the merger, Pibrex soon became a price leader in Russia to increase its profit margins. This strategy significantly decreased its sales volume and was difficult for the company's Russian production-oriented employees to understand.

Then, in the autumn of 1998, following the national financial crisis, Pibrex's market was reduced further. Many foreign firms fled the market. Some local firms defaulted on payments or turned to Pibrex competitors for better prices. Financial loss in Pibrex KZ's case intensified when the company was not able to effectively track its inventory, orders or payments. The future operating position of the plant became insecure, in stark contrast to the stability the well-known plant had enjoyed during communism.

Production under communism

Prior to the acquisition by Pibrex, the plant in Khemki (Khemki Zavod) operated as a traditional state-owned production facility. Under communism, the following operating environment characterized this plant along with most other manufacturing plants in Russia:

●   The state's full employment policy not only guaranteed jobs but also allowed for a sizeable support staff that could help out in the event of an emergency or an absence.

- Hiring was often based on whom one knew as opposed to skill, and salary was not based on performance.
- Communication was clear and reporting was direct.
- Socializing between staff and management was not encouraged to preserve a sense of authority.
- Employees enjoyed little flexibility or autonomy in their work.
- Production was the most important business function and everyone worked to fulfil production quotas set by the state regardless of ability to sell the products.
- Penalties for not meeting production targets were severe and, thus, people normally wanted to avoid responsibility.

While these characteristics created a secure and positive work environment on the one hand, they also led to inefficiencies. For instance, because the market was non-competitive, neither western business functions such as marketing and sales, nor western value-added product features such as quality and service were considered necessary. An absence of these features in turn led to poorly produced goods and product shortages/surpluses.

Pibrex structure

Shortly after Pibrex acquired the plants in 1994, they, along with the offices in St. Petersburg and Moscow, were incorporated into the corporate organizational structure and lumped together with the Scandinavian countries, the Baltic States, and the Ukraine to form Pibrex Region Europe North (PREN). Pibrex followed a decentralized structure worldwide wherein regional divisions like PREN could make most decisions autonomously from Pibrex headquarters in Gothenburg (see Exhibit 2). PREN, like all other Pibrex regions, was broken down into two business areas (manufacturing/supply and research/development) and four functions: (1) supply and technology, (2) marketing, (3) administration/finance and information technology (IT), (4) human resource management, safety, environment and quality. Manufacturing was further divided between two divisions: (1) adhesives and resins, and (2) plastic mouldings.

Corresponding managers within each subsidiary in the region reported to the functional manager in charge of the region, their business area manager in charge of the region, and to the general manager of Pibrex Russia. This very complicated and decentralized system allowed, in theory, for all subsidiaries to have access to excellent expertise. However, this structure caused problems for Pibrex Russia for several reasons. First, Russians were accustomed to working in organizations where power was very centralized and it was difficult for them to quickly adjust to and understand Pibrex's decentralized system. (Most Russians preferred to have one clear boss.) Second, functional managers in PREN were responsible for many profitable subsidiaries, unlike Pibrex Russia. As a result, it was often difficult for the Russian branch to attract the attention necessary from PREN's functional management. Third, projects that cut across functions required multiple approvals, sometimes slowing down the decision-making process. Thus, minimal operational control in conjunction with Pibrex's size, complicated organizational structure, and decreasing Pibrex commitment to the region limited the progress of the Russian subsidiaries.

The reduction period

Although it became apparent early on that the number of employees within the plant exceeded those needed, particularly since a more modern facility was brought in from Finland in 1995, the terms of the privatization agreement did not allow for staff reductions until 1997. By the end of 1997, Pibrex AB decided that the Russian economy would not develop fast enough to allow Russian operations to meet Pibrex's competitive standards of profitability and efficiency. Therefore, any hopes for further expansion in Russia were aborted and existing operations were reduced. The reduction period in Russia was characterized by two events in particular: the merger between Pibrex Russia and Pibrex KZ, and production layoffs. Both of these events, as Michailova discovered, had a significant negative effect on employee morale and necessitated a series of adjustments over the next few years.

The merger between Pibrex Russia and Pibrex KZ

The privatization agreement not only diminished Pibrex's commitment to Russia but also the commitment of Russian employees within the acquired plants to Pibrex. As well, according to the Pibrex Russia president, Kevin Donaldson, the initial setup of a head office in the centre of Moscow created a perception of Pibrex in Russia as an "investor," rather than a company committed to and responsible for managing production. For these reasons, when Pibrex Russia and Pibrex KZ merged in 1997, production employees felt a joint venture had been made only between Pibrex and the KZ management team (and not between the employees). The employees instead felt removed from the Pibrex entity and later reported to an external consultant, brought in to smooth the merger process, that they worked only for KZ and not Pibrex. These feelings were reinforced by a series of events following the merger.

First, Pibrex Russia brought in two new departments to the plant, sales and marketing. For some reason, however, these departments were separated and this created some role overlap. The merger created seven departments in total: (1) customer services and information technology; (2) supply; (3) safety, environment and quality; (4) human resources; (5) planning/economics; (6) sales and (7) marketing. To accommodate the new departments, the administration building was renovated, despite the poor state of production facilities and equipment. Employees of the post-Communist plant poorly understood the need for these departments and blamed the young and inexperienced sales and marketing executives for not only inequities, but also a decline in sales (i.e. miscommunications between the sales and supply departments led to missing or delayed deliveries). Executives were also seen as incompetent and arrogant as they drove company cars and spoke on cellular phones provided by the company. Although these fringe benefits were standard perquisites of an executive compensation package in Moscow, at the time, and were required to attract executives or good marketing and sales personnel, production workers, who were neither understanding nor comforted by this fact, soon referred to the new administration building and its staff as the "White House," after the parliament building in Russia.

Second, in 1997, Pibrex initiated two company-wide training programs held in Gothenburg, Sweden by the Pibrex Corporate Educational Institute, for top executives: (1) General Management—a five-course management program spread over three-week intervals; and (2) Pibrex in Depth—a shorter one-time product-training program for new members. Both programs were intended to instil within employees a sense of Pibrex pride and to educate them in terms of corporate strategy. According to one Russian Pibrex manager, by showing executives around plant facilities in Sweden, they could witness first hand what a well-run profitable Pibrex operation looked like, and they could also see how this differed from the Russian operations. Although Russian employees felt what they had learned was very useful, paradoxically, it also caused feelings of envy since Russian facilities were not as modern.

Third, following the merger, middle managers were required to report to both Pibrex Russia management and Pibrex KZ management. According to one manager, however, orders given by the former group were often ignored, and the traditional reporting structure was retained.

Fourth, Yuri Popov, a member of the Pibrex Russia team, replaced Vassily Simonov as plant director. Simonov had been director for the last 10 years. He was a traditional Russian leader, a strict and authoritative decision-maker who proved to be quite the opposite of his successor. Popov was considered by Pibrex KZ management to be a weak leader who preferred to delegate tasks and responsibility to others rather than take action.

Finally, Donaldson, an American Pibrex hire, was made technical manager of Pibrex Russia in 1996 and president in 1997. Donaldson became the supreme authority within the plant. And despite promoting an open-door policy following the merger, he was described as a "virtual" manager, unseen and untouched. This perception was created by several factors: his inability to speak Russian, his tendency to assign tasks from his office via intranet, and his infrequent visits to the factory floor, approximately once every six weeks. These things, in turn, kept him somewhat removed from the operating environment. The following example illustrates the problems this caused; an external consultant working for the company said:

> After speaking with some production workers, he discovered that there was no drinking water available in the main station. He proceeded to discuss the matter with Kevin Donaldson, who was very surprised by the information and grateful for being informed. Because KZ's pipes were so old and rusty, all agreed it was not possible to drink the orange water they emitted. As a result, in the weeks following the consultant's visit, a free bottled water dispenser

was provided. About six months later the external consultant returned to the factory and was thanked by the president for his recommendations regarding the water system which Kevin claimed the employees greatly appreciated. It was, therefore, rather ironic that immediately following this meeting, the consultant discovered that the water dispenser had been empty for almost five months. Workers accredited this as yet one more example of management's lack of regard for them.

Layoffs

As part of the privatization agreement, layoffs were approved to follow the investment period. According to Donaldson, the union was supportive of layoffs in 1994 for several reasons, including Pibrex's reputation as a reliable employer and the following:

- A full understanding and appreciation for the severity of the situation, in terms of job loss for the region and the financial repercussions for workers.
- An optimistic outlook illustrated by moderate salary increases in ruble terms despite widespread layoffs, wage decreases, and failure to pay salaries by other companies in the region and across the nation.
- Explanation that Pibrex believed in full support for a moderate number of employees, rather then partial-support for an excessive number of employees.
- An above-average layoff compensation package (beyond that required by law).

Pibrex was required by Russian labor code to give employees two months notice prior to laying them off. After this period, the official layoff policy was to relieve all pension-aged personnel first. Each Pibrex Russia employee was paid a large and extremely attractive severance package by Russian standards, between US$600 to US$1,000, in addition to two-months salary. (The severance package depended on the number of years of employment with the company.) One manager stressed that this policy was an act of "good will" by the company and not required by legislation. Pibrex KZ was responsible, however, for offering one possible vacancy per person (provided a respective position was to be reduced and such a vacancy could be found). The plant also worked with a local labor agency in Khemki to help those laid-off find employment alternatives. And on occasion, Pibrex rehired employees to fill temporary positions.

The reduction period created a situation whereby employees had to work much more than in the past for moderate pay. Then, in the summer of 1998, the situation took a turn for the worse. Exchange rate fluctuations in Russia led to diminished purchasing power. The work environment continued to deteriorate as finances tightened and no new investments were made. During this time, workers reported feeling "desperate," "frustrated" and "depressed." They could no longer envision a light at the end of the tunnel.

The market crash, August 17, 1998

Events leading up to the market crash on August 17, 1998, were precipitated six to seven years prior by the collapse of the Soviet Union, when price instability was rampant and inflation rates soared. The average Russian at this time, to hedge himself against further devastation, accumulated U.S. dollars as opposed to Russian rubles. (A reaction that could be explained by the greater stability the dollar enjoyed.) Rather than reinvest this money locally, it was often invested abroad or more commonly kept at home, stuffed away under the bed or in an old shoebox.

In an effort to reduce rampant inflation, the Russian government took two actions: the government set artificial limitations on the ruble's worth and privatized approximately 80 per cent of state-owned property. The stock market responded to such measures in turn by growing 165 per cent in one year. However, a lack of necessary reforms or reinvestment in the country led to the continued operation of factories that produced unwanted goods and a total loss of US$80 billion dollars to the economy. A failure to restructure the military complex, in conjunction with the government's inability to collect enough revenues, left the country in a state of arrears over wages and pension payments.

In 1997, falling oil and commodity prices reduced the country's export revenues. At the same time, interest rates rose and few people paid taxes. The government, still unable to collect sufficient revenues to cover the enormous debt, was forced to roll over US$1 billion a week in GKOs (ruble-denominated short-term debt). The international community was set to assist Russia, at this time, to prevent devaluation with a US$22 billion aid/loan package on the condition that the country undertake major tax reforms in conjunction with a voluntary debt restructuring scheme for GKO holders (to switch to long-term debt obligations). This rapidly increasing government borrowing created inflationary pressure that resulted in an overwhelming public preference against holding rubles. As a result, there was strong downward pressure on the ruble requiring the Russian government to invest increasingly large sums of foreign reserves to defend a ruble exchange rate that was not sustainable.

By August of 1998, the Russian government could no longer continue to spend the foreign currency required to defend the ruble and, thus, was forced to allow the ruble to devalue significantly. GKO restructuring was imposed uni-laterally by Russia—beginning with a temporary moratorium placed on private debt payments. The central bank stopped payment on the US$40 billion debt in ruble bonds, cancelling all agreed upon and future sales of dollars to banks and other institutions. Russian banks, which were not well regulated and had engaged in risky lending practices, began rapidly to experience cash flow problems. This event put some banks out of business, while others were forced to freeze all assets (a small portion of which was recovered and repaid to the original owners). In essence, the entire Russian banking system temporarily collapsed.

At the time, many Russians, who had traditionally been skeptical of banks but had invested in them nevertheless (since they were led to believe that the Russian banking system was a safe investment alternative), lost whatever remaining faith they had in banking and politics when they were unable to retrieve their deposited savings. The devaluation of the ruble increased the gap between dollar and ruble-denominated salaries, by reducing the purchasing power of the majority, who were paid in rubles. Many people turned to the streets in desperation to sell what they could to survive. Street markets, first initiated by earlier privatization in the late 1980s, now abounded. Businesses, unable to pay salaries, lost skilled personnel to such markets. Interest in Russia, by the international community, waned and the general attitude toward the crisis became one of reproach. Many foreign firms saw this event as the final straw and either pulled out of Russia or radically decreased their Russian activities. Russia was left, in relative isolation, to recover.

Elena's entrance

Shortly after the crisis began, Michailova began her financial audit of all of Pibrex's Russian operations, at the request of Pibrex Russia's steering committee. Michailova remembers arriving in Moscow to witness an overwhelming state of panic in the nation's capital. Many businesses had been forced into bankruptcy. Russians were unable to retrieve their savings and could be seen lined up for days outside banks and other financial institutions. Some slept in their cars, while others were forced to sleep in the streets waiting in line. Michailova, too, had financial problems due to the crisis when she was unable to use her line of credit.

Born and raised in southern Russia, she was well qualified for her new position as financial controller. She was well educated and fluent in both Russian and English. Prior to working with Pibrex, she owned a business in marketing and informational services. In 1995, Michailova was hired by Pibrex AO in St. Petersburg as the manager of sales and marketing, and through hard work, was promoted to managing director only two years later, while attending part-time MBA studies.

Audit of Pibrex Russia 1998

Michailova's audit of the Pibrex KZ plant coincided with a series of anti-crisis initiatives of the steering committee. The steering committee had worked intensively during the autumn of 1998 to formulate a survival strategy for Pibrex Russia. For instance, all highly paid expatriate management, with the exception of the president, Kevin Donaldson, were removed and redistributed throughout the worldwide Pibrex organization. In addition, a decision was made not to immediately replace Donaldson with another expat when his contract expired at the end of 1998. In fact, Donaldson stayed on at Pibrex Russia until February 1999 while he looked for another job within Pibrex. During this time, however, he began to slowly turn over responsibility to the steering committee and other Russian staff like Michailova. Once again, the management team of KZ was entirely of Russian origin. Next, all sales activity was limited to large, profitable customers. Other efforts were also made to reduce expenditures, where possible, and to carefully monitor and control all finances on both the part of Michailova and the steering committee. For example, daily reporting had been introduced whereby sales receipts of goods delivered, customer payments, money owed by each individual customer, and expenses were reported to minimize the likelihood of bad debts.

Michailova knew restructuring efforts had only just begun. More changes and reductions were to come and she watched as the mood within the plant reached an all-time low and faith in continued operations declined. Despite the visible drawbacks, she agreed with the overall need for restructuring Pibrex's Russian operations as required by headquarters in Sweden. Michailova's support for general restructuring stemmed not only from the obvious financial crisis in Russia, but also from constraints the Russian government had placed on Pibrex initially, preventing it from decreasing the workforce size due to efficiency increases. She had also observed that continuously, well-intended initiatives had not met with the anticipated results due to hurried and flawed implementation. As a result, a number of outstanding issues remained following the reduction period. Michailova believed that financial control, wage differentiation, management-employee relations, and working conditions were key issues that deserved special attention (see below).

With limited time, resources and support, Michailova was unsure of what she should do first and how she should solve the problems she chose to pursue. She felt it was critical to provide a clear long-term vision for Pibrex Russia employees. Michailova also was concerned that the steering committee and PREN seemed unclear of what it wanted to do to formulate such a message. The steering committee, however, felt that they had a clear strategy formulation that aimed to cut expenditures and increase income such that Pibrex Russia would at least break even in the near future. This, the steering committee felt, was the only hope for the company's continued survival in Russia.

Financial control

Michailova noticed immediately one of the biggest problems within the plant appeared to be a lack of order and financial control. This resulted from the absence of an integrated operating system and task redundancy across departments. For instance, accounting entries were made once by the planning department and again by customer services. One employee commented upon the problems encountered by the double-entry accounting system:

> Imagine that after receiving a daily bank statement two departments separately enter all payments into different systems. At the end of each month, each department reconcile their results and every time the results appear to be different. Then, some two to three people spend two to three days to fix discrepancies.

Customer accounts, in turn, were spread across numerous systems and management orders regarding credit allowances were sometimes lost. The company had tried repeatedly to implement the Concorde System, a tool for integrating financial items and implementing management orders since it would eliminate the need for a planning department. However, all attempts had been unsuccessful. Pibrex KZ finance/accounting department employees were neither equipped nor trained to deal with such issues. Michailova also learned most of the staff were computer illiterate and only administrative personnel had access to computer systems. Computer coverage in production, sales and logistics was particularly poor and this led to backups, improper orders and missed deliveries.

Finally, cost savings and losses were based on estimates because the planning department ineffectively covered budgeting in each department. (Managers were not made responsible for setting budgets within their own departments.) When Michailova asked one manager to report the losses in his department, he replied, "I feel the losses to be significant."

Staff divisions

Wage differentials were also an ongoing source of contention between staff and management and sales/marketing personnel and production personnel. Michailova knew that between 1996 and 1997, in an effort to boost sales and marketing coverage, Pibrex had recruited young talent with promises of training and above average U.S. dollar-based salaries to work for Pibrex Russia. Recruitment was aimed at young 20- to 30-year-old individuals, well educated with both English and computer skills. Demand for this group was high across all industries in Russia at the time, and salaries, therefore, needed to be competitive.

Problems arose when the Moscow office merged with the plant. It soon became evident two salary systems existed for the different groups, ruble salaries for old KZ employees (who basically worked in production) and U.S. dollar-equivalent salaries for sales employees and management hired by Pibrex. Production workers failed to understand the concept of paying individual specialists according to function and market demand. They complained, "Why should they be better paid than us? We're the ones producing!"

Despite the company's efforts to keep salaries confidential, it was common knowledge how much each person earned and a regular topic of discussion. Whereas an average production worker made about US$100 per month in 1998, most management and sales staff earned over US$1,000 per month (one-third of the company then made two-thirds the salary). To make matters worse, although the salaries of workers and middle management were not reduced in ruble terms following the crisis, rampant inflation led to their devaluation in purchasing power by more than 100 per cent.

To add equity to the system, top management's and sales/marketing employees' wages within Pibrex Russia were reduced in November 1998 by converting all salaries to rubles with an artificial exchange rate. (Although the actual exchange rate was RUB18/US$1, the conversion rate was set at RUB9.5/

US$1.) To eliminate the widespread knowledge of salaries, management considered the effects of outsourcing payroll as opposed to keeping the function within the plant despite the fact that this service was rather expensive. No final decision regarding the outcome of this issue had yet been made.

Management / employee relations

Michailova was also overwhelmed by the lack of communication between managers and subordinates. This could be blamed on the absence of a corporate culture and history. First, the merger had forced several new cultures to co-exist within the plant: small-town employees and big-city Moscovites, old production employees and young sales representatives, expatriates and locals, Pibrex and Khemki Zavod (KZ). No real attempts had yet been made to unify the company. Since 1997, profitability replaced market share as the strategic focus. However, old employees and KZ managers neither understood nor embraced this decision.

Second, Michailova was informed that despite the new additions, communications remained the most volatile between the original KZ workers and middle management. This ongoing feud dated back to the initial privatization when corporate shares were first divided. According to workers, management withheld shares intended for employees at this time, and since then had retained a reputation for thieving. Several managers were removed or demoted by Pibrex in turn. According to KZ workers however, punishments were "not severe enough!" When Michailova once asked an employee what he would have done differently as plant director, he responded, "I would have fired all people from Communist times . . . administration would be fired and young people hired." When asked why, he replied, "Because they are all robbers!"

Pibrex's practice of delegation/empowerment resulted in many new roles for employees within the organization. Following the merger, Michailova learned that middle managers were given the authority to delegate tasks to production workers. However, one top manager indicated that middle managers were proud and preferred to communicate only with top executives. On the other hand, many more traditional top managers did not want to delegate, seeing decision-making ability as power. Further, middle managers were not accustomed to making decisions, but rather to acquiring top management's approval for actions, so that it would be top management's fault if something went wrong. As a result, according to one senior manager, top managers were often forced to solve simple requests such as which gloves the cleaners should wear. Production employees, in turn, distrusted middle managers and felt uncomfortable when discussing concerns with this group. Workers were rarely given direction or feedback and this projected an image of corporate incompetence led by Pibrex.

Working conditions

Working conditions within the plant were very poor and had continued to deteriorate since Pibrex's acquisition. Typical of many factories in Russia, buildings and equipment were outdated and in desperate need of repair. Perhaps this was more noticeable at KZ than in other Russian factories due to spots of modernization, such as the plant from Finland brought over in 1995. Drinking water was still not available on the factory floor despite numerous requests. The water pipes were old and rusted and water had to be boiled or bottled water provided. Further, only one location where water was boiled was made available to workers from all buildings. Lighting was poor in most stations and employees complained of eyestrain. Workers were required to clean and make equipment repairs themselves after the layoff period had reduced mechanics and cleaning staff. Much of the work at Pibrex KZ was manual and muscle strain was common. Also, uniforms were badly stained. Finally, safety was a large concern within the plant. At one point, Pibrex workers had requested an expensive fire control system costing about US$20,000, but when the funds could not be provided, they never asked for additional fire extinguishers, which management claimed they would have provided gladly if it had been asked. Currently, there were few fire extinguishers and, thus, a water tub had been placed in the filling station for emergency purposes. However, in the winter, with temperatures reaching as low as −5 degrees Celsius within the station itself, the water often froze making the emergency bath unusable.

Employees informed Michailova they believed Pibrex had inherited a poor attitude towards them and bad working conditions. Simonov, the managing director prior to 1997, in response to complaints over working conditions once commented to a group of production workers that his job, too, was dangerous as he could break his legs walking up and down the stairs every day. Michailova knew significant investments would be needed to bring the factory up to western standards. However, the reduction period tightened all finances. After the crisis there was even less money available, and it was unclear where the money for the needed renovations would come from. In addition, Popov left the company about this time, and Pibrex KZ was in the market for a new managing director especially since the president, Donaldson, was also preparing to leave.

Elena's assignment

The findings from Michailova's audit were presented periodically over the fourth quarter of 1998. The steering committee's anti-crisis management proved successful and PREN appeared somewhat satisfied with results. To Michailova's surprise, on December 10, 1998, Virpi Vasilainen, human resource manager of PREN and a member of the steering committee, called Michailova to ask her whether or not she would consider becoming not only the new financial director for the Pibrex KZ plant, but also the managing director. She had until December 22, 1998, to decide whether or not she would accept the offer. Michailova knew she would need to develop her ideas of what to include in a basic restructuring plan by December 22, since she expected the steering committee would want to know her ideas prior to appointing her managing director. Michailova felt that in conducting the audit, she had been in a good position to monitor operations objectively, and this would assist her in suggesting how operations could be turned around by the year 2000.

Possible recommendations

Following the telephone call, Michailova flipped through her notes and jotted down a few ideas on paper. She sighed, crumpled the paper, and began again. Could she effectively lead the company through its restructuring period while balancing two top management positions, even with the steering committee's help? Michailova knew that if the answer to this question was "yes," she had to act quickly or risk further financial loss and serious damage to workforce morale. She would, therefore, need to highlight the most pressing points to the steering committee, crucial to efficiency and the plant's operating potential. She also knew that Pibrex, and, thus, the steering committee, was under significant pressure from shareholders to ensure Russian operations at least break even over the following year. Showing at least a small profit, however, would increase the likelihood that Pibrex shareholders would want to keep and invest further into Pibrex's Russian operations. Michailova knew that for now, finances would undoubtedly be tight, and developing a convincing plan over the next 12 days would not be easy.

Exhibit 1 Reporting between subsidiaries and Pibrex KZ, 1995

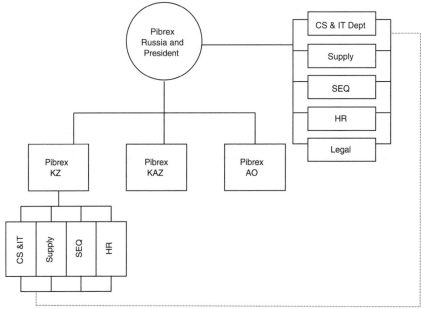

Exhibit 2 Pibrex regional divisions and turnover of operations (1999)

Region	Turnover US$*	Countries Included
Europe North	463 million	Denmark, Estonia, Finland, Iceland, Latvia, Lithuania, Norway, Russia Kaliningrad, Russia Moscow, Russia St. Petersburg, Sweden Goteborg, Sweden Sundbjberg, Ukraine
Europe South	220 million	France, Hungary, Italy, Romania, Slovakia, Spain
Europe Central	305 million	Germany, Netherlands, Poland, Switzerland
North America	366 million	Dominican Republic, Mexico, Puerto Rico, United States
South America	232 million	Ecuador, Peru, Uruguay, Venezuela

* Calculations were derived at an exchange rate of Sk8.2/US$1.
Source: Pibrex KZ, Finance Department 1999.

Notes

1.   The State Committee of Russian Statistics. 1999. "Russia in Figures", Moscow: *The State Committee of Russia Statistics*, (in Russian).
2.   Anonymous. 1998. "Plastics," *Scientific-Technical Journal*, (2): 23–25. (in Russian).

Chapter 9

Olly Racela in Bangkok

IN MAY 2000, AFTER living in Bangkok, Thailand for nearly three years, Olly Racela was slowly developing a tolerance for the local way of life. Finding herself stuck in one of the city's notorious traffic jams, Racela, a junior associate at a medium-sized Thai consulting firm, found herself thinking about a job offer she had recently received from a personal friend in Hawaii, her home state. Although the offer was "quite attractive," it was not without uncertainties. As well, Racela had developed a fondness for Thailand and had not entertained any serious thoughts about leaving the country prior to receiving the offer.

Dr. Hemant Merchant prepared this case solely to provide material for class discussion. The author does not intend to illustrate either effective or ineffective handling of a managerial situation. The author may have disguised certain names and other identifying information to protect confidentiality.

Richard Ivey School of Business
The University of Western Ontario

Racela debated whether she was ready to return to the United States. Should she stay or leave Thailand? Racela needed to convey her decision in three days.

A "farang" (foreigner) in Thailand

Racela's first trip to Thailand had been largely accidental. While earning her MBA at a reputed university in the midwest, Racela had made new friends, many of them from Thailand. She found her Thai friends to be good-natured and soon realized that they shared many of her own values and interests, including a love for travel. She bonded with them easily. During their travels together, the "Thai gang" told Racela much about their country and planted the idea that she should experience Thailand first-hand. The opportunity to visit Bangkok came shortly when, only a year after graduation, Racela became disillusioned with her first post-MBA position and sought "more fulfilling" employment elsewhere. In June 1997, Racela traveled to Bangkok to visit her friends for a few days and to ponder her career.

Less than a week after she landed at the Don Muang International Airport, Racela realized how little she knew about Bangkok and Thailand, despite everything her Thai friends had told her. For example, although Racela was generally familiar with the geography of Southeast Asia, she was unaware that the Thais called their capital city Krung Thep (City of Angels), and not Bangkok (City of Wild Plums). Racela found such details fascinating. To enrich her experience, she bought *Lonely Planet's Thailand Travel Guide*. The guide contained ample information about Thailand (see Exhibit 1). Moreover, the guide provided practical information of interest to tourists. For example, it mentioned many aspects of the Thai social etiquette (see Exhibit 2). It contained advice on ways to avoid Bangkok's legendary traffic jams (use *klongs*, i.e., canals) and suggested that most taxi fares within the city ought to be less than 200 bahts. The guide noted public buses to be the cheapest transportation mode (usually 3 bahts), but cautioned tourists about pickpockets who made a living on these buses. Finally, the guide listed numerous things to see and do in Bangkok and throughout Thailand. Racela found herself overwhelmed by so much information: Bangkok (and Thailand) seemed worlds apart from what she was accustomed to. Nonetheless, Racela looked forward to her stay, "The first time I came as a tourist, I was really excited. I was just thinking about all the different things that I'd be able to see and do."

Racela's first impressions of Bangkok were positive. For instance, she was pleasantly surprised that the Don Muang Airport was as modern and as clean as it was. The local personnel were courteous, and helpful, and all signs were in English as well as Thai. Racela found herself clearing Thailand's immigration and customs procedures quickly, and had no difficulty finding her friends who had come to receive her at the airport. Racela was equally impressed by what she saw enroute to the city. The freeway she traveled on was comparable to those in the United States, and billboards of many well-known multinationals lined both sides of the road. Racela spotted numerous high-rise towers in the distance, and marveled at the magnitude of ongoing construction everywhere. As they passed through Bangkok's main arteries, Racela was amazed at the number of large shopping centers she saw. Bangkok seemed to compare favorably with many large American cities Racela had visited. Moreover, everywhere she looked, there were countless food stalls, which, as her friends pointed out, offered an endless variety of inexpensive local Thai dishes. Racela was thrilled at what Bangkok seemed to offer and glad she had her friends to guide her during her stay in a city where English was not typically spoken. Her friends had taken time off work while she was visiting them. This meant that Racela did not have to worry about tourist-related issues, such as language or her personal safety.

Racela's experience as a tourist in Bangkok matched her first impressions of the city. There was a lot to see and do in the city itself, and Racela's friends made sure she enjoyed her stay. Together, they visited some of Asia's most magnificent *wats* (temples), among them Wat Arun (Temple of Dawn) and Wat Pra Keo (in the Grand Palace complex), and paid their homage to Lord Brahma (the Creator) at the famous Erawan shrine where also they watched free performances of Thai dances. They visited Jim Thomson's house and learned about the legendary American architect-entrepreneur who settled in Thailand after the Second World War and almost single-handedly revived the country's (then) moribund silk industry. They wandered in MBK (Mahaboonkrong, a mega-mall), window shopped in tourist districts along Sukhumvit Road and around Siam Square and haggled with vendors selling fake designer goods near Pratunum Market. They watched how the locals enjoyed themselves in traditional Thai sports at Sanam Luang (a large public park), relaxed in the oasis called Lumphini Park and how tourists enjoyed themselves on day-long boat trips on Chao Phraya River. They sampled the Thai cuisine at local food stalls and experienced the world-class Bangkok Oriental Hotel. Aside from spending time in Bangkok, Racela and her friends visited the surrounding countryside, which provided a glimpse into the Thai agrarian lifestyle. Here, shopping centers and high-rise towers gave way to rice fields and fallow lands. Life in this Thailand was noticeably different and considerably slower than in Bangkok. Racela enjoyed her stay in Thailand so much that she expressed a desire to visit the country again. Hearing this, one of her friends jokingly suggested she apply to local firms in Bangkok for work. Shortly after Racela returned home, she mailed her friend a copy of her resume. A few months later, in October 1997, Racela found herself back in Thailand having accepted a job offer from her current Thai employer.

From tourist to expatriate

Racela's position as an associate in a medium-sized consulting firm offered her an opportunity to engage her MBA more meaningfully than did her previous job. That job promised to be the best among all offers Racela had received upon her graduation. It offered US$ 36,000 plus benefits and met Racela's expectations in terms of organizational culture and potential for career growth. Yet, just six months after she began working, Racela realized this job could not provide her the challenges she was seeking. The consulting position seemed to address this important deficiency. Racela reflected on her decision to relocate to a new job in a foreign country:

What I was doing [in my previous job] wasn't rewarding. I wasn't using knowledge and skills I had gained in school. I wasn't really helping anyone. It was a satisfying and well-paying job, but I didn't feel it was productive in terms of personal satisfaction. I thought I could make a difference in Thailand. As an expatriate, I always hear the term "developing" country, meaning there is room for improvement. I interpret this as something that's in the process of starting . . . and trying to prosper.

Racela's friends in Hawaii thought she was crazy to give up a well-paying and secure job in Hawaii. However, as a young single woman, Racela had no obligations that could tie her down, and she thought that moving to Thailand would be a wonderful opportunity to live in an exotic land and travel within Asia. Racela had other personal reasons for accepting the Thai offer as well:

I've always thought about visiting other places but the thing that made me feel a little bit more comfortable about working here is that there were other people that I was placed with already. So I wouldn't really be alone. If I had gone to [another country], I would know some people but not as close as in Thailand. I knew I wanted to come back to Thailand, but when I found out about the possibility of working here, it was probably a lot more likely that I was drawn to it. And the timing was right. The timing was right for me to go.

Although knowing people in Bangkok facilitated Racela's return, she reflected on some challenges that lay before her. Racela sensed that living and working in Thailand was going to be different from being a tourist there:

Knowing I was going to be here for a long time I was a lot more worried and a little bit scared because I would be on my own. When I vacationed here, I was never separated from my friends. Now it will be different. None of my friends are working for the firm I am working for. Moreover, they live at home whereas I will be on my own. . . . I'm used to living on my own, but living on my own without being able to talk to anyone near or around is going to be a new experience.

Racela encountered other challenges. Her apartment did not have cooking facilities other than a rice cooker and a microwave, so Racela often ate out. However, because she could neither read nor speak Thai, even simple tasks (such as ordering food) often became difficult. Local vendors almost never had a menu, and when they did, it was in Thai. Consequently, Racela found herself eating at mid-priced to upscale restaurants, which not only were considerably more expensive (than the roadside vendors), but also, in Racela's opinion, served less tasty food. In a few days, Racela had her friends write the names of common Thai dishes on Post-it Notes so she could order food from local vendors. Over time, Racela memorized the pronunciation of her favorite dishes; sometimes, she just tried whatever looked interesting. Her friends always offered help, but this conflicted with Racela's need for independence.

> I have two very, very good friends. I know I can count on them, but I try not to depend on them. They would do anything for me if I asked for it. This feeling of dependence makes me uncomfortable. I always tell them, "Don't take away my freedom. It doesn't help me to always have the extra help." It took me a long time. It took me about eight months before I was really on my own.

Living in Bangkok

Independence turned out to be a double-edged sword for Racela. On one hand, it enabled her to travel on her own, permitted her to learn more about herself and allowed her to develop greater respect and tolerance for others. On the other hand, independence sometimes landed Racela in difficult situations, which made her wonder how much longer she could endure the seemingly minor, but frustrating, situations.

Being independent allowed Racela to discover many facets of Bangkok life without co-ordinating with her friends. Traveling around the city on weekends gave Racela an opportunity to better absorb Thailand's history and culture, and experience city life first-hand. Whenever possible, she traveled around Bangkok using its oldest transportation mode, *klongs*. The canals gave Racela a chance to experience the diversity of city life along their banks, from people tending to their huts on stilts to children playing in muddy waters to tugboats hauling large barges enroute to their destinations. Racela noticed many small *wats* along the klongs and wondered about their history. Indeed, Bangkok was full of ancient *wats* and boasted of many museums, such as the National Museum with its impressive collection of Thai art. Other areas of the city, such as Chinatown and the Indian and Italian districts, offered interesting glimpses into external influences on Thailand. When Racela wanted a change of scenery, she visited the expatriate zone on Silom Road or the tourist district on Sukhumvit Road where she could interact with nationals from other countries. Bangkok was also a shopper's paradise. It offered everything from pirated electronics to first-rate book selections to authentic luxury goods. Vendors selling fake versions of everything imaginable coexisted with upscale department stores, such as the Tokyu and Isetan. While such stores were comfortable and convenient, Racela found it more fun to bargain with countless smaller vendors that sold similar goods, albeit of inferior quality.

Racela's excursions into the city gave her the confidence to travel outside the city. There were many interesting places within a few hours of Bangkok. For example, Ayuthya, Thailand's former capital, was only a two-hour bus ride. The famous "Bridge on River Kwai" at Kanchanaburi was merely 150 kilometres from Bangkok, whereas Ko Samet, a popular island, was about four hours away. Racela enjoyed these travels as well:

The travel is great also, but I've been so busy that I can't travel as much as I'd like to. I've probably been to at least 20 destinations outside Bangkok. They're all very, very different—not just as destinations but also in terms of the local inhabitants. The Thais exhibit different degrees of friendliness, but all are generally friendly. Some are more intrigued by Westerners than others. If you go to Phuket [in southern Thailand], I think they're more used to Westerners and so less intrigued but they're still very hospitable. If you go to northern Thailand, you don't see that many Westerners, and so the locals there have the same curiosity that you have about them. But again, they're still very, very hospitable.

Travelling was something Racela didn't know if she could give up:

Despite my busy schedule, I still want to travel . . . It is one thing I don't want to give up. And it's just different for me. It's hard to explain. I know inside that maybe United States isn't the place for me to be. I think I'm of greater value somewhere else.

Racela benefited from her independence in other ways as well. Because of her travel experiences, she learned more about herself, her abilities and about others. Over time, Racela developed greater respect for others and cultivated tolerance for a different way of doing things. She began to see things from a Thai perspective:

Just the other day, I met a man for the first time. He said, "Let me tell you about some Thai behavior. I had a meeting with a Thai executive at six o'clock yesterday, and he didn't show up and didn't even call to apologize. Why can't these people pick up Western standards?" I was just sitting there thinking, "Oh my god, we're in Thailand. When in Thailand do as the Thais do." He continued, "When I saw him this morning, I said, 'Where were you at six o'clock?' and he replied, 'I went to get a haircut' . . . Can you believe this guy is a top Thai executive?" And on and on he went. I thought this is terrible. This is an expat working in Thailand and he expects Thai people to be Westerners. We shouldn't always have this sense of superiority. It seems that many foreigners lack that understanding. Even I do. I didn't realize how narrow my own thinking was until I had lived here for a few months.

Although Bangkok nurtured Racela in important ways, living in the city was not without its demerits. To the unaccustomed, Bangkok epitomized a hostile city: it was over-crowded, very polluted and unbearably hot. The city was infamous for its notorious traffic jams, albeit a recently constructed highway system around the city alleviated some traffic-related problems. The city's rapid growth was largely unplanned and created an urban chaos sprawling in every direction. Commuting under these conditions was never pleasant, even for the locals, except on weekends when the city's traffic congestion eased a bit.

Racela experienced the frustration of daily commute almost every day, calling it a nightmare. She did not own a car in Bangkok, nor did she have access to a company car. Hence, she depended on public transportation and taxis. Bangkok taxi drivers were known for overcharging unsuspecting passengers, usually by taking them via shortcuts that were not so. Consequently, Racela preferred the city's main arteries—which were invariably clogged—to the so-called shortcuts. A small consolation was that the taxis were air-conditioned and provided some quiet, albeit these comforts exacted a large price. Depending upon the distance travelled, taxis could cost almost 10 times as much as the city's most expensive air-conditioned Micro buses. Bangkok's public buses left much to be desired, at least in comparison with Western standards. The ubiquitous red buses were cheap (usually a 3½ baht fare), but dirty, over-crowded and known to host pickpockets. Racela never took these buses, preferring the relatively more expensive blue air-conditioned buses, which also plied along the city's congested main roads. Racela once wrote to her family:

> Buses are OK. I relied on buses for a long time, but the thing about buses here is that you don't know how long it's going to take getting from here to there. The only reason I took buses is because I knew exactly what route they would take so that I wouldn't be surprised . . . But buses here are so crowded. I have to wait at the bus stop on average for at least one hour to board a bus that was available. I don't take the red bus because of the pollution. I can't sit in them for 1½ hours because Bangkok is hot and polluted, and I have allergies.

Racela's general lack of the Thai language compounded the challenges of living in a foreign country. Although she taught herself bits and pieces of the language, it was far from what seemed necessary to get by, particularly outside the work environment. The lack of language skills occasionally landed Racela in unpleasant situations, exacerbating her frustration.

> One Sunday morning I needed to go to Silom, a very well-known road here . . . I don't know how but I ended up taking a taxi that didn't know where it was. The driver couldn't speak English. I couldn't speak Thai. He just kept saying, "Silom, Silom." After a few minutes, I knew he didn't know where Silom Road was. I knew how to get there because by then I had become somewhat familiar with the city. He was going to take a U-turn and go back to where we came from, so I asked him in broken Thai, "Where are you going?" He went down this wide street and pulled over on the side and was visibly upset. I didn't know what he was saying but guessed he was telling me to get out of the cab. Luckily he uttered a few Thai words I could recall, "Don't worry about the fare." At least I knew what that meant. So I got out in the middle of nowhere and was wondering how to get to where I need to go. I had to walk down this unknown street and was really scared because in Bangkok there are more crimes against women than against men . . . I've probably had my worst experiences with cab drivers. I'm not saying all of them are like that, but . . .

While Racela admitted that many of her problems stemmed from her lack of local language skills, she questioned whether being conversant in Thai would have made any real difference in her ability to better adapt to life in Bangkok. Besides, Racela had always found someone among city crowds who could understand and speak enough English to assist her. Racela believed she could get by in Bangkok without knowing Thai. The lack of language seemed to be a blessing for Racela:

> Since I don't know the language, I think I would want to stay. It would make it easier for me to stay. It is difficult for me to know whether I would appreciate knowing what the locals are saying. I'm at the point where I can tell if someone is talking about me. Maybe that's all I need to know.

Racela benefited from the city life in other ways as well. During the late 1990s, Bangkok had enhanced its public transportation system with the result that the city seemed a bit less congested and the air quality had improved slightly. To accommodate the anticipated increase in traffic due to Asian Games held in Bangkok, the Thai government had built many highways around the city and constructed an elevated transit system between major points. These upgrades reduced travel times for some trips as much as 75 per cent, and seemed to be well-received by the locals. Both toll highways and the transit system were relatively expensive by average Thai standards but not so by Western standards. For example, train fares ranged between 10 and 40 bahts, and could be easily paid with prepaid cards. It was estimated that the transit system alone led to 40,000 fewer cars per day. The congestion was expected to ease even more in 2002 when a subway system was expected to be in place. Racela expected to benefit from these improvements, but safety continued to be an issue for her if she was traveling alone. Racela tried to manage her travel risk. She bought herself a mobile phone that enabled her to call upon her friends when she found herself in unexpected situations:

> I've been really kind of cautious . . . I don't know how to use the public phones yet. Pretty pathetic. Three years and I still don't know how to use phones.

Racela's increased use of newer transportation modes and taxis and her concern for safety increased her living expenses in Bangkok. Occasionally, it also made her feel out-of-place and homesick, despite a busy work life, friends and colleagues, and myriad of activities that could be pursued in and around Bangkok:

> I miss my parents and family. I call home all the time. And I go home at least once a year. The thing is that I don't have cable TV. So all I have available on television is Thai, which I don't understand . . . It's driving me absolutely crazy. I get CNN, that's about it. So what did I do for loneliness? I bought a VCR and watch American movies all the

time. That's my entertainment now. Sad? Yeah. My personal life here is non-existent. If I'm looking for romance it would be very difficult . . . Thai men are kind of intimidated by my Western aggressiveness. I'm not sure how they interpret a woman that speaks loudly. I mean I'm not loud, but someone who speaks with confidence, is assertive, is very straightforward. I'm not sure if that's the kind of woman they're attracted to.

Working in Bangkok

Despite the challenges, Racela was slowly adjusting to a different way of life in Bangkok. However, her adjustment to the Thai workplace was more difficult than she had anticipated. The Thai and American workplaces were very different from each other in terms of autonomy, decision-making processes, acceptable office behavior and work ethic. These differences were a constant source of frustration and tension to Racela.

> When I first came here, I thought, "There are a lot of things I know. I hope to make a difference." I came as a cowgirl. That Western attitude: I'm gonna go and I want to make changes, suggest improvements. I soon realized that the Thais just really have a different way of doing things.

Racela recalled an encounter with one of the senior partners on her first day on the job. It was her first clue that the Thai work environment was unlike what she was accustomed to in the United States. Racela wondered how seriously she would be taken in her new role:

> When I first met my boss, it was kind of like an interview after I had been hired. Later, he described me as, "Oh yes! She's a very pretty girl." I thought that was a pretty strange thing to say. It made me wonder if I had been hired for my skills or for my good looks.

Over time, Racela developed a feeling that Thai males, especially those in higher positions, looked at her "in a certain way." She learned that it was not unusual for job ads to state the desired gender or age for a particular job, or request pretty job applicants. Such recruitment criteria would be considered discriminatory in the United States, but they seemed accepted in Thailand. Racela rationalized:

> Some Thai workplace behavior would be considered sexual harassment in the United States, but I let it go . . . I figure maybe they don't know what they are saying. Why rub elbows? Maybe that's just their way, their sense of humor, although it is with certain men in higher positions . . . they just make comments about women. Mind you, not all Thai males are like that. There is a social hierarchy based partly on gender, but most people are tolerant, respectful and courteous. I

really enjoy working with my colleagues and find them to be
extremely friendly.

Being a woman had one other disadvantage in the Thai workplace: Women
usually were paid less than men doing the same job. Racela found this was true
regarding her base salary. Although she did not usually discuss money with other
Westerners, Racela learned she was earning less than male Westerners. Some of
them had even urged her to ask for a raise in her gross compensation. Racela
learned that the Thai compensation system differed from its American counterpart in one other way: Performance bonuses were awarded more or less evenly
across the firm. These supposedly merit-based increases rarely differentiated
among individuals in terms of their performance; the differences seemed to be
driven by an individual's relative position within the firm:

> They evaluate your work, and as long as you perform your duties
> you get merit increases . . . Everyone gets the same amount, unless
> you do something severely bad then you don't get the bonus.

Despite her salary gap, Racela drew a comfortable paycheck. Her monthly salary
of 28,000 bahts (plus benefits) placed her in the upper-middle income bracket.
In contrast, the monthly minimum wage rate in Bangkok was approximately
4,800 bahts. Although Racela's salary was extremely modest by Western standards, she was not too concerned about her compensation as she had saved
US$15,000; these dollars would go a long way in Thailand. Racela felt pretty
secure financially. Her parents had always encouraged her to broaden her
horizons so she knew that they would be supportive if need arose. Moreover, the
purchasing power of Thai baht was relatively high. In that sense, Racela was
doing quite well. Yet, Racela had to be careful about how much she indulged
herself given the baht's recent decline in the foreign currency markets. On
June 15, 1997, the exchange rate was US$1 = Bht24.80; on October 15, 1997,
the exchange rate was US$1 = Bht36.78; on May 15, 2000, the exchange rate
was US$1 = Bht38.92.

Racela was glad she had negotiated that her company provide her with
accommodation; being a Westerner had helped her secure that benefit:

> I get better treatment, but not because I am a woman. They are nice
> to Westerners . . . We have expats here from developing countries
> and they don't get the same accommodations. I consider my accom-
> modations to be more than I ever expected. I was very pleasantly
> surprised at what they gave me.

Racela's one bedroom apartment had air conditioning, a refrigerator, a television
and a Western-style bathroom. It also had 24-hour running hot water, which was
unusual. Such an accommodation would have been standard in the United States,
but not in Thailand. It was much more than she had expected, and Racela clearly
preferred it that way. Coming from Hawaii, "where everyone is a minority,"
Racela enjoyed this new exalted experience:

I am used to a certain high standard of living now . . . I would exploit my Western status to retain it. If I were to go back to the United States, I would be like everyone else again.

Nonetheless, Racela's preferential accommodation treatment sometimes left her a little unsettled. It gave her a new perspective on minority issues:

> Being here has changed my opinion on discrimination because it actually became an advantage to be a Westerner. I don't like it deep inside me. I feel guilty, but I appreciate it all the same time. We shouldn't always have this sense of superiority. It seems that many foreigners—I won't say all—lack that understanding. Even I do. I didn't realize how narrow my own thinking was. When I first came I thought, "Why can't you Thais speak English?" Living here has mainly changed my opinion about the West. I think that's probably why I don't want to go back.

While Thailand influenced Racela in many ways, it had not altered her views about the Thai work ethic. Racela summarized her perceptions:

> Efficiency is different. There is a big difference between getting things done and *trying* to get something done and having to ask someone for help to get it done . . . The Thais don't really find the need to take care of things right away. So I have to adjust to that.

Over time, Racela had learned to accommodate her colleagues' work habits by planning her office work well in advance. For example, if she needed input on a client report by the 15th, she would ask for the feedback by the eighth. With any luck, she would get the feedback by the 13th so as to give her two days to incorporate the suggested changes. All this meant Racela had to start writing reports earlier than would otherwise be required, and still was constantly up against deadlines. Racela found this to be extremely frustrating and stressful. Racela's way of doing things was typical of most Americans: If it needs to be done, get it done now. However, in Thailand, it was difficult to get things done right away. Racela had to get used to the *mai pen rai* (do not worry) attitude of doing things.

Often, Racela felt that there wasn't much autonomy in her job. The decisions she made were often changed, which begged the question, "Why even ask me in the first place?" While she wasn't the only one this happened to, it really bothered her and left her feeling that her employers did not trust her professionally.

> They always ask a lot of questions. But I don't think they're willing to make a lot of changes. It's quite difficult to make changes here. For one thing, you don't tell someone that there is a better way to do something because that is kind of like an offense . . . It is perceived as the equivalent of saying, "You've been doing it wrong all along and I

have a better way. You should be doing it my way." I realized you should comment only when asked to . . . I was seldom asked, so my enthusiasm and my role as cowgirl just changed. I knew there wasn't much I could do.

Unlike the firm Racela previously worked for, her current firm lacked structure. For example, the firm had a Personnel Handbook that most people in the organization did not adhere to. There were few, if any, procedures for dealing even with routine tasks. Most staffers had multiple roles, with the result that no one individual could be held accountable for tardy work. Senior staff members were more concerned about preserving harmony and creating "good atmosphere" than about improving office productivity. Likewise, the firms' partners were busy socializing with important clients who could give them more business. Thus, most of the burden fell upon junior associates who sometimes came in on Sundays to catch up on pending work or simply organize their work for the following week. Having spent a few Sundays at work herself, Racela sometimes found herself so upset that she was ready to pack her bags and return home to a more predictable job. Once she confided to a close friend, "I just really get upset. Really upset. Yes, upset enough to go home . . . and get back into something that is a little more sensible." Yet, at the end of the day, there was still something keeping her in Thailand. Racela wasn't sure what it was.

Sensing Racela's disappointment, management encouraged her to take part in an expensive training program sponsored by the company. She thought this might give her a better chance of making an impact:

> I don't think I'm at that point of returning home yet. I still think that if I keep trying maybe I'll make a difference here, but I think the time might come soon when I'm ready to go home. I make recommendations on how to improve things but the senior partners always find a reason why it won't work . . . which is fine. It is a different perspective. They recommend that I enroll in a management development program. However, if they don't give me leeway after that and it still doesn't get me into a position to make a difference, I might leave.

The fact that Racela's employers were willing to sponsor her management development suggested the company saw her as more valuable than she often felt. It was likely that Racela would be offered more challenging assignments. Almost certainly, Racela would draw a higher salary. On the other hand, while the management program would benefit Racela's career prospects in Thailand, it would be of little value elsewhere. Additionally, Racela would have to sign a contract to work for her firm three more years. Racela wondered if she could commit herself to this obligation that would automatically require her to extend her stay in Thailand. Even if she did commit herself, it was quite possible that Thai workplace traditions would continue to stifle Racela in important ways. Yet, Racela drew some consolation in knowing that other people around her recognized the value of her ideas, even if management did not. Many of her clients admired her as well. Racela felt good to have people appreciate her and look up to her:

> My clients tell me all the time that I am very different from Thai women. That's why they are drawn to me. They always say, "I'd like to be like you." Even men tell me that. All of them say, "I want to be confident. I want to be straightforward." Confidence is the word they use when they talk about me.

The myriad of experiences had influenced Racela significantly in many ways. Racela reflected on how her three-year stay in Thailand had changed her.

> I have learnt to be tolerant. I hope I have a better understanding of another culture. In many, many ways, Thailand has changed me. I still try to make the most of every day. I am a lot easier going now. Nothing is a big deal. I always try to take it easy, no matter how much work is involved. I think their way of thinking has calmed me.

The decision

Living in Thailand apparently had shaped the person Racela had become. When she visited home, her friends often commented on how she had changed: "You know, you are different from what you were before. You are so easygoing now." The opportunity for personal growth and for contributing to the workplace had kept her in Bangkok, as had her education from traveling and the city itself. Racela had developed a life for herself here, but she also had a life at home in the United States. The job offer Racela had recently received would take her to her family. At home, in the United States, Racela would not have to constantly struggle with cultural issues, not to mention the traffic and pollution. The Hawaiian offer held promise for Racela's career, but the position itself was an unknown to a large extent. As the executive director of a startup eco-tourism company, Racela would partly be responsible for the company's internal operations and partly for setting its strategic direction. Racela would initially report to a retired marine engineer, who owned half of the company. Due to time and financial constraints, Racela and the firm's owners had conversed over the telephone for about half an hour. Racela gained as much insight into the job as could be expected from such a conversation, and reluctantly summarized her overall feeling as being "generally positive." There was so much to consider.

Racela's thoughts were interrupted by the sounds of car honks and roaring motorcycle engines. The city's traffic was crawling again. Everybody seemed eager to get home, if only to repeat their travails the next day. Racela herself needed the comfort of her apartment to think more clearly about what she wanted to do in the medium to long term. Would Thailand continue to be right for her, or was it time to move on?

Exhibit 1 Country information, Thailand

History

Thailand's earliest recorded inhabitants were Buddhist Mons who formed the loosely knit Dvaravati kingdom in the Chao Phraya basin from the 6th to 11th centuries. From the 8th to 12th centuries, Hindu Khmers expanded westward from Kampuchea and absorbed the Mons into their powerful empire. Mons today have largely disappeared in Thailand, although a sizable Mon community still exists in Myanmar. The Thai (Tai) people arrived later; two theories speculate as to their origins. Most believe they migrated from southern China during the 11th and 12th centuries and settled among the Khmers and Mons already residing in the central plains. Others argue that Neolithic cave settlements near Kanchanaburi and recent discoveries of a 6,000-year-old Bronze culture at Ban Chiang prove that the Thais preceded the Mons and Khmers.

Government

Thailand is a constitutional monarchy with a bicameral legislature consisting of a Senate appointed by the king and a National Assembly elected by the people. The National Assembly is composed primarily of the liberal-leaning Chart Thai, Social Action, and Democrat parties, three political groups who often form coalitions to work with the military. Both chambers elect a prime minister who chooses a cabinet of 20 ministers. Thailand's leading political figure of the early 1980s was smiling Prem Tinsulanonda, a handsome enigma who confounded the critics by holding the job of prime minister for almost 8 years—an amazing accomplishment when you consider that Thailand since 1932 has suffered through a dozen coups and 13 constitutions. Nineteen eighty-eight proved to be a watershed in Thai politics after public pressure for an elected leader brought the arrival of Chatichai Choonhavan, a business-minded politician who favors democracy over military rule. Chatichai fell from power in 1992 during a military coup in which dozens of citizens were murdered near Democracy Monument in Bangkok. Thailand today appears to be moving toward a compromise government of military influence but civilian control. The emerging hierarchy seems to be comprised of freely elected democratic leaders who work with ex-military leaders, the government bureaucracy, and powerful Chinese businessmen who control the economy.

Economy

Historically, Thailand's agrarian economy revolved around exports of commodities such as rubber, rice, and maize. In 1960s, a decision was made to begin a process of industrialization. This process gained momentum during 1980s as the Pacific Rim emerged as a significant economic force. Between 1991 and 1997 Thailand's exports doubled from US$28.2 billion to US$56.7 billion. During this time locally manufactured products accounted for approximately 80% of total exports which included computers and parts, textiles, jewelry, electronic and automotive parts. Despite this increasing role of manufacturing, about two-thirds of the country's labor force was still employed in the agricultural sector. The work-force in 1999 was about 32.9 million, most of it under the age of thirty.

Climate

Thailand's climate is ruled by monsoons that produce three seasons in northern, north-eastern, and central Thailand and two in southern Thailand. Generally the 'dry and wet' monsoon climate arrives sometime between May and July and lasts into November. It is followed by a dry season in which temperatures are relatively low until February and then begin to soar from March through May. Although some areas in northern Thailand are more temperate, the climate is best described as tropical—hot and humid. It rains the least during November through February when average temperatures are the most moderate, ranging from 18°C to 32°C (i.e., 65°F to 90°F). In Bangkok, March–June is the hottest period with average temperatures around 34°C (94°F).

Geography and demographics

Thailand is shaped like an elephant's head, and shares it borders with Myanmar, Laos, Cambodia, and Malaysia. The country's east coast borders the Gulf of Thailand and the west coast abuts the Andaman Sea. The country is divided into four main zones: the fertile, central plains of the Chao Phraya River; the poorer region of the 300m (985ft) high northeast plateau; the fertile valley and mountains of Northern Thailand; and the rain-forested southern peninsula. The country occupies 517,000 square kilometers of land, and is home to more than 60 million people, 80% of whom resided in rural areas in 1990. Approximately 75% of the country's population consists of Thais; the Chinese make up another 14% whereas the rest of the population is a mix of immigrants from India, Sri Lanka, and other countries.

Religion

Although Buddhism is Thailand's principal religion, there is complete religious freedom in the country. Modern Buddhism is divided into the Theravada school adopted in Sri Lanka, Thailand, and Burma, and the Mahayana version favored in China and Japan. Thais further subdivide Theravada into the less-rigorous Mahanikaya order, the majority cult, and the stricter Thammayut order followed by less than 10% of the population. Theravada Buddhism, the state religion of Thailand is practiced by 90% of the population. The king of Thailand, under the constitution and in practice, is patron of all major religions.

Language

The majority of the population speaks Thai, which is the country's official language. In addition to Thai, many people speak Chinese, and English is usually taught in primary and secondary schools. Thai is a monosyllabic and tonal language with 44 consonants, 24 vowels, and five tortes. Script is written from left to right without separation between words. There are no prefixes or suffixes, genders, articles, plurals, or verb conjugations. If this makes Thai appear to be a simple language, consider the following. Thai is a tonal language in which each word can be pronounced with five different tones: low, middle, high, rising, or falling. Each tone completely changes the meaning of the word. *Suay* with a rising tone means "wonderful" but with a falling tone means "bad fortune." Obviously, most

Thai words should be double-checked with a native speaker for correct pronunciation. The transliteration of Thai script into Romanized script is an inexact science and there is no accepted standardization of spelling. Each word can be spelled several different ways—such as the avenue in Bangkok variously rendered as Rajadamnern, Ratchadamnoen, and Rajdamnoen. Thai has several unique sounds that cannot properly be expressed with Roman letters. For example, there are sounds midway between D and T and others midway between B and P. Fortunately, Thai pronunciation is much more logical and consistent than English. Pity the poor Thai student studying English when confronted with cough, rough, though, thought, and through!

The Thai people

Thailand is one of the most racially homogeneous countries in Southeast Asia: about 82% of the country's 60 million inhabitants are Thai. Thais on the whole are a delightful race of people who believe life is to be enjoyed so long as no one impinges on another's rights. Many decline to be fanatical about productivity or deadlines. Foreign visitors are often perplexed with their stubborn resistance to the Westerner's fast-paced, ulcer-prone life. This attitude is epitomized by the phrase *mai pen rai* (never mind). Perhaps because of their Buddhist upbringings, Thais detest any form of conflict and will go to great pains to avoid confrontation and preserve harmony. This attitude—*jai yen* (cool heart)—is strongly favored over *jai rohn* (hot heart). One form of violence you *must* avoid is face-to-face criticism. Unlike Westerners, who criticize friends without ruining relationships, Thais see criticism as highly personal attacks. To make friends and enjoy yourself in Thailand, keep a *jai yen*. Thais are also a race of people obsessed with social ranking. Correct social conduct only happens after superior–inferior roles have been determined through direct questions such as "How much do you earn?" Westerners should consider such inquiries as friendliness or a form of flattery rather than an invasion of privacy. Social ranking is also reflected in the Thai language, including dozens of ways to say "I" depending on the speaker's social status. The top of the structure is fairly obvious: the king, his family, and the Buddhist priesthood. Below that are the variables of age, social connections, lineal descent, earnings, and education.

Sources: Cummings, 2001; Lonely Planet, 1994; Lonely Planet Online, 2001; Siengthai & Leelakulthanit, 1994.

Exhibit 2 Social etiquette in Thailand

Greetings and Gestures

- While most urban Thais are familiar with the Western-style hand-shake, the traditional Thai greeting is a with one's palms together in a prayer-like manner. This is known as *wâi*.
- When handing things to other people you should use both hands or your right hand only.

Do's

- Smile.
- Avoid disparaging comments about the royal family.
- Stand when you hear the national or royal anthems.

- Dress modestly.
- Dress neatly in temples, and elsewhere.
- Remove your shoes when entering a Thai home, or any building containing a Buddha image.
- Take what is offered in terms of food or drink if visiting someone's home.

Don'ts

- Don't pose for pictures in front of Buddha images as they are considered sacred.
- Don't wear short-sleeved or sleeveless shirts in temples.
- Monks should not touch or be touched by women.
- Don't use your feet to point at people, as this is the lowest part of the body spiritually.
- Don't put feet on table.
- Don't touch others with your feet.
- Don't touch anyone's head.

Face

It is important to not to embarrass oneself or others. Don't bring up negative topics when one notices stress in others' lives, and don't mention this stress unless the other person asks for help.

Status and obligation

Most relationships in Thai society are governed by the *phûu yai* (big person) *phûu náwy* (little person) connection. The status of this relationship is determined by age, wealth, status, and personal and political power. This is a reciprocal obligation wherein the younger are expected to show obedience and respect, but the older are expected to sponsor or take care of the *phûu náwy* they have constant contact with. For example *phûu yai* always pays for dinner, and for a *phûu náwy* to try to pay would risk losing face. Wealth is to be shared.

This concept explains why it is common for new acquaintances to ask, "How old are you?" as it helps determine the relative status of one person to another. It also explains why foreigners are often charged more, as they are seen as having more wealth than the most locals.

Sànùk

Sànùk means fun. There is an underlying concept in Thai culture which suggests that anything worth doing should contain an element of enjoyment or fun. This leads most Thais to approach tasks with a sense of playfulness and applies to labor jobs, as well as white-collar work in banks or offices. Sànùk finds its way into work through such means as singing, telling jokes or even flirtation between sexes.

Chapter 10

Distance still matters
The hard reality of global expansion

WHEN IT WAS LAUNCHED in 1991, Star TV looked like a surefire winner. The plan was straightforward: The company would deliver television programming to a media-starved Asian audience. It would target the top 5% of Asia's socioeconomic pyramid, a newly rich elite who could not only afford the services but who also represented an attractive advertising market. Since English was the second language for most of the target consumers, Star would be able to use readily available and fairly cheap English-language programming rather than having to invest heavily in creating new local programs. And by using satellites to beam programs into people's homes, it would sidestep the constraints of geographic distance that had hitherto kept traditional broadcasters out of Asia. Media mogul Rupert Murdoch was so taken with this plan—especially with the appeal of leveraging his Twentieth Century Fox film library across the Asian market—that his company, News Corporation, bought out Star's founders for $825 million between 1993 and 1995.

The results have not been quite what Murdoch expected. In its fiscal year ending June 30, 1999, Star reportedly lost $141 million, pretax, on revenues of $111 million. Losses in fiscal years 1996 through 1999 came to about $500 million all told, not including losses on joint ventures such as Phoenix TV in China. Star is not expected to turn in a positive operating profit until 2002.

Star has been a high-profile disaster, but similar stories are played out all the time as companies pursue global expansion. Why? Because, like Star, they routinely overestimate the attractiveness of foreign markets. They become so dazzled by the sheer size of untapped markets that they lose sight of the vast difficulties of pioneering new, often very different territories. The problem is rooted in the very analytic tools that managers rely on in making judgments about international investments, tools that consistently underestimate the costs of doing business internationally. The most prominent of these is country port-folio analysis (CPA), the hoary but still widely used technique for deciding where a company should compete. By focusing on national GDP, levels of consumer wealth, and people's propensity to consume, CPA places all the emphasis on potential sales. It ignores the costs and risks of doing business in a new market.

Most of those costs and risks result from barriers created by distance. By distance, I don't mean only geographic separation, though that is important. Distance also has cultural, administrative or political, and economic dimensions that can make foreign markets considerably more or less attractive. Just how much difference does distance make? A recent study by economists Jeffrey Frankel and Andrew Rose estimates the impact of various factors on a country's trade flows. Traditional economic factors, such as the country's wealth and size (GDP), still matter; a 1% increase in either of those measures creates, on average, a .7% to .8% increase in trade. But other factors related to distance, it turns out, matter even more. The amount of trade that takes place between countries 5,000 miles apart is only 20% of the amount that would be predicted to take place if the same countries were 1,000 miles apart. Cultural and adminis-trative distance produces even larger effects. A company is likely to trade ten times as much with a country that is a former colony, for instance, than with a country to which it has no such ties. A common currency increases trade by 340%. Common membership in a regional trading bloc increases trade by 330%. And so on. (For a summary of Frankel and Rose's findings, see the exhibit "Measuring the impact of distance.")

Much has been made of the death of distance in recent years. It's been argued that information technologies and, in particular, global communications are shrinking the world, turning it into a small and relatively homogeneous place. But when it comes to business, that's not only an incorrect assumption, it's a dangerous one. Distance still matters, and companies must explicitly and thoroughly account for it when they make decisions about global expansion. Traditional country portfolio analysis needs to be tempered by a clear-eyed evaluation of the many dimensions of distance and their probable impact on opportunities in foreign markets.

The four dimensions of distance

Distance between two countries can manifest itself along four basic dimensions: cultural, administrative, geographic, and economic. The types of distance influ-ence different businesses in different ways. Geographic distance, for instance, affects the costs of transportation and communications, so it is of particular importance to companies that deal with heavy or bulky products, or whose operations require a high degree of coordination among highly dispersed

Table 10.1 Measuring the impact of distance

Economists often rely on the so-called gravity theory of trade flows, which says there is a positive relationship between economic size and trade and a negative relationship between distance and trade. Models based on this theory explain up to two-thirds of the observed variations in trade flows between pairs of countries. Using such a model, economists Jeffrey Frankel and Andrew Rose[1] have predicted how much certain distance variables will affect trade.

Distance Attribute	Change in International Trade (%)
income level: GDP per capita (1% increase)	+0.7
economic size: GDP (1% increase)	+0.8
physical distance (1% increase)	−1.1
physical size (1% increase)*	−0.2
access to ocean*	+50
common border	+80
common language	+200
common regional trading bloc	+330
colony–colonizer relationship	+900
common colonizer	+190
common polity	+300
common currency	+340

1. Jeffrey Frankel and Andrew Rose, "An Estimate of the Effects of Currency Unions on Growth," unpublished working paper, May 2000.
* Estimated effects exclude the last four variables in the table.

people or activities. Cultural distance, by contrast, affects consumers' product preferences. It is a crucial consideration for any consumer goods or media company, but it is much less important for a cement or steel business.

Each of these dimensions of distance encompasses many different factors, some of which are readily apparent; others are quite subtle. (See the exhibit "The CAGE distance framework" for an overview of the factors and the ways in which they affect particular industries.) In the following pages, I will review the four principal dimensions of distance, starting with the two overlooked the most—cultural distance and administrative distance.

Cultural distance

A country's cultural attributes determine how people interact with one another and with companies and institutions. Differences in religious beliefs, race, social norms, and language are all capable of creating distance between two countries. Indeed, they can have a huge impact on trade: All other things being equal, trade between countries that share a language, for example, will be three times greater than between countries without a common language.

Some cultural attributes, like language, are easily perceived and understood. Others are much more subtle. Social norms, the deeply rooted system of unspoken principles that guide individuals in their everyday choices and

The CAGE *distance framework*

The cultural, administrative, geographic, and economic (CAGE) distance framework helps managers identify and assess the impact of distance on various industries. The upper portion of the table lists the key attributes underlying the four dimensions of distance. The lower portion shows how they affect different products and industries.

	Cultural Distance	Administrative Distance	Geographic Distance	Economic Distance
Attributes creating distance	different languages different ethnicities; lack of connective ethnic or social networks different religions different social norms	absence of colonial ties absence of shared monetary or political association political hostility government policies institutional weakness	physical remoteness lack of a common border lack of sea or river access size of country weak transportation or communication links differences in climates	differences in consumer incomes differences in costs and quality of: • natural resources • financial resources • human resources • infrastructure • intermediate inputs • information or knowledge
Industries or products affected by distance	products have high linguistic content (TV) products affect cultural or national identity of consumers (foods) product features vary in terms of: • size (cars) • standards (electrical appliances) • packaging products carry country-specific quality associations (wines)	government involvement is high in industries that are: • producers of staple goods (electricity) • producers of other "entitlements" (drugs) • large employers (farming) • large suppliers to government (mass transportation) • national champions (aerospace) • vital to national security (telecommunications) • exploiters of natural resources (oil, mining) • subject to high sunk costs (infrastructure)	products have a low value-to-weight or bulk ratio (cement) products are fragile or perishable (glass, fruit) communications and connectivity are important (financial services) local supervision and operational requirements are high (many services)	nature of demand varies with income level (cars) economies of standardization or scale are important (mobile phones) labor and other factor cost differences are salient (garments) distribution or business systems are different (insurance) companies need to be responsive and agile (home appliances)

interactions, are often nearly invisible, even to the people who abide by them. Take, for instance, the long-standing tolerance of the Chinese for copyright infringement. As William Alford points out in his book *To Steal a Book Is an Elegant Offense* (Stanford University Press, 1995), many people ascribe this social norm to China's recent communist past. More likely, Alford argues, it flows from a precept of Confucius that encourages replication of the results of past intellectual endeavors: "I transmit rather than create; I believe in and love the Ancients." Indeed, copyright infringement was a problem for Western publishers well before communism. Back in the 1920s, for example, Merriam Webster, about to introduce a bilingual dictionary in China, found that the Commercial Press in Shanghai had already begun to distribute its own version of the new dictionary. The U.S. publisher took the press to a Chinese court, which imposed a small fine for using the Merriam Webster seal but did nothing to halt publication. As the film and music industries well know, little has changed. Yet this social norm still confounds many Westerners.

Most often, cultural attributes create distance by influencing the choices that consumers make between substitute products because of their preferences for specific features. Color tastes, for example, are closely linked to cultural prejudices. The word "red" in Russian also means beautiful. Consumer durable industries are particularly sensitive to differences in consumer taste at this level. The Japanese, for example, prefer automobiles and household appliances to be small, reflecting a social norm common in countries where space is highly valued.

Sometimes products can touch a deeper nerve, triggering associations related to the consumer's identity as a member of a particular community. In these cases, cultural distance affects entire categories of products. The food industry is particularly sensitive to religious attributes. Hindus, for example, do not eat beef because it is expressly forbidden by their religion. Products that elicit a strong response of this kind are usually quite easy to identify, though some countries will provide a few surprises. In Japan, rice, which Americans treat as a commodity, carries an enormous amount of cultural baggage.

Ignoring cultural distance was one of Star TV's biggest mistakes. By supposing that Asian viewers would be happy with English-language programming, the company assumed that the TV business was insensitive to culture. Managers either dismissed or were unaware of evidence from Europe that mass audiences in countries large enough to support the development of local content generally prefer local TV programming. If they had taken cultural distance into account, China and India could have been predicted to require significant investments in localization. TV is hardly cement.

Administrative or political distance

Historical and political associations shared by countries greatly affect trade between them. Colony–colonizer links between countries, for example, boost trade by 900%, which is perhaps not too surprising given Britain's continuing ties with its former colonies in the commonwealth, France's with the franc zone

Industry sensitivity
to distance

The various types of distance affect different industries in different ways. To estimate industry sensitivity to distance, Rajiv Mallick, a research associate at Harvard Business School, and I regressed trade between every possible pair of countries in the world in each of 70 industries (according to their SIC designations) on each dimension of distance.

The results confirm the importance of distinguishing between the various components of distance in assessing foreign market opportunities. Electricity, for instance, is highly sensitive to administrative and geographic factors but not at all to cultural factors. The following table lists some of the industries that are more and less sensitive to distance.

	CULTURAL DISTANCE **Linguistic Ties**	ADMINISTRATIVE DISTANCE **Preferential Trading Agreements**	GEOGRAPHIC DISTANCE **Physical Remoteness**	ECONOMIC DISTANCE **Wealth Differences**
more sensitive	meat and meat preparations	gold, nonmonetary	electricity current	*(economic distance decreases trade)*
	cereals and cereal preparations	electricity current	gas, natural and manufactured	nonferrous metals
	miscellaneous edible products and preparations	coffee, tea, cocoa, spices	paper, paperboard	manufactured fertilizers
	tobacco and tobacco products	textile fibers	live animals	meat and meat preparations
	office machines and automatic data-processing equipment	sugar, sugar preparations, and honey	sugar, sugar preparations, and honey	iron and steel
				pulp and waste paper
less sensitive	photographic apparatuses, optical goods, watches	gas, natural and manufactured	pulp and waste paper	*(economic distance increases trade)*
	road vehicles	travel goods, handbags	photographic apparatuses, optical goods, watches	coffee, tea, cocoa, spices
	cork and wood	footwear	telecommunications and sound-recording apparatuses	animal oils and fats
	metalworking machinery	sanitary, plumbing, heating, and lighting fixtures	coffee, tea, cocoa, spices	office machines and automatic data-processing equipment
	electricity current	furniture and furniture parts	gold, nonmonetary	power-generating machinery and equipment
				photographic apparatuses, optical goods, watches

more sensitive ←→ *less sensitive*

of West Africa, and Spain's with Latin America. Preferential trading arrangements, common currency, and political union can also increase trade by more than 300% each. The integration of the European Union is probably the leading example of deliberate efforts to diminish administrative and political distance among trading partners. (Needless to say, ties must be friendly to have a positive influence on trade. Although India and Pakistan share a colonial history—not to mention a border and linguistic ties—their mutual hostility means that trade between them is virtually nil.)

Countries can also create administrative and political distance through unilateral measures. indeed, policies of individual governments pose the most common barriers to cross-border competition. In some cases, the difficulties arise in a company's home country. For companies from the United States, for instance, domestic prohibitions on bribery and the prescription of health, safety, and environmental policies have a dampening effect on their international businesses. More commonly, though, it is the target country's government that raises barriers to foreign competition: tariffs, trade quotas, restrictions on foreign direct investment, and preferences for domestic competitors in the form of subsidies and favoritism in regulation and procurement. Such measures are expressly intended to protect domestic industries, and they are most likely to be implemented if a domestic industry meets one or more of the following criteria:

- *It is a large employer.* Industries that represent large voting blocs often receive state support in the form of subsidies and import protection. Europe's farmers are a case in point.

- *It is seen as a national champion.* Reflecting a kind of patriotism, some industries or companies serve as symbols of a country's modernity and competitiveness. Thus the showdown between Boeing and Airbus in capturing the large passenger-jet market has caused feelings on both sides of the Atlantic to run high and could even spark a broader trade war. Also, the more that a government has invested in the industry, the more protective it is likely to be, and the harder it will be for an outsider to gain a beachhead.

- *It is vital to national security.* Governments will intervene to protect industries that are deemed vital to national security—especially in high tech sectors such as telecommunications and aerospace. The FBI, for instance, delayed Deutsche Telekom's acquisition of Voicestream for reasons of national security.

- *It produces staples.* Governments will also take measures to prevent foreign companies from dominating markets for goods essential to their citizens' everyday lives. Food staples, fuel, and electricity are obvious examples.

- *It produces an "entitlement" good or service.* Some industries, notably the health care sector, produce goods or services that people believe they are entitled to as a basic human right. In these industries, governments are prone to intervene to set quality standards and control pricing.

- *It exploits natural resources.* A country's physical assets are often seen as part of a national heritage. Foreign companies can easily be considered robbers.

Nationalization, therefore, is a constant threat to international oil and mining multinationals.

● *It involves high sunk-cost commitments.* Industries that require large, geography-specific sunk investments—in the shape, say, of oil refineries or aluminum smelting plants or railway lines—are highly vulnerable to interference from local governments. Irreversibility expands the scope for holdups once the investment has been made.

Finally, a target country's weak institutional infrastructure can serve to dampen cross-border economic activity. Companies typically shy away from doing business in countries known for corruption or social conflict. Indeed, some research suggests that these conditions depress trade and investment far more than any explicit administrative policy or restriction. But when a country's institutional infrastructure is strong—for instance, if it has a well-functioning legal system—it is much more attractive to outsiders.

How far away is China, really?

As Star TV discovered, China is a particularly tough nut to crack. In a recent survey of nearly 100 multinationals, 54% admitted that their total business performance in China had been "worse than planned," compared with just 25% reporting "better than planned." Why was the failure rate so high? The survey provides the predictable answer: 62% of respondents reported that they had overestimated market potential for their products or services.

A quick analysis of the country along the dimensions of distance might have spared those companies much disappointment. Culturally, China is a long way away from nearly everywhere. First, the many dialects of the Chinese language are notoriously difficult for foreigners to learn, and the local population's foreign-language skills are limited. Second, the well-developed Chinese business culture based on personal connections, often summarized in the term *guanxi*, creates barriers to economic interchange with Westerners who focus on transactions rather than relationships. It can even be argued that Chinese consumers are "home-biased"; market research indicates much less preference for foreign brands over domestic ones than seems to be true in India, for example. In fact, greater China plays a disproportionate role in China's economic relations with the rest of the world.

Administrative barriers are probably even more important. A survey of members of the American Chamber of Commerce in China flagged market-access restrictions, high taxes, and customs duties as the biggest barriers to profitability in China. The level of state involvement in the economy continues to be high, with severe economic strains imposed by loss-making state-owned enterprises and technically insolvent state-owned banks. Corruption, too, is a fairly significant problem. In 2000, Transparency International ranked the country 63rd out of 90, with a rating of one indicating the least perceived corruption. Considerations such as these led Standard & Poor's to assign China a political-risk ranking of five in 2000, with six being the worst possible score.

So, yes, China is a big market, but that is far from the whole story.

Distance matters, too, and along many dimensions.

Ignoring administrative and political sensitivities was Star TV's other big mistake. Foreign ownership of broadcasting businesses—even in an open society like the United States—is always politically loaded because of television's power to influence people. Yet shortly after acquiring the company, Rupert Murdoch declared on record that satellite television was "an unambiguous threat to totalitarian regimes everywhere" because it permitted people to bypass government-controlled news sources. Not surprisingly, the Chinese government enacted a ban on the reception of foreign satellite TV services soon thereafter. News Corporation has begun to mend fences with the Chinese authorities, but it has yet to score any major breakthroughs in a country that accounts for nearly 60% of Star TV's potential customers. Murdoch of all people should have foreseen this outcome, given his experience in the United States, where he was required to become a citizen in order buy the television companies that now form the core of the Fox network.

Geographic distance

In general, the farther you are from a country, the harder it will be to conduct business in that country. But geographic distance is not simply a matter of how far away the country is in miles or kilometers. Other attributes that must be considered include the physical size of the country, average within-country distances to borders, access to waterways and the ocean, and topography. Man-made geographic attributes also must be taken into account—most notably, a country's transportation and communications infrastructures.

Obviously, geographic attributes influence the costs of transportation. Products with low value-to-weight or bulk ratios, such as steel and cement, incur particularly high costs as geographic distance increases. Likewise, costs for transporting fragile or perishable products become significant across large distances.

Beyond physical products, intangible goods and services are affected by geographic distance as well. One recent study indicates that cross-border equity flows between two countries fall off significantly as the geographic distance between them rises. This phenomenon clearly cannot be explained by transportation costs—capital, after all, is not a physical good. Instead, the level of information infrastructure (crudely measured by telephone traffic and the number of branches of multinational banks) accounts for much of the effect of physical distance on cross-border equity flows.

Interestingly, companies that find geography a barrier to trade are often expected to switch to direct investment in local plant and equipment as an alternative way to access target markets. But current research suggests that this approach may be flawed: Geographic distance has a dampening effect, overall, on investment flows as well as on trade flows. In short, it is important to keep both information networks and transportation infrastructures in mind when assessing the geographic influences on cross-border economic activity.

Economic distance

The wealth or income of consumers is the most important economic attribute that creates distance between countries, and it has a marked effect on the levels of trade and the types of partners a country trades with. Rich countries, research suggests, engage in relatively more cross-border economic activity relative to their economic size than do their poorer cousins. Most of this activity is with other rich countries, as the positive correlation between per capita GDP and trade flows implies. But poor countries also trade more with rich countries than with other poor ones.

Of course, these patterns mask variations in the effects of economic disparities in the cost and quality of financial, human, and other resources. Companies that rely on economies of experience, scale, and standardization

Country portfolio analysis:
a flawed approach

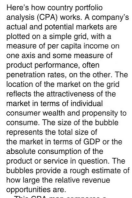

Here's how country portfolio analysis (CPA) works. A company's actual and potential markets are plotted on a simple grid, with a measure of per capita income on one axis and some measure of product performance, often penetration rates, on the other. The location of the market on the grid reflects the attractiveness of the market in terms of individual consumer wealth and propensity to consume. The size of the bubble represents the total size of the market in terms of GDP or the absolute consumption of the product or service in question. The bubbles provide a rough estimate of how large the relative revenue opportunities are.

This CPA map compares a number of non-U.S. markets for fast-food restaurants.

KEY: *(applies to both charts)*

① JAPAN	⑪ SAUDI ARABIA
② KOREA	⑫ POLAND
③ TAIWAN	⑬ BELGIUM
④ PUERTO RICO	⑭ FRANCE
⑤ MALAYSIA	⑮ GERMANY
⑥ AUSTRALIA	⑯ SPAIN
⑦ THAILAND	⑰ UK
⑧ NEW ZEALAND	⑱ CANADA
⑨ S. AFRICA	⑲ MEXICO
⑩ SINGAPORE	⑳ CHINA

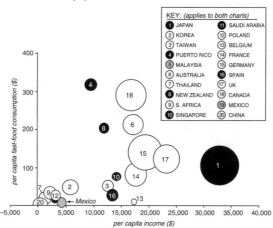

Country portfolio analysis:
adjusted for distance

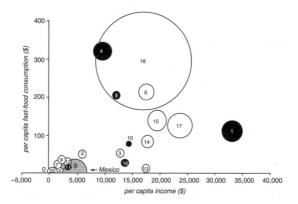

Taking distance into account dramatically changes estimates of market opportunities. In the chart at right, each of the fast-food markets has been adjusted for a number of distance attributes, based on the estimates by Frankel and Rose. The relative sizes of the bubbles are now very different. For example, Mexico, which was less than one-tenth the size of the largest international markets, Japan and Germany, ends up as the second largest opportunity. Clearly, the CPA approach paints an incomplete picture, unless it is adjusted for distance.

should focus more on countries that have similar economic profiles. That's because they have to replicate their existing business model to exploit their competitive advantage, which is hard to pull off in a country where customer incomes—not to mention the cost and quality of resources—are very different. Wal-Mart in India, for instance, would be a very different business from Wal-Mart in the United States. But Wal-Mart in Canada is virtually a carbon copy.

In other industries, however, competitive advantage comes from economic arbitrage—the exploitation of cost and price differentials between markets. Companies in industries whose major cost components vary widely across countries—like the garment and footwear industries, where labor costs are important—are particularly likely to target countries with different economic profiles for investment or trade.

Whether they expand abroad for purposes of replication or arbitrage, all companies find that major disparities in supply chains and distribution channels are a significant barrier to business. A recent study concluded that margins on distribution within the United States—the costs of domestic transportation, wholesaling, and retailing—play a bigger role, on average, in erecting barriers to imports into the United States than do international transportation costs and tariffs combined.

More broadly, cross-country complexity and change place a premium on responsiveness and agility, making it hard for cross-border competitors, particularly replicators, to match the performance of locally focused ones because of the added operational complexity. In the home appliance business, for instance, companies like Maytag that concentrate on a limited number of geographies produce far better returns for investors than companies like Electrolux and Whirlpool, whose geographic spread has come at the expense of simplicity and profitability.

A case study in distance

Taking the four dimensions of distance into account can dramatically change a company's assessment of the relative attractiveness of foreign markets. One company that has wrestled with global expansion is Tricon Restaurants International (TRI), the international operating arm of Tricon, which manages the Pizza Hut, Taco Bell, and KFC fast-food chains, and which was spun off from Pepsico in 1997.

When Tricon became an independent company, TRI's operations were farflung, with restaurants in 27 countries. But the profitability of its markets varied greatly: Two-thirds of revenues and an even higher proportion of profits came from just seven markets. Furthermore, TRI's limited operating cash flow and Tricon's debt service obligations left TRI with less than one-tenth as much money as archrival McDonald's International to invest outside the United States. As a result, in 1998, TRI's president, Pete Bassi, decided to rationalize its global operations by focusing its equity investments in a limited number of markets.

But which markets? The exhibit "Country portfolio analysis: a flawed approach" provides a portfolio analysis of international markets for the fast-food restaurant business, based on data used by TRI for its strategy discussions. The analysis suggests that the company's top markets in terms of size of opportunity would be the larger bubbles to the center and right of the chart. Applying the effects of distance, however, changes the map dramatically. Consider the Mexican market. Using the CPA method, Mexico, with a total fast-food consumption of $700 million, is a relatively small market, ranking 16th of 20. When combined with estimates of individual consumer wealth and per capita consumption, this ranking would imply that TRI should dispose of its investments there. But the exhibit "Country portfolio analysis: adjusted for distance" tells a different story. When the fast-food consumption numbers for each country are adjusted for their geographic distance from Dallas, TRI's home base, Mexico's consumption decreases less than any other country's, as you might expect, given Mexico's proximity to Dallas. Based on just this readjustment, Mexico leaps to sixth place in terms of market opportunity.

Further adjusting the numbers for a common land border and for membership in a trade agreement with the United States pushes Mexico's ranking all the way up to second, after Canada. Not all the adjustments are positive: adjusting for a common language—not a characteristic of Mexico—pushes Mexico into a tie for second place with the United Kingdom. Additional adjustments could also be made, but the overall message is plain. Once distance is taken into account, the size of the market opportunity in Mexico looks very different. If TRI had used the CPA approach and neglected distance, the company's planners might well have ended up abandoning a core market. Instead, they concluded, in Bassi's words, that "Mexico is one of TRI's top two or three priorities."

Factoring in the industry effects of distance is only a first step. A full analysis should consider how a company's own characteristics operate to increase or reduce distance from foreign markets. Companies with a large cadre of cosmopolitan managers, for instance, will be less affected by cultural differences than companies whose managers are all from the home country. In TRI's case, consideration of company-specific features made Mexico even more attractive. The company already owned more than four-fifths of its Mexican outlets and had a 38% share of the local market, well ahead of McDonald's.

Consideration of the interaction of company-specific features and distance is beyond the scope of this article. But whether the analysis is at the industry or company level, the message is the same: Managers must always be conscious of distance—in all its dimensions. The CAGE distance framework is intended to help managers meet that challenge. While it is necessarily subjective, it represents an important complement to the tools used by most companies seeking to build or rationalize their country market portfolios. Technology may indeed be making the world a smaller place, but it is not eliminating the very real—and often very high—costs of distance.

Chapter 11

Strategy under uncertainty

WHAT MAKES FOR GOOD strategy in highly uncertain business environments? Some executives seek to shape the future with high-stakes bets. Eastman Kodak Company for example, is spending $500 million per year to develop an array of digital photography products that it hopes will fundamentally change the way people create, store, and view pictures. Meanwhile, Hewlett-Packard Company is investing $50 million per year to pursue a rival vision centered around home-based photo printers. The business press loves to hype such industry-shaping strategies because of their potential to create enormous wealth, but the sober reality is that most companies lack the industry position, assets, or appetite for risk necessary to make such strategies work.

More risk-averse executives hedge their bets by making a number of smaller investments. In pursuit of growth opportunities in emerging markets, for example, many consumer-product companies are forging limited operational or distribution alliances. But it's often difficult to determine if such limited investments truly reserve the right to play in these countries or just reserve the right to lose.

Alternatively, some executives favor investments in flexibility that allow their companies to adapt quickly as markets evolve. But the costs of establishing such flexibility can be high. Moreover, taking a wait-and-see strategy—

postponing large investments until the future becomes clear—can create a window of opportunity for competitors.

How should executives facing great uncertainty decide whether to bet big, hedge, or wait and see? Chances are, traditional strategic-planning processes won't help much. The standard practice is to lay out a vision of future events precise enough to be captured in a discounted-cash-flow analysis. Of course, managers can discuss alternative scenarios and test how sensitive their forecasts are to changes in key variables, but the goal of such analysis is often to find the most likely outcome and create a strategy based on it. That approach serves companies well in relatively stable business environments. But when there is greater uncertainty about the future, it is at best marginally helpful and at worst downright dangerous.

One danger is that this traditional approach leads executives to view uncertainty in a binary way—to assume that the world is either certain, and therefore open to precise predictions about the future, or uncertain, and therefore completely unpredictable. Planning or capital-budgeting processes that require point forecasts force managers to bury underlying uncertainties in their cash flows. Such systems clearly push managers to underestimate uncertainty in order to make a compelling case for their strategy.

Underestimating uncertainty can lead to strategies that neither defend against the threats nor take advantage of the opportunities that higher levels of uncertainty may provide. In one of the most colossal underestimations in business history, Kenneth H. Olsen, then president of Digital Equipment Corporation, announced in 1977 that "there is no reason for any individual to have a computer in their home." The explosion in the personal computer market was not inevitable in 1977, but it was certainly within the range of possibilities that industry experts were discussing at the time. At the other extreme, assuming that the world is entirely unpredictable can lead managers to abandon the analytical rigor of their traditional planning processes altogether and base their strategic decisions primarily on gut instinct. This "just do it" approach to strategy can cause executives to place misinformed bets on emerging products or markets that result in record write-offs. Those who took the plunge and invested in home banking in the early 1980s immediately come to mind.

Risk-averse managers who think they are in very uncertain environments don't trust their gut instincts and suffer from decision paralysis. They avoid making critical strategic decisions about the products, markets, and technologies they should develop. They focus instead on reengineering, quality management, or internal cost-reduction programs. Although valuable, those programs are not substitutes for strategy.

Making systematically sound strategic decisions under uncertainty requires a different approach—one that avoids this dangerous binary view. It is rare that managers know absolutely nothing of strategic importance, even in the most uncertain environments. In fact, they usually can identify a range of potential outcomes or even a discrete set of scenarios. This simple insight is extremely powerful because determining which strategy is best, and what process should be used to develop it, depend vitally on the level of uncertainty a company faces. What follows, then, is a framework for determining the level of uncertainty surrounding strategic decisions and for tailoring strategy to that uncertainty. No approach can make the challenges of uncertainty go away, but this one offers practical guidance that will lead to more informed and confident strategic decisions.

Four levels of uncertainty

Even the most uncertain business environments contain a lot of strategically relevant information. First, it is often possible to identify clear trends, such as market demographics, that can help define potential demand for future products or services. Second, there is usually a host of factors that are currently *unknown* but that are in fact *knowable*—that could be known if the right analysis were done. Performance attributes for current technologies, elasticities of demand for certain stable categories of products, and competitors' capacity-expansion plans are varieties that are often unknown, but not entirely unknowable.

The uncertainty that remains after the best possible analysis has been done is what we call *residual uncertainty*—for example, the outcome of an ongoing regulatory debate or the performance attributes of a technology still in development. But often, quite a bit can be known about even those residual uncertainties. In practice, we have found that the residual uncertainty facing most strategic-decision makers falls into one of four broad levels:

Level 1: a clear-enough future

At level 1, managers can develop a single forecast of the future that is precise *enough* for strategy development. Although it will be inexact to the degree that all business environments are inherently uncertain, the forecast will be sufficiently narrow to point to a single strategic direction. In other words, at level 1, the residual uncertainty is irrelevant to making strategic decisions.

Consider a major airline trying to develop a strategic response to the entry of a low-cost, no-frills competitor into one of its hub airports. Should it respond with a low-cost service of its own? Should it cede the low-cost niche segments to the new entrant? Or should it compete aggressively on price and service in an attempt to drive the entrant out of the market?

To make that strategic decision, the airline's executives need market research on the size of different customer segments and the likely response of each segment to different combinations of pricing and service. They also need to know how much it costs the competitor to serve, and how much capacity the competitor has for, every route in question. Finally, the executives need to know the new entrant's competitive objectives to anticipate how it would respond to any strategic moves their airline might make. In today's U.S. airline industry such information is either known already or is possible to know. It might not be easy to obtain—it might require new market research, for example—but it is inherently knowable. And once that information is known, residual uncertainty would be limited, and the incumbent airline would be able to build a confident business case around its strategy.

Level 2: alternate futures

At level 2, the future can be described as one of a few alternate outcomes, or *discrete scenarios*. Analysis cannot identify which outcome will occur, although it may help establish probabilities. Most important, some, if not all, elements of the strategy would change if the outcome were predictable.

Many businesses facing major regulatory or legislative change confront level 2 uncertainty. Consider U.S. long-distance telephone providers in late 1995, as they began developing strategies for entering local telephone markets. By late 1995, legislation that would fundamentally deregulate the industry was pending in Congress, and the broad form that new regulations would take was fairly clear to most industry observers. But whether or not the legislation was going to pass and how quickly it would be implemented in the event it did pass were uncertain. No amount of analysis would allow the long-distance carriers to predict those outcomes, and the correct course of action—for example, the timing of investments in network infrastructure—depended on which outcome occurred.

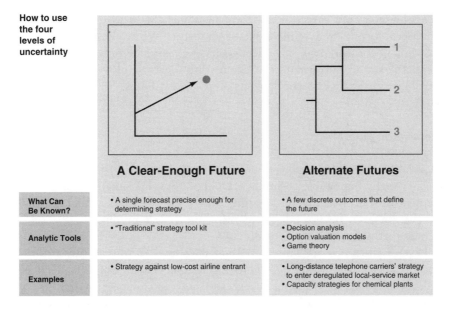

How to use the four levels of uncertainty	A Clear-Enough Future	Alternate Futures
What Can Be Known?	• A single forecast precise enough for determining strategy	• A few discrete outcomes that define the future
Analytic Tools	• "Traditional" strategy tool kit	• Decision analysis • Option valuation models • Game theory
Examples	• Strategy against low-cost airline entrant	• Long-distance telephone carriers' strategy to enter deregulated local-service market • Capacity strategies for chemical plants

In another common level 2 situation, the value of a strategy depends mainly on competitors' strategies, and those cannot yet be observed or predicted. For example, in oligopoly markets, such as those for pulp and paper, chemicals, and basic raw materials, the primary uncertainty is often competitors' plans for expanding capacity; Will they build new plants or not? Economies of scale often dictate that any plant built would be quite large and would be likely to have a significant impact on industry prices and profitability. Therefore, any one company's decision to build a plant is often contingent on competitors' decisions. This is a classic level 2 situation: The possible outcomes are discrete and clear. It is difficult to predict which one will occur. And the best strategy depends on which one does occur.

Level 3: a range of futures

At level 3, a range of potential futures can be identified. That range is defined by a limited number of key variables, but the actual outcome may lie anywhere along a continuum bounded by that range. There are no natural discrete scenarios. As in level 2, some, and possibly all, elements of the strategy would change if the outcome were predictable.

Companies in emerging industries or entering new geographic markets often face level 3 uncertainty. Consider a European consumer-goods company deciding whether to introduce its products to the Indian market. The best possible market research might identify only a broad range of potential customer-penetration rates—say, from 10% to 30%—and there would be no obvious scenarios within that range. Such a broad range of estimates would be common when introducing completely new products and services to a market, and therefore determining the level of latent demand is very difficult. The company entering India would be likely to follow a very different and more aggressive entry strategy if it knew for certain that its customer penetration rates would be closer to 30% than to 10%.

Analogous problems exist for companies in fields driven by technological innovation, such as the semiconductor industry. When deciding whether to invest in a new technology, producers can often estimate only a broad range of potential cost and performance attributes for the technology, and the overall profitability of the investment depends on those attributes.

Level 4: true ambiguity

At level 4, multiple dimensions of uncertainty interact to create an environment that is virtually impossible to predict. Unlike in level 3 situations, the range of potential outcomes cannot be identified, let alone scenarios within that range. It might not even be possible to identify, much less predict, all the relevant variables that will define the future.

Level 4 situations are quite rare, and they tend to migrate toward one of the other levels over time. Nevertheless, they do exist. Consider a telecommunications company deciding where and how to compete in the emerging consumer-multimedia market. It is confronting multiple uncertainties concerning technology, demand, and relationships between hardware and content providers, all of which may interact in ways so unpredictable that no plausible range of scenarios can be identified.

Companies considering making major entry investments in post-Communist Russia in 1992 faced level 4 uncertainty. They could not outline the potential laws or regulations that would govern property rights and transactions. That central uncertainty was compounded by additional uncertainty over the viability of supply chains and the demand for previously unavailable consumer goods and services. And shocks such as a political assassination or a currency default could have spun the whole system toward completely unforeseen outcomes.

Those examples illustrate how difficult strategic decisions can be at level 4,

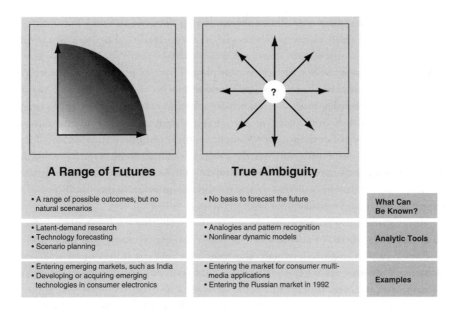

A Range of Futures	**True Ambiguity**
• A range of possible outcomes, but no natural scenarios	• No basis to forecast the future
• Latent-demand research • Technology forecasting • Scenario planning	• Analogies and pattern recognition • Nonlinear dynamic models
• Entering emerging markets, such as India • Developing or acquiring emerging technologies in consumer electronics	• Entering the market for consumer multi-media applications • Entering the Russian market in 1992

What Can Be Known?

Analytic Tools

Examples

but they also underscore their transitory nature. Greater political and regulatory stability has turned decisions about whether to enter Russian markets into level 3 problems for the majority of industries today. Similarly, uncertainty about strategic decisions in the consumer multimedia market will migrate to level 3 or to level 2 as the industry begins to take shape over the next several years.

Tailoring strategic analysis to the four levels of uncertainty

Our experience suggests that at least half of all strategy problems fall into levels 2 or 3, while most of the rest are level 1 problems. But executives who think about uncertainty in a binary way tend to treat all strategy problems as if they fell into either level 1 or level 4. And when those executives base their strategies on rigorous analysis, they are most likely to apply the same set of analytic tools regardless of the level of residual uncertainty they face. For example, they might attempt to use standard, quantitative market-research techniques to forecast demand for data traffic over wireless communications networks as far out as ten years from now.

But, in fact, a different kind of analysis should be done to identify and evaluate strategy options at each level of uncertainty. All strategy making begins with some form of situation analysis—that is, a picture of what the world will look like today and what is likely to happen in the future. Identifying the levels of uncertainty thus helps define the best such an analysis can do to describe each possible future an industry faces.

To help generate level 1's usefully precise prediction of the future, managers can use the standard strategy tool kit—market research, analyses of competitors' costs and capacity, value chain analysis, Michael Porter's five-forces framework, and so on. A discounted-cash-flow model that incorporates those predictions can then be used to determine the value of various alternative strategies. It's not surprising that most managers feel extremely comfortable in level 1 situations—these are the tools and frameworks taught in every leading business program in the United States.

Level 2 situations are a bit more complex. First, managers must develop a set of discrete scenarios based on their understanding of how the key residual uncertainties might play out—for example, whether deregulation occurs or not, a competitor builds a new plant or not. Each scenario may require a different valuation model—general industry structure and conduct will often be fundamentally different depending on which scenario occurs, so alternative valuations can't be handled by performing sensitivity analyses around a single baseline model. Getting information that helps establish the relative probabilities of the alternative outcomes should be a high priority.

After establishing an appropriate valuation model for each possible outcome and determining how probable each is likely to be, a classic decision-analysis framework can be used to evaluate the risks and returns inherent in alternative strategies. This process will identify the likely winners and losers in alternative scenarios, and perhaps more important, it will help quantify what's at stake for companies that follow status quo strategies. Such an analysis is often the key to making the case for strategic change. In level 2 situations, it is important not only to identify the different possible future outcomes but also to think through the likely paths the industry might take to reach those alternative futures. Will change occur in major steps at some particular point in time, following, for example, a regulatory ruling or a competitor's decision to enter the market? Or will change occur in a more evolutionary fashion, as often happens after a resolution of competing technology standards? This is vital information because it determines which market signals or trigger variables should be monitored closely. As events unfold and the relative probabilities of alternative scenarios change, it is likely that one's strategy will also need to be adapted to these changes.

At one level, the analysis in level 3 is very similar to that in level 2. A set of scenarios needs to be identified that describes alternative future outcomes, and analysis should focus on the trigger events signaling that the market is moving toward one or another scenario. Developing a meaningful set of scenarios, however, is less straightforward in level 3. Scenarios that describe the extreme points in the range of possible outcomes are often relatively easy to develop, but these rarely provide much concrete guidance for current strategic decisions. Since there are no other natural discrete scenarios in level 3, deciding which possible outcomes should be fully developed into alternative scenarios is a real art. But there are a few general rules. First, develop only a limited number of alternative scenarios—the complexity of juggling more than four or five tends to hinder decision making. Second, avoid developing redundant scenarios that have no unique implications for strategic decision making; make sure each scenario offers a distinct picture of the industry's structure, conduct, and performance. Third, develop a set of scenarios that collectively account for the *probable* range of future outcomes and not necessarily the *entire possible* range.

Because it is impossible in level 3 to define a complete list of scenarios and related probabilities, it is impossible to calculate the expected value of different strategies. However, establishing the range of scenarios should allow managers to determine how robust their strategy is, identify likely winners and losers, and determine roughly the risk of following status quo strategies.

Situation analysis at level 4 is even more qualitative. Still, it is critical to avoid the urge to throw one's hands up and act purely on gut instinct. Instead, managers need to catalog systematically what they know and what is possible to know. Even if it is impossible to develop a meaningful set of probable, or even possible, outcomes in level 4 situations, managers can gain valuable strategic perspective. Usually, they can identify at least a subset of the variables that will determine how the market will evolve over time—for example, customer penetration rates or technology performance attributes. And they can identify favorable and unfavorable indicators of these variables that will let them track the market's evolution over time and adapt their strategy as new information becomes available.

Managers can also identify patterns indicating possible ways the market may evolve by studying how analogous markets developed in other level 4 situations, determining the key attributes of the winners and losers in those situations and identifying the strategies they employed. Finally, although it will be impossible to quantify the risks and returns of different strategies, managers should be able to identify what information they would have to believe about the future to justify the investments they are considering. Early market indicators and analogies from similar markets will help sort out whether such beliefs are realistic or not.

Uncertainty demands a more flexible approach to situation analysis. The old one-size-fits-all approach is simply inadequate. Over time, companies in most industries will face strategy problems that have varying levels of residual uncertainty, and it is vitally important that the strategic analysis be tailored to the level of uncertainty.

Postures and moves

Before we can talk about the dynamics of formulating strategy at each level of uncertainty, we need to introduce a basic vocabulary for talking about strategy. First, there are three *strategic postures* a company can choose to take vis-à-vis uncertainty: shaping, adapting, or reserving the right to play. Second, there are three types of moves in *the portfolio of actions* that can be used to implement that strategy: big bets, options, and no-regrets moves.

Strategic posture

Any good strategy requires a choice about strategic posture. Fundamentally, *posture* defines the intent of a strategy relative to the current and future state of an industry. *Shapers* aim to drive their industries toward a new structure of their own devising. Their strategies are about creating new opportunities in a market—either by shaking up relatively stable level 1 industries or by trying to control the direction of the market in industries with bigger levels of uncertainty. Kodak, for example, through its investment in digital photography, is pursuing a shaping strategy in an effort to maintain its leadership position, as a new technology supersedes the one currently generating most of its earnings. Although its product technology is new, Kodak's strategy is still based on a traditional model in which the company provides digital cameras and film while photo-processing stores provide many of the photo-printing and storage functions for the consumer. Hewlett-Packard also seeks to be a shaper in this market, but it is pursuing a radically different model in which high quality, low-cost photo printers shift photo processing from stores to the home.

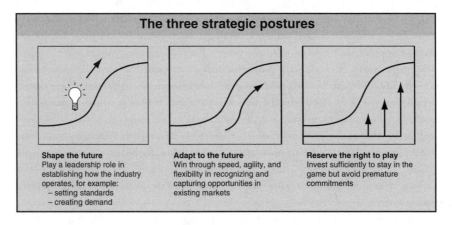

The three strategic postures

Shape the future
Play a leadership role in establishing how the industry operates, for example:
  – setting standards
  – creating demand

Adapt to the future
Win through speed, agility, and flexibility in recognizing and capturing opportunities in existing markets

Reserve the right to play
Invest sufficiently to stay in the game but avoid premature commitments

In contrast, *adapters* take the current industry structure and its future evolution as givens, and they react to the opportunities the market offers. In environments with little uncertainty, adapters choose a strategic positioning— that is, where and how to compete—in the current industry. At higher levels of uncertainty, their strategies are predicated on the ability to recognize and respond quickly to market developments. In the highly volatile telecommunications-service industry, for example, service resellers are adapters. They buy and resell the latest products and services offered by the major telecom providers, relying on pricing and effective execution rather than on product innovation as their source of competitive advantage.

The third strategic posture, *reserving the right to play*, is a special form of adapting. This posture is relevant only in levels 2 through 4; it involves making incremental investments today that put a company in a privileged position, through either superior information, cost structures, or relationships between customers and suppliers. That allows the company to wait until the environment becomes less uncertain before formulating a strategy. Many pharmaceutical companies are reserving the right to play in the market for gene therapy applications by acquiring or allying with small biotech firms that have relevant expertise. Providing privileged access to the latest industry developments, these are low-cost investments compared with building a proprietary, internal gene-therapy R&D program.

A portfolio of actions

A posture is not a complete strategy. It clarifies strategic intent but not the actions required to fulfill that intent. Three types of moves are especially relevant to implementing strategy under conditions of uncertainty: big bets, options, and no-regrets moves.

Big bets are large commitments, such as major capital investments or acquisitions, that will result in large payoffs in some scenarios and large losses in others. Not surprisingly, shaping strategies usually involve big bets, whereas adapting and reserving the right to play do not.

Options are designed to secure the big payoffs of the best-case scenarios while minimizing losses in the worst-case scenarios. This asymmetric payoff structure makes them resemble financial options. Most options involve making modest initial investments that will allow companies to ramp up or scale back the investment later as the market evolves. Classic examples include conducting pilot trials before the full-scale introduction of a new product, entering into limited joint ventures for distribution to minimize the risk of breaking into new markets, and licensing an alternative technology in case it proves to be superior to a current technology. Those reserving the right to play rely heavily on options, but shapers use them as well, either to shape an emerging but uncertain market as an early mover or to hedge their big bets.

Finally, *no-regrets moves* are just that—moves that will pay off no matter what happens. Managers often focus on obvious no-regrets moves like initiatives aimed at reducing costs, gathering competitive intelligence, or building skills. However, even in highly uncertain environments, strategic decisions like investing in capacity and entering certain markets can be no-regrets moves. Whether or not they put a name to them, most managers understand intuitively that no-regrets moves are an essential element of any strategy.

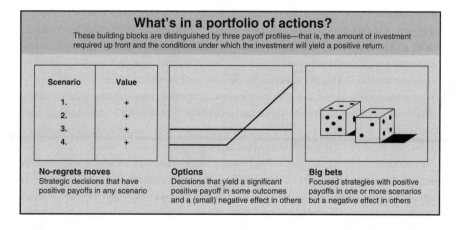

The choice of a strategic posture and an accompanying portfolio of actions sounds straightforward. But in practice, these decisions are highly dependent on the level of uncertainty facing a given business. Thus the four-level framework can help clarify the practical implications implicit in any choice of strategic posture and actions. The discussion that follows will demonstrate the different strategic challenges that each level of uncertainty poses and how the portfolio of actions may be applied.

Strategy in level 1's clear-enough future

In predictable business environments, most companies are adapters. Analysis is designed to predict an industry's future landscape, and strategy involves making positioning choices about where and how to compete. When the underlying analysis is sound, such strategies are by definition made up of a series of no-regrets moves.

Adapter strategies in level 1 situations are not necessarily incremental or boring. For example, Southwest Airlines Company's no-frills, point-to-point service is a highly innovative, value-creating adapter strategy, as was Gateway 2000's low-cost assembly and direct-mail distribution strategy when it entered the personal computer market in the late 1980s. In both cases, managers were able to identify unexploited opportunities in relatively low-uncertainty environments within the existing market structure. The best level 1 adapters create value through innovations in their products or services or through improvements in their business systems without otherwise fundamentally changing the industry.

It is also possible to be a shaper in level 1 situations, but that is risky and rare, since level 1 shapers increase the amount of residual uncertainty in an otherwise predictable market—for themselves and their competitors—in an attempt to fundamentally alter long-standing industry structures and conduct. Consider Federal Express Corporation's overnight-delivery strategy. When it entered the mail-and-package delivery industry, a stable level 1 situation, FedEx's strategy in effect created level 3 uncertainty for itself. That is, even though CEO Frederick W. Smith commissioned detailed consulting reports that confirmed the feasibility of his business concept, only a broad range of potential demand for overnight services could be identified at the time. For the industry incumbents like United Parcel Service, FedEx created level 2 uncertainty. FedEx's move raised two questions for UPS: Will the overnight-delivery strategy succeed or not? and Will UPS have to offer a similar service to remain a viable competitor in the market?

Over time, the industry returned to level 1 stability, but with a fundamentally new structure. FedEx's bet paid off, forcing the rest of the industry to adapt to the new demand for overnight services.

What portfolio of actions did it take to realize that strategy? Like most shaper strategies, even in level 1 situations, this one required some big bets. That said, it often makes sense to build options into a shaper strategy to hedge against bad bets. Smith might have hedged his bets by leasing existing cargo airplanes instead of purchasing and retrofitting his original fleet of Falcon "minifreighters," or he could have outsourced ground pickup and delivery services. Such moves would have limited the amount of capital he would have needed to sink into his new strategy and facilitated a graceful exit had his concept failed. However, that kind of insurance doesn't always come cheap. In FedEx's case, had Smith leased standard-size cargo planes, he would have come under the restrictive regulations of the Civil Aeronautics Board. And outsourcing local pickups and deliveries would have diluted FedEx's unique door-to-door value to customers. Thus Smith stuck mainly to big bets in implementing his strategy, which drove him to the brink of bankruptcy in his first two years of operation but ultimately reshaped an entire industry.

Strategy in level 2's alternate futures

If shapers in level 1 try to raise uncertainty, in levels 2 through 4 they try to lower uncertainty and create order out of chaos. In level 2, a shaping strategy is designed to increase the probability that a favored industry scenario will occur. A shaper in a capital-intensive industry like pulp and paper, for example, wants to prevent competitors from creating excess capacity that would destroy the industry's profitability. Consequently, shapers in such cases might commit their companies to building new capacity far in advance of an upturn in demand to preempt the competition, or they might consolidate the industry through mergers and acquisitions.

Consider the Microsoft Network (MSN). A few years ago, one could identify a discrete set of possible ways in which transactions would be conducted between networked computers. Either proprietary networks such as MSN would become the standard, or open networks like the Internet would prevail. Uncertainty in this situation was thus at level 2, even though other related strategy issues—such as determining the level of consumer demand for networked applications—were level 3 problems.

Microsoft could reasonably expect to shape the way markets for electronic commerce evolved if it created the proprietary MSN network. It would, in effect, be building a commerce hub that would link both suppliers and consumers through the MSN gateway. The strategy was a big bet: the development costs were significant and, more important, involved an enormously high level of industry exposure and attention. In effect, for Microsoft, it constituted a big credibility bet. Microsoft's activities in other areas—such as including one-button access to MSN from Windows95—were designed to increase the probability that this shaping bet would pay off.

But even the best shapers must be prepared to adapt. In the battle between proprietary and open networks, certain trigger variables—growth in the number of Internet and MSN subscribers, for example, or the activity profiles of early MSN subscribers—could provide valuable insight into how the market was evolving. When it became clear that open networks would prevail, Microsoft refocused the MSN concept around the Internet. Microsoft's shift illustrates that choices of strategic posture are not carved in stone, and it underscores the value of maintaining strategic flexibility under uncertainty. Shaping strategies can fail, so the best companies supplement their shaping bets with options that allow them to change course quickly if necessary. Microsoft was able to do just that because it remained flexible by being willing to cut its losses, by building a cadre of engineers who had a wide range of general-programming and product-development skills, and by closely monitoring key trigger variables. In uncertain environments, it is a mistake to let strategies run on autopilot, remaining content to update them only through standard year-end strategy reviews.

Because trigger variables are often relatively simple to monitor in level 2, it can be easy to adapt or reserve the right to play. For instance, companies that generate electricity—and others whose business depends on energy-intensive production processes—often face level 2 uncertainty in determining the relative cost of different fuel alternatives. Discrete scenarios can often be identified—for example, either natural gas or oil will be the low-cost fuel. Many companies thus choose an adapter strategy when building new plants: they construct flexible manufacturing processes that can switch easily between different fuels.

Chemical companies often choose to reserve the right to play when facing level 2 uncertainty in predicting the performance of a new technology. If the technology performs well, companies will have to employ it to remain competitive in the market. But if it does not fulfill its promise, incumbents can compete effectively with existing technologies. Most companies are reluctant to bet several hundred million dollars on building new capacity and retrofitting old plants around a new technology until it is proven. But if they don't make at least incremental investments in the short run, they risk falling too far behind competitors should the technology succeed. Thus many will purchase options to license the new technology within a specified time frame or begin retrofitting a proportion of existing capacity around the new technology. In either case, small, up-front commitments give the companies privileged positions, but not obligations, to ramp up or discontinue development of the new technology as its performance attributes become clearer over time.

Strategy in level 3's range of futures

Shaping takes a different form in level 3. If at level 2, shapers are trying to make a discrete outcome occur, at level 3, they are trying to move the market in a general direction because they can identify only a range of possible outcomes. Consider the battle over standards for electronic cash transactions, currently a level 3 problem since one can define a range of potential products and services that fall between purely paper-based and purely electronic cash transactions, but it is unclear today whether there are any natural discrete scenarios within that range. Mondex International, a consortium of financial services providers and technology companies, is attempting to shape the future by establishing what it hopes will become universal electronic-cash standards. Its shaping posture is backed by big-bet investments in product development, infrastructure, and pilot experiments to speed customer acceptance.

In contrast, regional banks are mainly choosing adapter strategies. An adapter posture at uncertainty levels 3 or 4 is often achieved primarily through investments in organizational capabilities designed to keep options open. Because they must make and implement strategy choices in real time, adapters need quick access to the best market information and the most flexible organizational

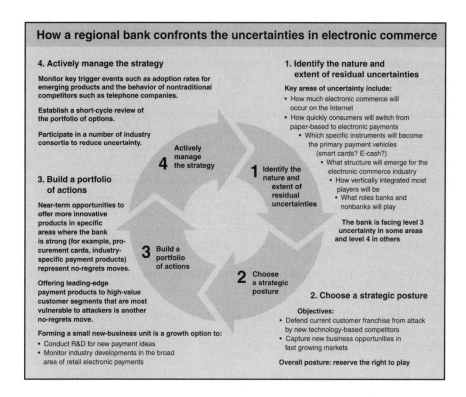

How a regional bank confronts the uncertainties in electronic commerce

4. Actively manage the strategy

Monitor key trigger events such as adoption rates for emerging products and the behavior of nontraditional competitors such as telephone companies.

Establish a short-cycle review of the portfolio of options.

Participate in a number of industry consortia to reduce uncertainty.

3. Build a portfolio of actions

Near-term opportunities to offer more innovative products in specific areas where the bank is strong (for example, pro-curement cards, industry-specific payment products) represent no-regrets moves.

Offering leading-edge payment products to high-value customer segments that are most vulnerable to attackers is another no-regrets move.

Forming a small new-business unit is a growth option to:
- Conduct R&D for new payment ideas
- Monitor industry developments in the broad area of retail electronic payments

1. Identify the nature and extent of residual uncertainties

Key areas of uncertainty include:
- How much electronic commerce will occur on the Internet
- How quickly consumers will switch from paper-based to electronic payments
  - Which specific instruments will become the primary payment vehicles (smart cards? E-cash?)
    - What structure will emerge for the electronic commerce industry
      - How vertically integrated most players will be
        - What roles banks and nonbanks will play

The bank is facing level 3 uncertainty in some areas and level 4 in others

2. Choose a strategic posture

Objectives:
- Defend current customer franchise from attack by new technology-based competitors
- Capture new business opportunities in fast growing markets

Overall posture: reserve the right to play

(Diagram labels: 4 Actively manage the strategy; 1 Identify the nature and extent of residual uncertainties; 3 Build a portfolio of actions; 2 Choose a strategic posture)

structures. Many regional banks, for example, have put in place steering committees focused on electronic payments, R&D projects, and competitive-intelligence systems so that they can constantly monitor developments in electronic payment technology and markets. In addition, many regional banks are making small investments in industry consortia as another way to monitor events. This adapter approach makes sense for most regional banks—they don't have the deep pockets and skills necessary to set standards for the electronic payment market, yet it is essential that they be able to offer the latest electronic services to their customers as such services become available.

Reserving the right to play is a common posture in level 3. Consider a telecommunications company trying to decide whether to make a $1 billion investment in broadband cable networks in the early 1990s. The decision hinged on level 3 uncertainties such as demand for interactive TV service. No amount of solid market research could precisely forecast consumer demand for services that didn't even exist yet. However, making incremental investments in broadband-network trials could provide useful information, and it would put the company in a privileged position to expand the business in the future should that prove attractive. By restructuring the broadband-investment decision from a big bet to a series of options, the company reserved the right to play in a potentially lucrative market without having to bet the farm or risk being preempted by a competitor.

Strategy in level 4's true ambiguity

Paradoxically, even though level 4 situations contain the greatest uncertainty, they may offer higher returns and involve lower risks for companies seeking to shape the market than situations in either level 2 or 3. Recall that level 4 situations are transitional by nature, often occurring after a major technological, macroeconomic, or legislative shock. Since no player necessarily knows the best strategy in these environments, the shaper's role is to provide a vision of an industry structure and standards that will coordinate the strategies of other players and drive the market toward a more stable and favorable outcome.

Needed: a more comprehensive strategy tool kit

In order to perform the kinds of analyses appropriate to high levels of uncertainty, many companies will need to supplement their standard strategy tool kit. Scenario-planning techniques are fundamental to determining strategy under conditions of uncertainty. Game theory will help managers understand uncertainties based on competitors' conduct. Systems dynamics and agent-based simulation models can help in understanding the complex interactions in the market. Real-options valuation models can help in correctly valuing investments in learning and flexibility. The following sources will help managers get started:

- **Scenario Planning.** Kees van der Heijden, *Scenarios: The Art of Strategic Conversation* (New York: John Wiley & Sons, 1996); Paul J.H. Schoemaker, "Scenario Planning: A New Tool for Strategic Thinking," *Sloan Management Review*, Winter 1995.
- **Game Theory.** Avinash K. Dixit and Barry J. Nalebuff, *Thinking Strategically: The Competitive Edge in Business, Politics, and Everyday Life* (New York: W.W. Norton, 1991); Adam M. Brandenburger and Barry J. Nalebuff, "The Right Game: Use Game Theory to Shape Strategy," HBR July–August 1995.
- **System Dynamics.** Peter N. Senge, *Fifth Discipline: The Art and Practice of the Learning Organization* (New York: Doubleday, 1990); Arie de Geus, "Planning as Learning," HBR March–April 1988.
- **Agent-Based Models.** John L. Casti, *Would-Be Worlds: How Simulation Is Changing the Frontiers of Science* (New York: John Wiley & Sons, 1997).
- **Real Options.** Avinash K. Dixit and Robert S. Pindyck, "The Options Approach to Capital Investment," HBR May–June 1995; Timothy A. Luehrman, "What's It Worth?" HBR May–June 1997.

Mahathir bin Mohamad, Malaysia's prime minister, is trying to shape the future of the multimedia industry in the Asian Pacific Rim. This is truly a level 4 strategy problem at this point. Potential products are undefined, as are the players, the level of customer demand, and the technology standards, among other factors. The government is trying to create order out of this chaos by investing at least $15 billion to create a so-called Multimedia Super Corridor (MSC) in Malaysia. The MSC is a 750-square-kilometer zone south of Kuala Lumpur that will include state-of-the-art "smart" buildings for software companies, regional headquarters for multinational corporations, a "Multimedia University," a paperless government center called Putrajaya, and a new city called Cyberjaya. By leveraging incentives like a ten-year exemption from the tax on profits, the MSC has received commitments from more than 40 Malaysian and foreign companies so far, including such powerhouses as Intel, Microsoft, Nippon Telegraph and Telephone, Oracle, and Sun Microsystems. Mahathir's shaping strategy is predicated on the notion that the MSC will create a web of relationships between content and hardware providers that will result in clear industry standards and a set of complementary multimedia products and services. Intel's Malaysia managing director, David B. Marsing, recognized Mahathir's shaping aspirations when he noted, "If you're an evolutionist, it's strange. They're [the Malaysian government] trying to intervene instead of letting it evolve."

Shapers need not make enormous bets as the Malaysian government is doing to be successful in level 3 or 4 situations, however. All that is required is the credibility to coordinate the strategies of different players around the preferred outcome. Netscape Communications Corporation, for example, didn't rely on deep pockets to shape Internet browser standards. Instead, it leveraged the credibility of its leadership team in the industry so that other industry players thought, "If these guys think this is the way to go, they must be right."

Reserving the right to play is common, but potentially dangerous, in level 4 situations. Oil companies believed they were reserving the right to compete in China by buying options to establish various beachheads there some 20 years ago. However, in such level 4 situations, it is extremely difficult to determine whether incremental investments are truly reserving the right to play or simply the right to lose. A few general rules apply. First, look for a high degree of leverage. If the choice of beachhead in China comes down to maintaining a small, but expensive, local operation or developing a limited joint venture with a local distributor, all else being equal, go for the low-cost option. Higher cost options must be justified with explicit arguments for why they would put the company in a better position to ramp up over time. Second, don't get locked into one position through neglect. Options should be rigorously reevaluated whenever important uncertainties are clarified—at least every six months. Remember, level 4 situations are transitional, and most will quickly move toward levels 3 and 2.

The difficulty of managing options in level 4 situations often drives players toward adapter postures. As in level 3, an adapter posture in level 4 is frequently implemented by making investments in organizational capabilities. Most potential players in the multimedia industry are adopting that posture today but will soon be making bigger bets as the industry moves into level 3 and 2 uncertainty over time.

A new approach to uncertainty

At the heart of the traditional approach to strategy lies the assumption that by applying a set of powerful analytic tools, executives can predict the future of any business accurately enough to allow them to choose a clear strategic direction. In relatively stable businesses, that approach continues to work well. But it tends to break down when the environment is so uncertain that no amount of good analysis will allow them to predict the future.

Levels of uncertainty regularly confronting managers today are so high that they need a new way to think about strategy. The approach we've outlined will help executives avoid dangerous binary views of uncertainty. It offers a discipline for thinking rigorously and systematically about uncertainty. On one plane, it is a guide to judging which analytic tools can help in making decisions at various levels of uncertainty and which cannot. On a broader plane, our framework is a way to tackle the most challenging decisions that executives have to make, offering a more complete and sophisticated understanding of the uncertainty they face and its implications for strategy.

This article is based on research sponsored by McKinsey's ongoing Strategy Theory Initiative (STI). The authors would like to thank their STI colleagues for their significant contributions to this article.

Chapter 12

Harnessing the science of persuasion

A LUCKY FEW HAVE it; most of us do not. A handful of gifted "naturals" simply know how to capture an audience, sway the undecided, and convert the opposition. Watching these masters of persuasion work their magic is at once impressive and frustrating. What's impressive is not just the easy way they use charisma and eloquence to convince others to do as they ask. It's also how eager those others are to do what's requested of them, as if the persuasion itself were a favor they couldn't wait to repay.

The frustrating part of the experience is that these born persuaders are often unable to account for their remarkable skill or pass it on to others. Their way with people is an art, and artists as a rule are far better at doing than at explaining. Most of them can't offer much help to those of us who possess no more than the ordinary quotient of charisma and eloquence but who still have to wrestle with leadership's fundamental challenge: getting things done through others. That challenge is painfully familiar to corporate executives, who every day have to figure out how to motivate and direct a highly individualistic workforce. Playing the "Because I'm the boss" card is out. Even if it weren't demeaning and demoralizing for all concerned, it would be out of place in a world where cross-functional teams, joint ventures, and inter-company partnerships have blurred the lines of authority. In such an environment, persuasion skills exert far greater influence over others' behavior than formal power structures do.

Which brings us back to where we started. Persuasion skills may be more necessary than ever, but how can executives acquire them if the most talented practitioners can't pass them along? By looking to science. For the past five decades, behavioral scientists have conducted experiments that shed considerable light on the way certain interactions lead people to concede, comply, or change. This research shows that persuasion works by appealing to a limited set of deeply rooted human drives and needs, and it does so in predictable ways. Persuasion, in other words, is governed by basic principles that can be taught, learned, and applied. By mastering these principles, executives can bring scientific rigor to the business of securing consensus, cutting deals, and winning concessions. In the pages that follow, I describe six fundamental principles of persuasion and suggest a few ways that executives can apply them in their own organizations.

The principle of liking: *people like those who like them*

The application: uncover real similarities and offer genuine praise

The retailing phenomenon known as the Tupperware party is a vivid illustration of this principle in action. The demonstration party for Tupperware products is hosted by an individual, almost always a woman, who invites to her home an array of friends, neighbors, and relatives.

The guests' affection for their hostess predisposes them to buy from her, a dynamic that was confirmed by a 1990 study of purchase decisions made at demonstration parties. The researchers, Jonathan Frenzen and Harry Davis, writing in the *Journal of Consumer Research*, found that the guests' fondness for their hostess weighed twice as heavily in their purchase decisions as their regard for the products they bought. So when guests at a Tupperware party buy something, they aren't just buying to please themselves. They're buying to please their hostess as well.

What's true at Tupperware parties is true for business in general: If you want to influence people, win friends. How? Controlled research has identified several factors that reliably increase liking, but two stand out as especially compelling—similarity and praise. Similarity literally draws people together. In one experiment, reported in a 1968 article in the *Journal of Personality*, participants stood physically closer to one another after learning that they shared political beliefs and social values. And in a 1963 article in *American Behavioral Scientists*, researcher F. B. Evans used demographic data from insurance company records to demonstrate that prospects were more willing to purchase a policy from a salesperson who was akin to them in age, religion, politics, or even cigarette smoking habits.

Managers can use similarities to create bonds with a recent hire, the head of another department, or even a new boss. Informal conversations during the workday create an ideal opportunity to discover at least one common area of enjoyment, be it a hobby, a college basketball team, or reruns of *Seinfeld*. The important thing is to establish the bond early because it creates a presumption of goodwill and trustworthiness in every subsequent encounter. It's much easier to build support for a new project when the people you're trying to persuade are already inclined in your favor.

Praise, the other reliable generator of affection, both charms and disarms. Sometimes the praise doesn't even have to be merited. Researchers at the University of North Carolina writing in the *Journal of Experimental Social Psychology* found that men felt the greatest regard for an individual who flattered them unstintingly even if the comments were untrue. And in their book *Interpersonal Attraction* (Addison-Wesley, 1978), Ellen Berscheid and Elaine Hatfield Walster presented experimental data showing that positive remarks about another person's traits, attitude, or performance reliably generates liking in return, as well as willing compliance with the wishes of the person offering the praise.

Along with cultivating a fruitful relationship, adroit managers can also use praise to repair one that's damaged or unproductive. Imagine you're the manager of a goodsized unit within your organization. Your work frequently brings you into contact with another manager—call him Dan—whom you have come to dislike. No matter how much you do for him, it's not enough. Worse, he never seems to believe that you're doing the best you can for him. Resenting his attitude and his obvious lack of trust in your abilities and in your good faith, you don't spend as much time with him as you know you should; in consequence, the performance of both his unit and yours is deteriorating.

The research on praise points toward a strategy for fixing the relationship. It may be hard to find, but there has to be something about Dan you can sincerely admire, whether it's his concern for the people in his department, his devotion to his family, or simply his work ethic. In your next encounter with him, make an appreciative comment about that trait. Make it clear that in this case at least, you value what he values. I predict that Dan will relax his relentless negativity and give you an opening to convince him of your competence and good intentions.

The principle of reciprocity: *people repay in kind*

The application: give what you want to receive

Praise is likely to have a warming and softening effect on Dan because, ornery as he is, he is still human and subject to the universal human tendency to treat people the way they treat him. If you have ever caught yourself smiling at a coworker just because he or she smiled first, you know how this principle works.

Charities rely on reciprocity to help them raise funds. For years, for instance, the Disabled American Veterans organization, using only a well-crafted fund-raising letter, garnered a very respectable 18% rate of response to its appeals. But when the group started enclosing a small gift in the envelope, the response rate nearly doubled to 35%. The gift—personalized address labels—was extremely modest, but it wasn't what prospective donors received that made the difference. It was that they had gotten anything at all.

What works in that letter works at the office, too. It's more than an effusion of seasonal spirit, of course, that impels suppliers to shower gifts on purchasing departments at holiday time. In 1996, purchasing managers admitted to an interviewer from *Inc.* magazine that after having accepted a gift from a supplier, they were willing to purchase products and services they would have otherwise declined. Gifts also have a startling effect on retention. I have encouraged readers of my book to send me examples of the principles of influence at work in their own lives. One reader, an employee of the State of Oregon, sent a letter in which she offered these reasons for her commitment to her supervisor:

> He gives me and my son gifts for Christmas and gives me presents on my birthday. There is no promotion for the type of job I have, and my only choice for one is to move to another department. But I find myself resisting trying to move. My boss is reaching retirement age, and I am thinking I will be able to move out after he retires . . . [F]or now, I feel obligated to stay since he has been so nice to me.

Ultimately, though, gift giving is one of the cruder applications of the rule of reciprocity. In its more sophisticated uses, it confers a genuine first-mover advantage on any manager who is trying to foster positive attitudes and productive personal relationships in the office: Managers can elicit the desired behavior from coworkers and employees by displaying it first. Whether it's a sense of trust, a spirit of cooperation, or a pleasant demeanor, leaders should model the behavior they want to see from others.

The same holds true for managers faced with issues of information delivery and resource allocation. If you lend a member of your staff to a colleague who is shorthanded and staring at a fast-approaching deadline, you will significantly increase your chances of getting help when you need it. Your odds will improve even more if you say, when your colleague thanks you for the assistance, something like, "Sure, glad to help. I know how important it is for me to count on your help when I need it."

The principle of social proof: *people follow the lead of similar others*

The application: use peer power whenever it's available

Social creatures that they are, human beings rely heavily on the people around them for cues on how to think, feel, and act. We know this intuitively, but intuition has also been confirmed by experiments, such as the one first described in 1982 in the *Journal of Applied Psychology*. A group of researchers went door-to-door in Columbia, South Carolina, soliciting donations for a charity campaign and displaying a list of neighborhood residents who had already donated to the cause. The researchers found that the longer the donor list was, the more likely those solicited would be to donate as well.

To the people being solicited, the friends' and neighbors' names on the list were a form of social evidence about how they should respond. But the evidence would not have been nearly as compelling had the names been those of random strangers. In an experiment from the 1960s, first described in the *Journal of Personality and Social Psychology*, residents of New York City were asked to return a lost wallet to its owner. They were highly likely to attempt to return the wallet when they learned that another New Yorker had previously attempted to do so. But learning that someone from a foreign country had tried to return the wallet didn't sway their decision one way or the other.

The lesson for executives from these two experiments is that persuasion can be extremely effective when it comes from peers. The science supports what most sales professionals already know: Testimonials from satisfied customers work best when the satisfied customer and the prospective customer share similar circumstances. That lesson can help a manager faced with the task of selling a new corporate initiative. Imagine that you're trying to streamline your department's work processes. A group of veteran employees is resisting. Rather than try to convince the employees of the move's merits yourself, ask an old-timer who supports the initiative to speak up for it at a team meeting. The compatriot's testimony stands a much better chance of convincing the group than yet another speech from the boss. Stated simply, influence is often best exerted horizontally rather than vertically.

The principle of consistency: *people align with their clear commitments*

The application: make their commitments active, public, and voluntary

Liking is a powerful force, but the work of persuasion involves more than simply making people feel warmly toward you, your idea, or your product. People need not only to like you but to feel committed to what you want them to do. Good turns are one reliable way to make people feel obligated to you. Another is to win a public commitment from them.

My own research has demonstrated that most people, once they take a stand or go on record in favor of a position, prefer to stick to it. Other studies reinforce that finding and go on to show how even a small, seemingly trivial commitment can have a powerful effect on future actions. Israeli researchers writing in 1983 in the *Personality and Social Psychology Bulletin* recounted how they asked half the residents of a large apartment complex to sign a petition favoring the establishment of a recreation center for the handicapped. The cause was good and the request was small, so almost everyone who was asked agreed to sign. Two weeks later, on National Collection Day for the Handicapped, all residents of the complex were approached at home and asked to give to the cause. A little more than half of those who were not asked to sign the petition made a contribution. But an astounding 92% of those who did sign donated money. The residents of the apartment complex felt obligated to live up to their commitments because those commitments were active, public, and voluntary. These three features are worth considering separately.

There's strong empirical evidence to show that a choice made actively—

one that's spoken out loud or written down or otherwise made explicit—is considerably more likely to direct someone's future conduct than the same choice left unspoken. Writing in 1996 in the *Personality and Social Psychology Bulletin*, Delia Cioffi and Randy Garner described an experiment in which college students in one group were asked to fill out a printed form saying they wished to volunteer for an AIDS education project in the public schools. Students in another group volunteered for the same project by leaving blank a form stating that they didn't want to participate. A few days later, when the volunteers reported for duty, 74% of those who showed up were students from the group that signaled their commitment by filling out the form.

The implications are clear for a manager who wants to persuade a subordinate to follow some particular course of action: Get it in writing. Let's suppose you want your employee to submit reports in a more timely fashion. Once you believe you've won agreement, ask him to summarize the decision in a memo and send it to you. By doing so, you'll have greatly increased the odds that he'll fulfill the commitment because, as a rule, people live up to what they have written down.

Research into the social dimensions of commitment suggests that written statements become even more powerful when they're made public. In a classic experiment, described in 1955 in the *Journal of Abnormal and Social Psychology*, college students were asked to estimate the length of lines projected on a screen. Some students were asked to write down their choices on a piece of paper, sign it, and hand the paper to the experimenter. Others wrote their choices on an erasable slate, then erased the slate immediately. Still others were instructed to keep their decisions to themselves.

The experimenters then presented all three groups with evidence that their initial choices may have been wrong. Those who had merely kept their decisions in their heads were the most likely to reconsider their original estimates. More loyal to their first guesses were the students in the group that had written them down and immediately erased them. But by a wide margin, the ones most reluctant to shift from their original choices were those who had signed and handed them to the researcher.

This experiment highlights how much most people wish to appear consistent to others. Consider again the matter of the employee who has been submitting late reports. Recognizing the power of this desire, you should, once you've successfully convinced him of the need to be more timely, reinforce the commitment by making sure it gets a public airing. One way to do that would be to send the employee an e-mail that reads, "I think your plan is just what we need. I showed it to Diane in manufacturing and Phil in shipping, and they thought it was right on target, too." Whatever way such commitments are formalized, they should never be like the New Year's resolutions people privately make and then abandon with no one the wiser. They should be publicly made and visibly posted. More than 300 years ago, Samuel Butler wrote a couplet that explains succinctly why commitments must be voluntary to be lasting and effective: "He that complies against his will/Is of his own opinion still." If an undertaking is forced, coerced, or imposed from the outside, it's not a commitment; it's an unwelcome burden. Think how you would react if your boss pressured you to donate to the campaign of a political candidate. Would that make you more apt to opt for that candidate in the privacy of a voting booth? Not likely. In fact, in their 1981 book *Psychological Reactance* (Academic Press), Sharon S. Brehm and Jack W. Brehm present data that suggest you'd vote the opposite way just to express your resentment of the boss's coercion.

This kind of backlash can occur in the office, too. Let's return again to that tardy employee. If you want to produce an enduring change in his behavior, you should avoid using threats or pressure tactics to gain his compliance. He'd likely view any change in his behavior as the result of intimidation rather than a personal commitment to change. A better approach would be to identify something that the employee genuinely values in the workplace—high-quality workmanship, perhaps, or team spirit—and then describe how timely reports are consistent with those values. That gives the employee reasons for improvement that he can own. And because he owns them, they'll continue to guide his behavior even when you're not watching.

The principle of authority: *people defer to experts*

The application: expose your expertise; don't assume it's self-evident

Two thousand years ago, the Roman poet Virgil offered this simple counsel to those seeking to choose correctly: "Believe an expert." That may or may not be good advice, but as a description of what people actually do, it can't be beaten. For instance, when the news media present an acknowledged expert's views on a topic, the effect on public opinion is dramatic. A single expert-opinion news story in the *New York Times* is associated with a 2% shift in public opinion nationwide, according to a 1993 study described in the *Public Opinion Quarterly*. And researchers writing in the *American Political Science Review* in 1987 found that when the expert's view was aired on national television, public opinion shifted as much as 4%. A cynic might argue that these findings only illustrate the docile submissiveness of the public. But a fairer explanation is that, amid the teeming complexity of contemporary life, a well-selected expert offers a valuable and efficient shortcut to good decisions. Indeed, some questions, be they legal, financial, medical, or technological, require so much specialized knowledge to answer, we have no choice but to rely on experts.

Since there's good reason to defer to experts, executives should take pains to ensure that they establish their own expertise before they attempt to exert influence. Surprisingly often, people mistakenly assume that others recognize and appreciate their experience. That's what happened at a hospital where some colleagues and I were consulting. The physical therapy staffers were frustrated because so many of their stroke patients abandoned their exercise routines as soon as they left the hospital. No matter how often the staff emphasized the importance of regular home exercise—it is, in fact, crucial to the process of regaining independent function—the message just didn't sink in.

Interviews with some of the patients helped us pinpoint the problem. They were familiar with the background and training of their physicians, but the patients knew little about the credentials of the physical therapists who were urging them to exercise. It was a simple matter to remedy that lack of information: We merely asked the therapy director to display all the awards, diplomas, and certifications of her staff on the walls of the therapy rooms. The result was startling: Exercise compliance jumped 34% and has never dropped since.

What we found immensely gratifying was not just how much we increased compliance, but how. We didn't fool or browbeat any of the patients. We *informed* them into compliance. Nothing had to be invented; no time or resources had to be spent in the process. The staff's expertise was real—all we had to do was make it more visible.

The task for managers who want to establish their claims to expertise is somewhat more difficult. They can't simply nail their diplomas to the wall and wait for everyone to notice. A little subtlety is called for. Outside the United States, it is customary for people to spend time interacting socially before getting down to business for the first time. Frequently they gather for dinner the night before their meeting or negotiation. These get-togethers can make discussions easier and help blunt disagreements—remember the findings about liking and similarity—and they can also provide an opportunity to establish expertise. Perhaps it's a matter of telling an anecdote about successfully solving a problem similar to the one that's on the agenda at the next day's meeting. Or perhaps dinner is the time to describe years spent mastering a complex discipline—not in a boastful way but as part of the ordinary give-and-take of conversation.

Granted, there's not always time for lengthy introductory sessions. But even in the course of the preliminary conversation that precedes most meetings, there is almost always an opportunity to touch lightly on your relevant background and experience as a natural part of a sociable exchange. This initial disclosure of personal information gives you a chance to establish expertise early in the game, so that when the discussion turns to the business at hand, what you have to say will be accorded the respect it deserves.

Persuasion experts, safe at last

Thanks to several decades of rigorous empirical research by behavioral scientists, our understanding of the how and why of persuasion has never been broader, deeper, or more detailed. But these scientists aren't the first students of the subject. The history of persuasion studies is an ancient and honorable one, and it has generated a long roster of heroes and martyrs.

A renowned student of social influence, William McGuire, contends in a chapter of the *Handbook of Social Psychology*, 3rd ed. (Oxford University Press, 1985) that scattered among the more than four millennia of recorded Western history are four centuries in which the study of persuasion flourished as a craft. The first was the Periclean Age of ancient Athens, the second occurred during the years of the Roman Republic, the next appeared in the time of the European Renaissance, and the last extended over the hundred years that have just ended, which witnessed the advent of large-scale advertising, information, and mass media campaigns. Each of the three previous centuries of systematic persuasion study was marked by a flowering of human achievement that was suddenly cut short when political authorities had the masters of persuasion killed. The philosopher Socrates is probably the best known of the persuasion experts to run afoul of the powers that be.

Information about the persuasion process is a threat because it creates a base of power entirely separate from the one controlled by political authorities. Faced with a rival source of influence, rulers in previous centuries had few qualms about eliminating those rare individuals who truly understood how to marshal forces that heads of state have never been able to monopolize, such as cleverly crafted language, strategically placed information, and, most important, psychological insight.

It would perhaps be expressing too much faith in human nature to claim that persuasion experts no longer face a threat from those who wield political power. But because the truth about persuasion is no longer the sole possession of a few brilliant, inspired individuals, experts in the field can presumably breathe a little easier. Indeed, since most people in power are interested in remaining in power, they're likely to be more interested in acquiring persuasion skills than abolishing them.

The principle of scarcity: *people want more of what they can have less of*

The application: highlight unique benefits and exclusive information

Study after study shows that items and opportunities are seen to be more valuable as they become less available. That's a tremendously useful piece of information for managers. They can harness the scarcity principle with the organizational equivalents of limited-time, limited supply, and one-of-a-kind offers. Honestly informing a coworker of a closing window of opportunity—the chance to get the boss's ear before she leaves for an extended vacation, perhaps—can mobilize action dramatically.

Managers can learn from retailers how to frame their offers not in terms of what people stand to gain but in terms of what they stand to lose if they don't act on the information. The power of "loss language" was demonstrated in a 1988 study of California home owners written up in the *Journal of Applied Psychology*. Half were told that if they fully insulated their homes, they would save a certain amount of money each day. The other half were told that if they failed to insulate, they would lose that amount each day. Significantly more people insulated their homes when exposed to the loss language. The same phenomenon occurs in business. According to a 1994 study in the journal *Organizational Behavior and Human Decision Processes*, potential losses figure far more heavily in managers' decision making than potential gains.

In framing their offers, executives should also remember that exclusive information is more persuasive than widely available data. A doctoral student of mine, Amram Knishinsky, wrote his 1982 dissertation on the purchase decisions of wholesale beef buyers. He observed that they more than doubled their orders when they were told that, because of certain weather conditions overseas, there was likely to be a scarcity of foreign beef in the near future. But their orders increased 600% when they were informed that no one else had that information yet.

The persuasive power of exclusivity can be harnessed by any manager who comes into possession of information that's not broadly available and that supports an idea or initiative he or she would like the organization to adopt. The next time that kind of information crosses your desk, round up your organization's key players. The information itself may seem dull, but exclusivity will give it a special sheen. Push it across your desk and say, "I just got this report today. It won't be distributed until next week, but I want to give you an early look at what it shows." Then watch your listeners lean forward.

Allow me to stress here a point that should be obvious. No offer of exclusive information, no exhortation to act now or miss this opportunity forever should be made unless it is genuine. Deceiving colleagues into compliance is not only ethically objectionable, it's foolhardy. If the deception is detected—and it certainly will be—it will snuff out any enthusiasm the offer originally kindled. It will also invite dishonesty toward the deceiver. Remember the rule of reciprocity.

Putting it all together

There's nothing abstruse or obscure about these six principles of persuasion. Indeed, they neatly codify our intuitive understanding of the ways people evaluate information and form decisions. As a result, the principles are easy for most people to grasp, even those with no formal education in psychology. But in the seminars and workshops I conduct, I have learned that two points bear repeated emphasis.

First, although the six principles and their applications can be discussed separately for the sake of clarity, they should be applied in combination to compound their impact. For instance, in discussing the importance of expertise, I suggested that managers use informal, social conversations to establish their credentials. But that conversation affords an opportunity to gain information as well as convey it. While you're showing your dinner companion that you have the skills and experience your business problem demands, you can also learn about your companion's background, likes, and dislikes—information that will help you locate genuine similarities and give sincere compliments. By letting your expertise surface and also establishing rapport, you double your persuasive power. And if you succeed in bringing your dinner partner on board, you may encourage other people to sign on as well, thanks to the persuasive power of social evidence.

The other point I wish to emphasize is that the rules of ethics apply to the science of social influence just as they do to any other technology. Not only is it ethically wrong to trick or trap others into assent, it's ill-advised in practical terms. Dishonest or high-pressure tactics work only in the short run, if at all. Their long-term effects are malignant, especially within an organization, which can't function properly without a bedrock level of trust and cooperation.

That point is made vividly in the following account, which a department head for a large textile manufacturer related at a training workshop I conducted. She described a vice president in her company who wrung public commitments from department heads in a highly manipulative manner. Instead of giving his subordinates time to talk or think through his proposals carefully, he would approach them individually at the busiest moment of their workday and describe the benefits of his plan in exhaustive, patience-straining detail. Then he would move in for the kill. "It's very important for me to see you as being on my team on this," he would say. "Can I count on your support?" Intimidated, frazzled, eager to chase the man from their offices so they could get back to work, the department heads would invariably go along with his request. But because the commitments never felt voluntary, the department heads never followed through, and as a result the vice president's initiatives all blew up or petered out.

This story had a deep impact on the other participants in the workshop. Some gulped in shock as they recognized their own manipulative behavior. But what stopped everyone cold was the expression on the department head's face as she recounted the damaging collapse of her superior's proposals. She was smiling.

Nothing I could say would more effectively make the point that the deceptive or coercive use of the principles of social influence is ethically wrong and pragmatically wrongheaded. Yet the same principles, if applied appropriately, can steer decisions correctly. Legitimate expertise, genuine obligations, authentic similarities, real social proof, exclusive news, and freely made commitments can produce choices that are likely to benefit both parties. And any approach that works to everyone's mutual benefit is good business, don't you think? Of course, I don't want to press you into it, but, if you agree, I would love it if you could just jot me a memo to that effect.

Chapter 13

Achieving business success in Confucian societies

The importance of *Guanxi* (Connections)

IN LIGHT OF THE remarkable economic transformation that has taken place in East and Southeast Asia in the past several decades, there is a consensus among government and business leaders that significant business opportunities will abound in this region. Economists project that China will be one of the world's four largest economies by the year 2010. If China's economy were to be combined with that of Hong Kong and Taiwan—greater China, in short—the economic implications would be even more staggering.

Many have attributed this phenomenal success to Confucianism, which stresses scholarship, hard work, thrift, and perseverance. Societies influenced by the teachings of Confucius (551–478 B.C.) include China, Hong Kong, Taiwan, Japan and Korea—all countries with prospects for sustained economic growth.

Rosabeth Moss Kanter, among others, asserts that in order to establish a world class organization, it is imperative that the firm maintain an extensive web of worldwide connections. This takes on a special significance in Confucian societies. As one popular saying in these societies puts it, "Who you know is more important than what you know." "Who you know" refers to personal connections with the appropriate authorities or individuals. These connections are known in Chinese as *guanxi*. Japanese refer to this web of connections as *kankei*; Koreans, *kwankye*. "What you know" refers to technological expertise, including the price and quality of a tendered product or service.

Reprinted from *Organizational Dynamics*, Vol. 25, Yeung and Tung, "Achieving Business Success in Confucian Societies: The Importance of *Guanxi* (Connections)," pp. 54–65, Copyright © 1996, with permission from Elsevier.

Despite widespread belief among Asians and non-Asians alike that *guanxi* is important (perhaps more important than price and quality), its relationship with business performance has not been verified empirically. In general, there is a dearth of research on the subject. This can be attributed to two primary reasons: One, Westerners often regard *guanxi* as a sordid form of favoritism and nepotism; it may be viewed as an inferior construct not worthy of investigation. Two, because Chinese consider *guanxi* as a personal asset, they are usually reluctant to talk openly about their connections.

This article investigates the importance of *guanxi* by proposing answers to four questions: (1) What is *guanxi* and how is it different from friendship or networking patterns in the Western world? (2) Why does *guanxi* assume such a significant role in Confucian societies? (3) How does *guanxi* affect long-term business success in China? (4) How does one build and maintain *guanxi*? The analysis is based on literature review and an empirical study of *guanxi* that investigated its relationship with the financial performance of 19 firms that have business dealings with China.

The meaning of *guanxi*

In Chinese, *guanxi* is a general term for social networking and is often translated as "relationship" or "connection." The two Chinese characters that make up the term mean a "gate/pass" or "to connect." Thus, *guanxi* refers to the establishment of a connection between two independent individuals to enable a bilateral flow of personal or social transactions. However, both parties must derive benefits from the transaction to ensure the continuation of such a relationship. Louis Kraar has dubbed this the "Chinese art of reciprocal back-scratching."

An important question can be raised as to how *guanxi* compares with friendship and networking patterns in the West, specifically the United States. The similarities and differences can be analyzed along six paths: the motives for engaging in social relations, reciprocation in social exchanges, time orientation, pattern of differentiation, nature of power, and sanction practice.

1. Motives: role obligations vs. self-interest

One basic tenet of Confucianism stresses the importance of an individual's place in the hierarchy of social relationships: individuals are part of a system of inter-dependent relationships, not isolated entities. The system includes five types of relationships: ruler–subject, father–son, husband–wife, brother–brother, and friend–friend. A person's fulfillment of the responsibilities of a given role ensures the smooth functioning of society. In the West, however, the primary influence on human behavior is self-interest. This dissimilarity between the two cultures has led to the development of very different attitudes about reciprocation.

2. Reciprocation: self-loss vs. self-gain

Confucianism encourages each individual to become a *yi-ren* (righteous person). To become a *yi-ren*, a person must repay favors and increase the value of the favor given. The Chinese saying, "If someone pays you an honor of a linear foot, you should reciprocate by honoring the giver with ten linear foot," captures the essence of this principle. According to Peter M. Blau's social exchange theory, while there is also unequal reciprocity in Western social transactions, the tilt of disadvantage is directed at the other party, not the self.

3. Time orientation: long-term vs. short-term perspective

Strategic management thought in East Asia includes an understanding of the relationship between situations and time. This perspective stems from the East Asian belief that duality and contradictions (yin/yang) are inherent in all aspects of life. Members of Confucian societies assume the interdependence of events, and understand all social interactions within the context of a long-term balance sheet. In the words of one executive, "Every *guanxi* relationship is regarded as 'stock' to be put away in times of abundance and plenty. The 'stock' will then be at their disposal in times of need and trouble." The debit and credit sides of this balance sheet are never in equilibrium, since such a status often means the end of a *guanxi* relationship. *Guanxi* is maintained and reinforced through continuous, long-term association and interaction.

In contrast, social transactions in the West are usually seen as isolated occurrences. The objective is to maintain balance in each transaction, with great emphasis placed on immediate gains from the interaction.

4. Power differentiation: xia vs. power

Another basic tenet of Confucianism is *xia*, a term that carries the same connotations as "knight" in the Western world. In striving to become a "righteous individual," each person must become a knight, and attempt to right the wrongs of the world. Thus, those in positions of power and authority must assist the disadvantaged. In return, the former gains face and a good reputation. This perspective on the appropriate relationship between the strong and the weak explains, in part, why the Chinese often feel that investors from industrialized countries should make concessions to help developing nations.

While social conscience may be strong in the West, the powerful are under no obligation to assist those who are disadvantaged.

5. Nature of power: personal power vs. institutional authority

Under Confucianism, governance by ethics (*li zhi*) is preferred over governance by law (*fa zhi*). This accounts for the general aversion to law and litigation in

Confucian societies. The disregard for institutional law means tha[...] occupy positions of authority (*ren zhi*) have power of influence.

Emphasis on personal power promotes the practice of *guanxi*, since [...] vidual (rather than institutional authority) defines what is permissible in a [...] context at a particular time. According to Lee Kuan Yew, founding father o[...] Republic of Singapore, the Chinese use *guanxi* "to make up for the lack of t[...] rule of law and transparency in rules and regulations." For example, the Chinese authorities forced McDonald's to relocate in Beijing to accommodate real estate development by Hong Kong billionaire Li Ka Shing. The latter is well-connected to high-ranking officials in China.

In contrast, Western society relies primarily on institutional law to ensure smooth and orderly progress.

6. Sanction: shame vs. guilt

In Confucian societies, the primary deterrent against immoral or illegal behavior is shame. Two factors have contributed to this: (1) the absence of indigenous religions such as Judaism and Christianity, and (2) the emphasis on "face" and "face-saving."

While the latter principle is important in all countries, both are essential in Confucian societies. Face implies more than reputation. There is a Chinese saying that "Face is like the bark of a tree; without its bark, the tree dies." People who have lost face in Confucian societies are more than social outcasts: a loss of face brings shame not only to individuals, but also to family members. Because of this shame, the family members are unable to function in society.

In Confucian societies, face is contextual; it can be given and taken away only within the broader context of social interactions. Thus, to maintain *guanxi*, extra care must be taken in the acquisition and maintenance of face, generally referred to as "face works."

The West, under the influence of Judeo-Christianity, operates primarily on the basis of guilt. Because of an internalized understanding of sin, individuals feel guilty if their behavior deviates from the cultural standards of morality.

The differences are important

While there are parallels between *guanxi* and networking patterns in the West, there are fundamental differences in the principles that guide their implementation. In practice, *guanxi* appears to resemble nepotism in the West. *Guanxi* and nepotism share some characteristics: both involve situations where someone in authority will make decisions—perhaps about employment or the awarding of business deals or contracts—based on family ties or connections instead of an objective evaluation of ability.

In his recent book, *China: The Next Economic Superpower* (New York: Norton, 1993) William Overholt, a senior financial manager in Hong Kong, described this nepotism as a "particularly corrupt form of neo-feudalism." The Western

ncelings," family members of senior officials in
guanxi to engage in varied activities, including
to export Chinese military armaments; the
state-subsidized prices for sale in the open
ritable foundations where the delineation
t best; and the use of assets of state-owned
seas.

ng, son of Zhou Guanwu (who is a close
cquired several Hong Kong companies
ese enterprises. At its height, this group of
value of $1.4 billion. In February 1995, Zhou Beifang
or "serious economic crimes" as part of an anti-corruption
paign launched by Communist Party Chairman Jiang Zemin.

The significance of *guanxi*

Gordon C. Chu and Yanan Ju surveyed 2,000 Chinese from Shanghai (the hub of
commercial activities in China) and Qingpu (a rural county outside of Shanghai)
on the significance of *guanxi* in daily living. Some pertinent findings in their
survey were:

- An overwhelming majority of those polled (92.4 percent) affirmed the
  importance of *guanxi* in their daily lives.
- A strong majority (84.5 percent) indicated that they do not trust strangers
  until they have had the opportunity to get to know them better.
- Not surprisingly, 71.7 percent preferred to use *guanxi* connections over
  normal bureaucratic channels to advance personal interests and solve
  problems.
- The younger generation tended to place greater emphasis on *guanxi* than
  older people.

Given the significance of *guanxi*, Thomas B. Gold has coined the term
guanxixue (relationology) to describe the art of establishing and maintaining
guanxi.

Why does *guanxi* assume such central importance in the Chinese society?
The answer lies in Confucianism. As noted earlier, each individual occupies
one or more roles in a hierarchy of social relationships and takes on that role's
obligations. Three of the five relationships pertain to the family, accounting for
the strong emphasis on family in Confucian societies. Most Chinese businesses
are still family-run concerns. For example, Formosa Plastics in Taiwan, a highly
successful conglomerate that employs 30,000 people, is essentially run as a
family business. This emphasis on the family results in a clear distinction between
members of the in-group and the out-group.

John Kao has attributed this phenomenon to the "life-raft" mentality characteristic of most overseas Chinese. Because of the political and economic
uncertainty in China, most Chinese believe that the only people they can trust

are family members. According to Lee Shau Kee, who has amassed a family fortune of $6 billion, "The success of the overseas Chinese is the result of bad times in China itself. . . . Because we have no social security, the overseas Chinese habit is to save a lot and make a lot of friends." Kao refers to this worldwide circle of business friends as the "Chinese commonwealth."

Patterns of social interaction in China have undergone fundamental changes under communism, especially during the Cultural Revolution (1966–1976). Shortly after the establishment of the People's Republic of China in 1949, the Chinese Communist Party encouraged each person to become an idealistic socialist. Confucian social relationships came under attack because they ran contrary to the ideology of comradeship, which stresses equality among individuals. Comradeship called for an abolition of the in-group and out-group distinctions. This new ideology even questioned the bonds that had traditionally cemented families. For example, children were taught that worthy comrades had to report their family affairs to their teachers.

According to Gordon Redding, communist ideology produced two unexpected changes in social relations. To buffer overwhelming state control, some found solace and security in their own private spheres of *guanxi* networks. While the ideal of communism is to promote selflessness, it actually had the opposite effect: because individuals could no longer trust family or friends, they began to see social relations as the means to advance personal interests. Thus, an extreme form of instrumentalism began to emerge in *guanxi* relations during the Cultural Revolution.

Ambrose King, for example, found that Chinese respondents use "relationology" (or "using people") to gain special privileges and career advancement and terminate such relationships once their usefulness is at an end. David Ralston of the University of Connecticut, working with a group of international researchers, found that there was a significant increase in Chinese managers' scores on the Machiavellianism dimension after June 4, 1989, another watershed in the evolution of present-day Chinese society. The Machiavellianism dimension is a "measure of the degree to which a person places self-interest above the interest of the group . . . self-interest may be the individual or extended family set against those beyond the intimacy of family relationships."

ABOUT THE RESEARCH

The national origins of the 19 companies included in this study were as follows: Hong Kong (11), U.S. (5), Canada (1), Germany (1), and Sweden (1). The companies were engaged in a diverse range of industries and services, including real estate, finance, import/exports, and the manufacture of toys, electronic products, and telecommunication equipment. These companies employed between four and over 10,000 people in China. The heads of China operations in all 19 companies were ethnic Chinese. While constituting a sampling bias, the fact that even non-Chinese firms chose to head their China operations with an ethnic Chinese reveals the perceived importance of hiring someone who can fit easily into the Chinese circle of connections. The majority of the interviews took place in Hong Kong and all were conducted in Chinese. Each interview ran for 90 to 120 minutes.

Guanxi and long-term business success

Although prior research provides considerable insight into contemporary Confucian society, it deals only indirectly with the role of *guanxi* in business relationships. To investigate the relationship, we conducted semi-structured interviews with the heads of China operations of 19 companies, who were referred to the interviewer through friends and relatives. Given the sensitive nature of the *guanxi* construct, it was easier to elicit such information when the interviewer was someone with whom the respondent felt comfortable. The box (above) provides information about the respondents and their companies.

Guanxi *as key success factor*

The executives were presented with a list of 11 factors and were asked to rank them in order of importance to long-term business success in China. These 11 factors were: choosing the right business location, choosing the right entry strategy, competitive prices, complementarity of goals, familiarity with Chinese negotiation style, flexibility in business operations, *guanxi* with Chinese business associates, long-term commitment to the China market, management control, product differentiation and quality, and understanding of China's policy. Long-term business success was measured in terms of the growth of annual net income or pretax profits of the firm between 1991 to 1994. The firm's financial performance was compared to corresponding performance norms for the industry in China.

Of this list, *guanxi* was the only item which was consistently chosen as a key success factor (mean=0.83). The respondents attributed the importance of *guanxi* to the ambiguity of Chinese legislation. Despite the enactment of new legislation in the past decade and a half, Chinese business laws remain vague. In the absence of explicit guidelines, directives and policies are open to interpretation by those who occupy positions of authority and/or power.

While recognizing the importance of *guanxi* in financial affairs, most of the executives agreed that *guanxi* alone is not enough to guarantee long-term success in China. The significance of *guanxi* in ensuring continued success decreased over the life of the venture. Once the operation is established, other conditions must be met to sustain success, and of these conditions, technical competence is most important. The business must supply high-quality products, adopt suitable business strategies, and possess in-depth knowledge of the market. Venturetech, a Chinese state enterprise staffed by "princelings," collapsed because of poor product quality.

One respondent characterized *guanxi* as only one of three cardinal requisites for business success in China. He called these requisites the three "Cs": capital, capability and connections (*guanxi*). Another respondent drew the analogy between *guanxi* and a piece of wood thrown to a drowning swimmer: "The wood does not have inherent magical properties which will automatically rescue the swimmer. Whether the swimmer is ultimately saved depends upon how he utilizes it." Yet another respondent likened *guanxi* to a boarding pass that enables the bearer to explore a treasure island. "There is no guarantee that they will find wealth even if they are permitted access."

This finding about the relationship between *guanxi* and long-term business success parallels earlier work on business negotiations between U.S. and Chinese firms conducted by one of the authors for this article. These studies found that while knowledge of cultural differences on the part of the Americans will not always guarantee success, its absence (ignorance of Chinese culture, including the role of *guanxi*) usually leads to failure.

The relationship between *guanxi* and long-term business success was further moderated by the nationality of the firm, years of experience, firm size, and industry type.

- Despite the fact that all interviewees were ethnic Chinese, the representatives from Hong Kong firms assigned a higher significance to *guanxi* than non-Hong Kong firms. This difference may stem from the fact that the Hong Kong firms derived 100 percent of their revenues from China while the non-Hong Kong firms were more diversified in their investment portfolio. For the non-Hong Kong firms, revenues from their China operations accounted for 5 to 45 percent of their total sales from the Asia-Pacific region.
- Those with ten or more years of experience in China assigned lower priority to *guanxi* than those with less experience. Years of experience is a reflection of the age of the business's establishment in China. As noted earlier, *guanxi* is of paramount importance in the initial stages of entering the China market. Beyond a certain threshold level, however, other factors assume greater significance.
- Small- and medium-sized firms tended to place greater emphasis on *guanxi* than large companies. Since large firms can contribute substantially to the local economy, the Chinese authorities are keen to attract their investment in the first place. One company invested over $50 million in two communities in Guandong province (south China) and was thus hailed as a "savior" by the local government officials. Similarly, the local government courted the investment of another company, which hired 7,000 local Chinese in their manufacturing plant and built railways and bridges to improve the local infrastructure.
- Firms in the tertiary and exporting sectors assigned greater importance to *guanxi* than those engaged in manufacturing and importing. This appears to stem from the fact that firms engaged in manufacturing and importing were more localized in their operations; once they were established in a specific business location, they did not have to expand and/or shift their *guanxi* networks continuously. Those in the tertiary and exporting sectors had to frequently broaden their base of operations and search for new suppliers.

Right and strong guanxi

The theoretical literature suggests that building strong *guanxi* relations with the right persons is crucial to the attainment of long-term business success in China. The two components ("strong" and "right") were treated as two separate variables in the initial analysis of our interview data. It was found that companies that had developed the right *guanxi* networks tended to perform better financially than those which had not. No statistically significant relationship was found between those firms that had established strong *guanxi* networks and those with moderate or weak *guanxi* relations.

When the two components were combined, however, a statistically significant pattern emerged. In other words, in order to attain business success in China, it is important for the company to maintain a strong and right *guanxi* network. Consequently, to succeed in China, an investor has to identify the right parties to establish connections with. Furthermore, these relationships must be nourished and maintained over time.

How to build and maintain *guanxi*

Since *guanxi* is essential to the initial set-up of business operations in China, it is important to understand the dynamics of *guanxi* building and maintenance. Mayfair M. H. Yang has described guanxi building as the transformation process whereby two discrete individuals construct a basis of familiarity to enable the subsequent development of relationships. In this process, the gap between two hitherto unrelated individuals is bridged so that an outsider becomes part of the inside social circle of another person.

As Kao described it, the Chinese commonwealth has an "open architecture." The network has permeable borders where connections can be established or discontinued. *Guanxi* is embedded in dyadic relationships between two people, not organizational entities. Hence *guanxi* is a personal asset that cannot be transferred. Consequently, when a person with the right and strong *guanxi* leaves an organization, the latter loses the *guanxi* or goodwill. According to Kwek Leng Joo, whose family's business has assets over $5 billion, "Who I know is exclusive information. I hardly make it known even to friends."

There are two ways to facilitate the transformation process: group identification and altercasting.

Group identification

Group identification can be of two types: ascribed and achieved. The two most common forms of ascribed *guanxi* bases are kinship and locality. Kinship refers to members of a person's immediate and extended families. As Gordon C. Chu and Yanan Ju report from their research, an overwhelming majority of the respondents (70.9 percent) stated that they would offer help to a relative rather than a friend. Locality refers to the ancestral village or province. Many overseas

Chinese who may not have visited their ancestral village still feel a strong affinity to others whose forefathers are also from that locality. Locality is believed to be the most important *guanxi* base in Chinese politics.

Achieved *guanxi*, on the other hand, is based on common or shared experience, such as going to the same school, serving in the same military unit, or working in the same organization or organizational unit.

Altercasting

Since the majority of non-Chinese investors are not related to the Chinese by blood and locality, most have to rely on the second mechanism, altercasting, for establishing *guanxi*. Altercasting refers to the establishment of *guanxi* between two individuals who have no ascribed commonalty. The objective of altercasting is to rearrange the targeted person's social network in such a way as to involve the individual who wishes to be included in it. An effective way of attaining this goal is to use an intermediary who is a mutual friend of both parties. The intermediary can vouch for the behavior and sincerity of either party. According to Victor Fung, chairman of Prudential Asia, a Hong Kong investment bank, "If you are being considered for a new partnership, a personal reference from a respected member of the Chinese business community is worth more than any amount of money you could throw on the table."

In his research, A. De Keijzer found that 42 percent of non-Chinese investors used intermediaries to locate suitable joint venture partners. Similarly, many of the non-Hong Kong firms included in this study used intermediaries to establish connections in China. Many of these intermediaries are ethnic Chinese who have been educated abroad and who have a good knowledge of both Chinese and Western cultures. One executive characterized the role of the intermediary as follows: "The China market is like a pond full of hidden delicious food. A new fish in the pond can starve to death because he doesn't know how to locate the food. Your intermediary is an old fish who knows where every plant and plankton is. He can show you the precise location of this food so you can eat to your heart's satisfaction."

Since *guanxi* is a gate that can be open or shut, it needs to be propped wide once opened; otherwise, it can slam shut again. There are essentially four strategies for maintaining *guanxi* relationships: tendering favors, nurturing long-term mutual benefits, cultivating personal relationships, and cultivating trust.

Tendering favors

Given the instrumental nature of *guanxi*, one way to establish relations is to offer immediate rewards. Gift-giving, entertainment at lavish banquets, questionable payments, overseas trips, and sponsoring and supporting the children of Chinese officials at universities abroad are common. Many respondents perceived this to be the quickest way to build *guanxi* relations in China. According to Yang, when a gift has been received or a request for a favor has been granted, there is a "symbolic breaking down of the boundaries between persons." In fact, one respondent indicated that "no *guanxi* can be built without meat and wine." This refers to the practice of throwing lavish banquets accompanied by expensive gifts.

As explained in a prior article published in this journal (see Selected Bibliography), a number of popular stratagems derived from ancient military classics continue to guide strategic management thought in East Asia. Two of these 36 stratagems describe the distribution of favors to gain even bigger advantages or successes: "Trade a brick for a piece of jade" and "sacrifice the plum tree for the peach tree." All 19 companies interviewed in this study had tendered favors in the course of *guanxi* building and maintenance.

Many study participants also felt that while short-term favors can open doors, thus initiating the cycle of guanxi development, these favors cannot be the basis for long-term *guanxi*. This is true for three reasons: One, since these favors can be duplicated readily by others, any relationship that is based exclusively on short-term gains will be unstable. Two, the use of questionable payments connotes a sense of cheating. Two companies asserted that, "If your products are good, you don't have to bribe." Since technical competence gains ascendancy in the established phase of a business operations in China, questionable payments cannot substitute indefinitely for poor product quality. Three, the high costs of offering short-term gains erode profit margin, and thus affect financial performance.

Nurturing long-term mutual benefits

There are two essential components to this strategy: long-term and mutual interests. The intent of this approach is to create an interdependence between the two parties in the relationship so that there will be a great cost to either side in severing such ties. As Lucian W. Pye puts it, "Each can tax the other and expect automatic special considerations." This interdependence increases over time. The primary goal of the foreign investor is to attain business success in China; the principal gains for the Chinese partner are the acquisition of materialistic rewards and/or enhancement of a political career. Those officials who are able to attract foreign investment—which contributes substantially to employment and development of infrastructure—will have a better chance of advancing their political careers.

Cultivating personal relationships

Many of the respondents felt that since short- and long-term gains can be duplicated by others, *guanxi* relations that are premised exclusively on material benefits can be fragile. Consequently, to maintain *guanxi* relationships, many feel that it is important to develop a personal relationship with the partner that cannot be readily imitated by others. "Personal" implies something specific to the two parties in the relationship, such as sharing inner feelings or personal secrets. To build an intimate relationship with the Chinese, most respondents indicated that sincerity and frankness were absolutely essential. To do this, one must acquire an in-depth knowledge of the Chinese business associate and know what appeals to his or her personal needs. One-half of the companies interviewed in this study felt that this strategy is less feasible in present-day China because of the strong emphasis on utilitarian gains.

Cultivating trust

Almost 85 percent of the companies included in this study indicated that trust was an essential condition for building and maintaining *guanxi* relationships. Without trust, many felt that it was virtually impossible to build *guanxi*. According to one executive, "Trust is very important in China because it is a relation-based society." Many interviewees adopted the following two mottoes for cultivating trust: "Deliver what you have promised" and "don't cheat." Another effective way of building trust is to learn the Chinese culture, including its language. Many Chinese reason that if investors genuinely try to understand the Chinese culture, they should not be considered outsiders.

These four strategies for building and maintaining *guanxi* reflect the five fundamental dimensions of *guanxi*: instrumentalism, personal relationships, trust, reciprocity, and longevity. The strategies are not mutually exclusive; they should be viewed as complementary. Alone, none of the strategies is capable of building and maintaining strong *guanxi* relations. Given the emphasis on material gains, the development of personal and trusting relationships alone, without an accompanying gift of benefits, cannot sustain *guanxi* ties. In other words, no *guanxi* connection can exist in the absence of utilitarian gains to the Chinese partner. However, the mere tendering of favors alone is insufficient to maintain the *guanxi* relationship since such efforts can be readily duplicated by others. Six of the 19 companies included in this study had adopted an integrated approach to *guanxi* building and maintenance, using all four strategies. These companies experienced significantly higher levels of financial performance. In general, those companies that were engaged in the exporting and service sectors tended to rely more heavily on tendering favors, whereas those in importing and manufacturing emphasized long-term mutual benefits. Those companies with more years of experience in China usually used an integrated approach.

Besides adopting an integrated approach to building and maintaining *guanxi*, it is also more effective to establish multiplex rather than single-stranded relationships. Multiplex relationships cultivate more commonalties—more *guanxi* bases—between two parties, so that the ties become stronger, more permanent, and more irreplaceable.

Conclusion and discussion

The findings in this study suggest that there is indeed a correlation between the possession of "right and strong" *guanxi* and a firm's financial performance. While the focus of this article has been on China, other research suggests that having good connections is equally important to business success in other Confucian societies, such as Japan, Korea, Hong Kong, Taiwan, Singapore and overseas Chinese communities. The chairman of the Lippo Group, an Indonesian conglomerate, has stated that he devotes his time exclusively to cultivating relationships while delegating the daily operations of the group's business to his two sons. In his words, "I open the door, and others walk through." Under the influence of Confucianism, these societies share the following characteristics: disdain for institutional law; strong bonds on the basis of blood, ancestral village, and school and military ties; a clear demarcation between members of the in-versus out-groups; an ability to grasp the interdependent relationship of situations that may not be obvious to Westerners; and a tendency to view matters from a long-term perspective. These characteristics contribute to the significance of connections in virtually all social functions, business being one of them. While relationships and networking are also important in the West, their role is often overshadowed by institutional law, which establishes what can and should be done.

The findings on the 19 Hong Kong and non-Hong Kong firms that have business dealings in China point to several conclusions about *guanxi* connections: One, *guanxi* is a necessary but insufficient condition to long-term business success in China. Two, in the established phase of business operations in China, technical competence gains importance. Three, to be successful, it is important to build strong relationships with the right individuals. Four, *guanxi* relationships are person-specific and cannot be transferred. Five, non-Chinese firms often have to resort to intermediaries to gain the proper connections in China. Six, the tendering of favors, particularly the offer of short-term gains, is essential, but not powerful enough to maintain long-term *guanxi* relationships alone. To maintain long-term relationships, an integrated approach is more effective. Seven, trust is essential to long-term *guanxi* maintenance. This can only come about if there is a genuine attempt on the part of the foreign investor to understand Chinese culture.

The practice of *guanxi* has come under attack in the recent past, primarily in connection with the current attempts by the Chinese government to eradicate widespread corruption. Some believe that as China's economy develops, greater emphasis should be placed on institutional law. However, a cursory review of the situations in other economically advanced or more developed Confucian societies—Japan, South Korea and Hong Kong—will show that the establishment of institutional law will not displace the reliance on connections. Relationships and connections are among the core values upheld by these societies. Geert Hofstede used the "onion" analogy to characterize the manifestations of culture in a given society. The outer layers of the onion, such as symbols, heroes, and rituals, are more susceptible to change. Consequently, Chinese youth may desire the same clothing and music popular in the West. The core of the onion, where values reside, is most resistant to change. As such, it appears that *guanxi* will continue to be a dominant aspect of society for some time in China. There is a continuing need for foreign investors who seek to do business in China to understand the dynamics of *guanxi* building and maintenance.

From the Western perspective, there are obvious pros and cons associated with doing business with *guanxi* societies. On the negative side, decision making in such networks tends to be highly centralized; decisions are generally made by the patriarch of the group. Management processes are neither clearly defined nor formalized, and thus tend to be conducted on an ad hoc basis. Furthermore, such networks are mistrustful of outsiders. It is difficult to gather information about such groups because their operations are often highly secretive—"all within the family." These characteristics have accounted for the fact that despite the entrepreneurial ingenuity of many overseas Chinese, to date there is no Chinese organization that has approached the rank of a world class organization, such as Sony Corporation in Japan.

On the positive side, however, centralized control by the group's patriarch allows for speed in decision making, thus enabling the group to seize business opportunities where expediency is of crucial importance. Another advantage associated with such family-oriented businesses is that they are able to adopt a long-term perspective in their business strategies rather than being overly concerned with manipulating profit-and-loss statements to make the group's shares more attractive to outsiders. Foreign investors who know the pros and cons associated with *guanxi* societies can capitalize on the strengths of the system and ride the wave of economic prosperity in the Asian Pacific region.

Selected bibliography

To better understand the evolution of societal values in modern China, read Thomas B. Gold, "After Comradeship: Personal Relations in China Since the Cultural Revolution," *China Quarterly*, Vol. 104 (1985), pp. 657–675; Ambrose King, "*Guanxi* and Network Building: A Sociological Interpretation," *Daedalus*, Vol. 10, No. 2 (1991), pp. 63–82; S. Gordon Redding, *The Spirit of Chinese Capitalism* (Walter de Gruyter Press, 1990); Gordon C. Chu and Yanan Ju, *The Great Wall in Ruins* (State University of New York Press, 1993); and Mayfair M. H. Yang, *Gifts, Favors and Banquets* (Cornell University Press, 1994).

To learn more about the Chinese mindset as it affects business dealings with Westerners, read John Kao, "The Worldwide Web of Chinese Business," *Harvard Business Review*, March–April 1993, pp. 24–36; A. De Keizer, *China: Business Strategies for the 1990s* (Pacific View Press, 1992); and Rosalie L. Tung, "Strategic Management Thought in East Asia," *Organizational Dynamics*, Vol. 22, No. 4 (1994), pp. 55–65. See also Rosalie L. Tung, "A Longitudinal Study of U.S.-China Business Negotiations," *China Economic Review*, Vol. 1, No. 2 (1989), pp. 57–71.

Chapter 14

The role of family conglomerates in emerging markets

What Western companies should know

Executive summary

Large, diversified, family-owned businesses are dominant players in the economies of most emerging markets and can be excellent business partners for Western companies. This article highlights the evolutionary patterns of family conglomerates (FCs) and delineates principal drivers of their growth, expansion, and internationalization. Those aspects of FCs examined in this study include early mover advantages, foreign alliances, competitive market positioning, and diversification. Also discussed are entry-mode considerations for Western companies contemplating doing business in the fast-growth markets of East Asia, Latin America, and elsewhere.

Introduction

THE HYUNDAI GROUP, one of the top five conglomerates (*chaebols*) in Korea, recently experienced a financial crisis. In response, the Korean government and Hyundai's major creditors provided well over $300 million in

Thunderbird International Review, Vol. 46(1) 13–38, January–February 2004 © 2004 Wiley Periodicals, Inc. Reprinted with permission of John Wiley & Sons, Inc.

THUNDERBIRD
SCHOOL OF GLOBAL MANAGEMENT

assistance, including credit extension and short-term loans, to save some of the major business units of the group from bankruptcy (Donga, 2001). It is not easy for most small and medium-sized firms in Korea to obtain that type of assistance, but the family-owned and -operated Hyundai Group secured the considerable financial assistance successfully (Chung, 2000). Historically, the group was led by its founder, Joo Young Chung, in all strategic moves, which included diversifying into many different industries, but the business is in the process of transition to the second generation (Drozdow & Carroll, 1997). The recent crisis resulted from a battle for power among the founder's sons, and the bailout reflects the heavy dependence of the Korean economy on this major family conglomerate (FC) (Chung, 2000; Donga, 2001; Hwang, 2000).

Several months earlier, the Daewoo Group, another top chaebol and FC, also experienced a severe financial crisis and was restructured. Creditors and the government sought the highest bidder for one of the group's major business arms, Daewoo Motors. Despite successful growth at home and abroad, the group's inefficient and exuberant business expansion—financed largely by loans (Chung, 2000; Hwang, 2000)—drove the conglomerate to the brink of ruin (Donga, 2001; Khanna & Palepu, 1999; Nachum, 1999).

Large, diversified FCs are not unique to Korea. Indeed, they are dominant players in many emerging markets (EMs). Known as chaebols in Korea, business houses in India, holding companies in Turkey, and *grupos* in Latin America, huge FCs represent a unique business enterprise in such countries. Table 1 provides a sample of FCs from selected EMs. The role of such groups is substantial. For example, the top 30 FCs in Korea generate more than 46% of industry revenues, and their combined assets account for 47% of the whole economy. Andrade, Barra, and Elstrodt (2001) describe grupos as "the backbone of the economies in Latin America." The origin and growth of FCs can be attributed to a special relationship with government and with the economy itself.

Several aspects of FCs contribute to their relative success (Andrade et al., 2001). Their informal structure facilitates quick decision making, a key attribute in rapidly growing and often turbulent economies. FCs also exhibit strong shared values, often rooted in the founder's vision and legacy. Loyalty of workers is high, and management turnover tends to be low. Equally important is a deep understanding of local markets and customers. Furthermore, close ties with

Table 1 Sample of family conglomerates in select emerging markets

Country of Origin	Group Name
India	Tata, Reliance, Mahindra
Indonesia	Astra
Korea	Hyundai, Daewoo, LG, Samsung
Mexico	Desc, Alfa, Vitro
Philippines	Ayala, San Miguel
Taiwan	Formosa Plastics, Tatung
Thailand	Siam Cement
Turkey	Koc, Sabanci, Alarko

governmental agencies and ruling political parties translate into competitive advantage and staying power.

Because FCs play such a significant role in many emerging markets, it is critical for Western companies that aspire to enter these markets to develop a comprehensive understanding of their nature and impact. The objective of this article is to contribute to such an understanding through a study of 19 FCs in eight emerging markets: India, Indonesia, Korea, Mexico, the Philippines, Taiwan, Thailand, and Turkey.

Family conglomerates in emerging markets

Emerging markets exhibit high growth potential and present a mixture of opportunities and risks for Western companies. (Cavusgil, 1997; Garten, 1997a; Kock & Guillen, 2001). Their attractiveness lies not only in cheap raw materials and labor but also in the potential to generate revenue. Companies in industrialized countries depend on overseas markets for economies of scale in production as well as profits. EMs are not just suppliers but also buyers of goods and services.

There are risks to doing business in the EMs. These include an inadequate marketing infrastructure, such as poorly developed distribution systems; limited communication channels; lack of regulatory discipline and frequent changes in regulation; a high level of product diversion; various market failures; and political and economic instability (Arnold & Quelch, 1998; Garten, 1997a; Khanna & Palepu, 1997, 2000). In many EMs, Western companies have poor market information, and sometimes regulation misguides foreign businesses (Khanna & Palepu, 1997). Consequently, strategic alliances are an important entry mode in these markets (Kock & Guillen, 2001; Lane & Beamish, 1990; Osborn & Hagedoorn, 1997). Through alliances, Western companies can share risk and resources, gain knowledge, and obtain access to markets (Kock & Guillen, 2001).

FCs are potential allies and are a universally observed ownership type across many EMs (Andrade et al., 2001; Khanna & Palepu, 1997; Kock & Guillen, 2001). In this study, we characterize an FC by referring to specific attributes. The typical FC is owned and controlled by a family (Ben-Porath, 1980) and has a single founder who dominates, although family members may serve as executives in the business (Church, 1993; Drozdow & Carroll, 1997). Traditionally, the family holds the majority of controlling rights (Church, 1993; Khanna & Palepu, 1999; Kock & Guillen, 2001). Therefore, FCs are not the same as business groups, which are not necessarily owned by a family (Granovetter, 1995). Business groups may include firms linked by personal relationships that stem from a similar personal, ethnic, and/or regional background (Granovetter, 1995; Leff, 1978). FCs also differ from family businesses (FBs), though they possess several similar characteristics. For example, both FCs and FBs are owned and controlled by a family (Davis & Harveston, 2000), and inherit similar behaviors such as leadership and entrepreneurship (Dyer, 1986; Sorenson, 2000). Nevertheless, FCs are considered to be a large network of corporations that are owned by the same family. They are more diversified and have a larger size when compared to the family businesses. Their economic impact (jobs, revenues, branches of activity, technology, etc.) in the respective countries is much more substantial. The present study attempts to examine the characteristics of FCs, considering the relatively significant impact they have on their respective economies.

Another feature of FCs is that they have been operating for many years and have a substantial history (Ben-Porath, 1980). In the second and third generations, FC owners may become more removed from management, and this gap may gradually widen (Drozdow & Carroll, 1997). Eventually, few family members may actually work in the company, but the family tends to control the board of directors. Also, they are highly dominant in their home markets (Granovetter, 1995). The typical FC has significant investments in a wide variety of businesses, ranging from manufacturing to banking to construction. Finally, FCs tend to use internally generated capital as well as government loans for expansion and growth.

The contribution of FCs to their home economies is considerable (Granovetter, 1995; Kock & Guillen, 2001; Nachum, 1999), and they can add value to it in several ways (Khanna & Palepu, 1999). For example, the subsidiaries of the top 30 Korean conglomerates numbered more than 600 in 2000, and the top five chaebols accounted for 59% of total value of firms listed on the Korean Stock Exchange. The conglomerates in Korea, which are mostly FCs, make a significant contribution in terms of employment, tax revenues, foreign currency generation, and general economic growth (Hwang, Lee, Seo, Lee, & Han, 2000). More specifically, as of the late 1990s, the annual revenue of the Samsung chaebol in Korea exceeded $70 billion whereas Daewoo employs more than 265,000 employees. Koc accounts for 19% of Istanbul (Stock) Market trading, while Sabanci is responsible for 5.3% of Turkey's tax revenue. Furthermore, Siam Cement in Thailand has 64 subsidiaries, and Tata in India has around 300,000 employees with eight percent of total public capitalization in the country.

FCs tap funds and management talent from within their operations to start new ventures rather than relying on intermediaries (Khanna & Palepu, 1999). Guillen (2000) suggests that those who learn to combine their resources will be able to create new business ventures across a wide variety of industries, and the expansion capability of FCs encourages them to diversify, rather than specialize in one product line, and take advantage of scale and scope. As a result, FCs hold the largest market share in many sectors of the economy. For example, Mahindra & Mahindra focuses on automobiles and related businesses in India but invests in a range of other projects. In most cases, FCs command assets that give them a competitive edge. Also, they invest in training programs and education (Khanna & Palepu, 1999). In addition, they seek partnerships with foreign firms because these may bring new managerial or technical know-how, insights, and experience.

Indigenous FCs have several advantages over foreign companies intent on entering EMs. They have a well-established local distribution network that would take years for Western companies to replicate. Their longstanding relationships with government officials are not available to foreign companies ("Links with the First Family," 1994; Kock & Guillen, 2001). Their distinctive products appeal to local tastes (Ger, 1999). FCs also access natural resources or labor that can give them a cost advantage (Dawar & Frost, 1999) and competitive prices (Prahalad & Lieberthal, 1998). Usually, FCs become aware of a Western company's new product strategy long before the brand is launched in the local market and can adjust their product line accordingly. In sum, FCs play an important role in the industrialization of their country and make ideal partners for Western companies as they tend to possess valuable local market expertise and understand local preferences (Kock & Guillen, 2001).

An FC can use its group name to advantage when entering into new businesses (Khanna & Palepu, 1997). Hyundai, Samsung, and Koc are examples. The goodwill, reputation, and the positive image that surround the name, even if limited to the local market, often symbolize world-class quality and customer service (Khanna & Palepu, 1999), and can help FCs compete with well-established multinational brands (Prahalad & Lieberthal, 1998). In contrast, it is costly for Western companies to build a credible brand identity in markets with relatively poor communication infrastructure (Khanna & Palepu, 1997; Kock & Guillen, 2001).

The present study addresses three basic questions. Why are FCs so important to their home economy? What advantages do FCs offer to Western companies? What does the future hold for FCs? Our research provides a better understanding of the concept of FCs and identifies similarities as well as differences with respect to their origins, governance, drivers, foreign partnerships, internationalization, and transition to professional management.

The study

Content analysis

A replicable experiment is essential for a reliable and objective analysis, and categorizations should be consistent with the applied rules to avoid researcher bias (Holsti, 1968). Since this is an exploratory investigation, we specified the scale and scope of the study in advance, according to a set of qualitative and quantitative factors. First, the investigation excludes non-family conglomerates, i.e., those that are publicly- and/or state-owned. For example, in some emerging markets such as China or countries in Africa, the majority of conglomerates are owned by the state. These are not the focus of present inquiry. Second, the selection of FCs and EMs was based largely on quantitative factors, such as economic, financial, and business-related indicators.

In classifying EMs, most observers tend to include Argentina, Brazil, Chile, China, Colombia, the Czech Republic, Egypt, Hong Kong, Hungary, India, Indonesia, Israel, Malaysia, Mexico, Peru, the Philippines, Poland, Russia, Singapore, South Africa, South Korea, Taiwan, Thailand, Turkey, and Venezuela (see, e.g., "Emerging Market indicators," 2001; Garten, 1997b). Initially, we ranked these countries by growth in GDP, industrial production, and consumer prices. Eight were eventually selected: India, Indonesia, Korea, Mexico, the Philippines, Taiwan, Thailand, and Turkey. The selection criteria were as follows: large population and resource base; major participant in the critical political, economic, and social activities taking place on the world scene; among world's fastest expanding markets and responsible for the growth of global trade; and GDP increasing two or three times faster than that of developed countries.

The FCs were selected based on their origin, revenues, diversification, foreign partnership, and internationalization. The following criteria were used: founded by a family; have a number of subsidiaries and businesses; year-end sales in 1998; mode of market entry; formation of joint ventures; and existence in foreign markets. The FCs we analyzed have 10–400 domestic or foreign subsidiaries with annual sales of $0.85–72 billion. They maintain joint ventures ranging from 1 to 23, while the number of foreign markets they operate ranges from 6 to more than 130. In each EM, we selected from one to four FCs that were usually among the top ten such companies in the country. In the final analysis, nineteen FCs were classified into different stages (introduction, growth, and maturity) based on certain indicators (such as sales and number of products). We then verified the drivers for each stage and determined those for each company.

Secondary research

Websites, annual reports, press releases, and financial records of the companies were content-analyzed. Biographies of founders, which provided some important insights about an FC's evolution, were also consulted. Several directories were used, such as *Wright Investors' Service, Hoover's Handbook of World Business, Lexis & Nexis Corporate Affiliations—International Public and Private Companies, International Directory of Company Histories, Principal International Business*, and *Asia's 7500 Largest Companies*. Business periodicals and newspapers were examined, including *Harvard Business Review, The Economist*, and *The Wall Street Journal*. Scholarly journals were also consulted.

The formation of family conglomerates

Several factors seem to characterize the formation of FCs in EMs. Especially significant is the role of founders and some unique country features such as employee work ethic and source of capital.

Founders

The critical role of the founder has been noted in the literature. Certain aspects are noteworthy. Founders usually start the business with some capital when they are young. Through foresight and strategic decision-making ability, they become market leaders (Drozdow & Carroll, 1997), although in most cases they are not highly educated. Generally, they are entrepreneurs and risk takers who become nationally prominent (Davis, 1968; Mariussen, Wheelock, & Baines, 1997).

Within the organization, they are portrayed as having strong personal ties with employees (Schein, 1983), and their dominant position is rarely challenged (Steers, Shin, & Ungson, 1989). They assume social responsibilities by endowing schools, cultural and sports centers, and health care facilities ("Import-Import," 1997). They also play an inspirational role in the advancement of business groups (Dent & Randerson, 1997). Typical founders are Joo Young Chung of Hyundai, Byung Chull Lee of Samsung, Vehbi Koc of Koc, and Haci Omer Sabanci of Sabanci; they are well-known for their creativity, proactive and arduous effort, aggressive and anticipatory decision making, and successful achievements.

Country-specific factors

Each country is a unique environment (Woodall, 1998) depending on the evolutionary stage of the economy, political system, government influence, natural resources, work ethic, financial resources, and endowments in land and labor (Kock & Guillen, 2001; Nachum, 1999). Some of these factors may cause the decay of family businesses ("Manila Moves In," 1982), others may foster their growth (Khanna & Palepu, 1999), and each may play a different role in various evolutionary stages of the FC.

Drivers of family conglomerates

At each stage of FC evolution—introduction, growth, and maturity—certain drivers are influential, as shown in Exhibit 1. We also attempted to assess the relative importance of these drivers in each stage. The following sections are organized chronologically, that is, according to drivers that are prominent in the early, middle, and late stages of FC development.

Early mover advantage

Early in their formation, FCs tend to be very good at translating market needs into business opportunities. FCs are generally the first players in many industries to cater to the local market. As early movers, they can capture a high market share and build brand equity ahead of competitors. For example, Koc was the first producer of automobiles, washing machines, and refrigerators in Turkey; it played an important role in the country's industrialization and in the development of those sectors. Mahindra & Mahindra was the first manufacturer of tractors in India and currently has the largest facility. Hyundai Group, one of the early movers among Korean automobile manufacturers, now has the largest share of the country's auto market (Guillen, 2001). The early mover advantage establishes market position for many FCs as they expand into various sectors throughout the subsequent growth stage. Typical expansion sectors include consumer durables, automotive, electronics, construction, information technology, food and confectionery, beverages, retailing, tourism, and education. These companies often were involved in import substitution activities early in their evolution.

Government protection

In EMs, the government is heavily involved in business decisions (Granovetter, 1995; Kock & Guillen, 2001; Steers et al., 1989). In some cases, it even initiates the FC (e.g., Siam Cement Group in Thailand and the Indonesian FCs of Salim, Astra, and Lippo) (Shin, 1993). Government protection may take the form of special loans, subsidies, market entry barriers for competitors, and tax incentives, among others (Jones & Rose, 1993). For example, the Indian government regulates commodity prices, raw material imports, and business exit. In most of the countries we examined, government protection has played a significant role in the growth of FCs. LG group in Korea benefited from elevated import barriers until the government opened the toothpaste market to the world in the 1980s. Previously, LG made and marketed toothpaste products without any major competition in the domestic market. The following excerpt from *Inside-Indonesia* (Mulholland & Thomas, 1999) indicated the relationship between Salim and the government.

Exhibit 1 Drivers of family conglomerates

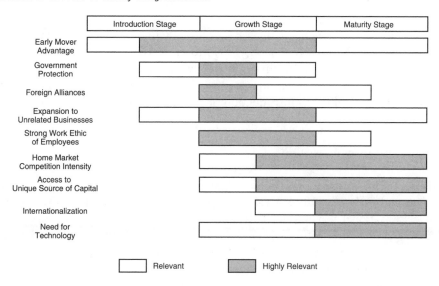

Since the late 1950s the success of particular business groups in Indonesia has generally been linked to powerful political actors. Bulog, the national logistics board that controls the supply of rice and other basic commodities, functioned as a "centre of the state" during the New Order in the country. Ever since its operations from May 1967, especially in the food sector, Bulog has been playing an important role in promoting private businesses that could help the state in return. At the same time, it accelerated the growth of the Salim Group, which is owned by Suharto's long-time friend, Liem Sioe Liong. The Salim Group's expansion and growth into many unrelated industries, from shipping to banking, all started with flour. Ever since 1969, the Salim subsidiary PT Bogasari Flour Mills has monopolized the import, milling and distribution of wheat. It became the largest domestic wheat flour producer, and one of the largest instant noodle producers and exporters in the world. It achieved this prominence because of support from Bulog. In return, the Salim group became one of the strongest private supporters of the New Order's high economic growth.

An important part of New Order capitalism in Indonesia was the "tax free charitable foundation," known as the yayasan. Controlled by top New Order officials, several of these bodies served as financial centres for the repayment of Salim's "gratitude" (hutang budi) to Suharto and his regime. The diversified Yayasan Harapan Kita (controlled by Suharto himself) and the Yayasan Dharma Putra Kostrad (run by the elite military unit Kostrad) received huge "financial contributions"—purportedly 26% of their incomes—from Bogasari Flour Mills. The expectation of such a quid pro quo among friends was presumably the reason why Bulog helped accelerate the Salim Group's growth in the first place and was an important element in the creation of a powerful network of conglomerates.

As FCs grow, maintaining a tight relationship with the governmental sector becomes easier (Khanna & Palepu, 1997; Kock & Guillen, 2001). Experience and connections with officials give FCs an advantage in managing their business. Government protection is an important driver in the growth stage and is less frequently observed in the introduction or maturity stages of FC evolution.

Foreign alliances

Alliances with international business partners prove critical to an FC in the growth and early maturity stages. The need for expansion, access to resources, and organizational learning leads to joint ventures, international alliances, and licensing agreements with Western companies (Kock & Guillen, 2001). Because of poorly developed financial markets, weak institutions for capital distribution, and volatility in economic development, FCs need access to capital at a reasonable cost (Hitt, Dacin, Levitas, Arregle, & Borza, 2000). They also require multiple forms of technological capability and may seek partners who can provide experience and knowledge (Amsden & Hikino, 1994; Kock & Guillen, 2001). For example, joint ventures between Ford and Koc, Vitro, and Alfa as well as between DuPont and Sabanci, seek complementarities of benefit to each party. Also, Mahindra & Mahindra is licensed by Peugeot to produce automobile parts.

Through their maturity, the need to enhance managerial skills becomes another reason for seeking foreign alliances. These capabilities and decision-making processes are not always well-developed in FCs. Hitt et al. (2000) suggest that the need to compete in market-oriented economies and with more managerially sophisticated companies prompts FCs to seek partners. In the initial stage of the relationship, FCs provide a dealer/distribution network, market information, and institutional knowledge about local regulations and laws, as well as language competency. The Western partner requires local know-how, and the FC seeks advanced technology or industry know-how (Kock & Guillen, 2001). It can be expected for the Western partner to seek closer business relationships with FCs as they perceive greater uncertainty about the local market. The nature of the arrangement may move over time—from supplier to licensing agreements, to joint ventures, and to technology/know-how transfers.

Expansion to unrelated businesses

Companies grow in many different ways. As they evolve, FCs tend to diversify. This may happen partially because of the entrepreneurial orientation of the owners. Some expand production capacity to meet excess demand, enter new markets, develop new products, form mergers, or make acquisitions (Hwang, 2000). Some diversify within an industry, and others expand across sectors. Although patterns depend on the unique business environment (Kock & Guillen, 2001; Markides, 1997), they also may be a function of internal factors, such as the founder's business philosophy, financial soundness, and latent connections with other businesses. The following quotation concerns the LG group in Korea.

> My father and I started a cosmetic cream factory in the late 1940s. At the time, no company could supply us with plastic caps of adequate quality for cream jars, so we had to start a plastic business. Plastic caps alone were not sufficient to run the plastic-molding plant, so we added combs, toothbrushes, and soapboxes. This plastic business also led us to manufacture electric fan blades and telephone cases, which in turn led us to manufacture electrical and electronic products and telecommunication equipment. The plastic business also took us into oil refining, which needed a tanker-shipping company. The oil refining company alone was paying an insurance premium amounting to more than half of the total revenue of the largest insurance company in Korea. Thus, an insurance company was started. This natural step-by-step evolution through related businesses resulted in the Lucky-Goldstar group (now LG) as we see it today (Koo, Cha-Kyung, son of the LG founder, as quoted in Milgrom & Roberts, 1992, pp. 542–543).

There is some question as to whether FCs tend to overdiversify in their home markets (Church, 1993; Hwang, 2000; Kock & Guillen, 2001), but it is clear that an expansion strategy is one of the most important drivers of their growth

(Amsden & Hikino, 1994; Kock & Guillen, 2001). Even though expansion also occurs in the early and late stages, it is a major driver in the growth stage. FCs tend to deepen their involvement in one industry during the early stage, and they expand into different industries in the late growth and maturity stages (Amsden & Hikino, 1994). For example, Daewoo began as a textile exporting company and moved into clothing manufacturing, garnering Sears, JCPenney, and Montgomery Ward as accounts. As the Korean economy took off, it entered construction and heavy industries, then automobile manufacturing and financial services.

In EMs, FCs tend to expand as a way to cope with a poor communication structure, misguided regulations, and an inefficient judicial system (Khanna & Palepu, 1997), as well as to realize some economic benefits from internalizing transactions (Hwang, 2000). In addition, they have to perform the basic functions of several institutions in order to do business effectively. Sabanci in Turkey, for example, has its own private bank and university. Another reason for expansion is exit barriers in EMs. Most FCs, including the Tata companies in India, continue to stay in business to leverage their large scale and wide scope.

How does investment in unrelated businesses affect FC performance in EMs? Khanna and Palepu (2000) report a curvilinear relationship in their research on Chilean business groups. That is, performance declines until unrelated diversification reaches a certain threshold, beyond which point further increases will improve firm performance. Surprisingly, Hwang (2000) reports that failed chaebols tend to have a higher level of related diversification than do successful FCs in Korea, which implies that the problem may be a lack of institutional infrastructure and individual chaebol competence (Khanna & Palepu, 1999), rather than unrelated diversification.

Strong work ethic of employees

A cornerstone of Korean FCs seems to be the work ethic of employees. For instance, during the 1980s and 1990s, they were willing to work overtime, to achieve assigned goals in a shorter period than expected, and to put the employer first. Biggart (1990) describes this phenomenon as institutionalized patrimonialism. The work ethic has contributed to the growth of FCs in most Asian countries. Indeed there are remarkable stories about the unusual degree of attachment these employees feel toward their companies.

Home market competitive intensity

Later in the growth and maturity stages, FCs encounter domestic and even some foreign competition. As the market becomes crowded, FCs must serve customers better than rivals do, create new markets, and develop their own technologies (Kock & Guillen, 2001). They diversify and internationalize their businesses, seeking a competitive edge in the global arena. Goldstar, now part of the LG group, enjoyed an early mover position in the Korean electronics market until Daewoo and Samsung entered the industry. As the competition grew fierce, Goldstar merged with Lucky, and the new group acquired Zenith, a major TV manufacturer in the United States, in order to penetrate the North American market.

Access to unique source of capital

Unique sources of capital play an important role in the formation of FCs, including government loans at very favorable interest rates and special investment opportunities (e.g., land and/or real estate investments with extremely high annual returns). Special loans are an outcome of the close FC/government relationship (Dent & Randerson, 1997; Nachum, 1999). In Korea, cross-equity investments and cross-debt guarantees are widely used to finance FC business expansions (Hwang, 2000). Some Mexican FCs, such as Desc and Alfa, listed on the New York Stock Exchange to obtain financing. All of the FCs we analyzed in Korea, plus Koc and Sabanci in Turkey, Vitro in Mexico, and Astra in Indonesia, have their own financial arms (e.g., insurance, banking, and securities brokerage), which are sources of capital (Granovetter, 1995). Even though the capital sources cannot be identified for all FCs, all have various types of financial resources available to them. In addition, unique capital markets in each country contribute to the formation and growth of FCs in various ways.

Internationalization

As a business matures, it seeks growth opportunities outside national borders. Some companies are "born global" and internationalize early, but many others take the gradual approach. Depending on the nature of the company and the type of industry in which it is engaged, some will do business abroad in the introduction stage, and others will wait until the growth or maturity stage. Exhibit 2 indicates typical internationalization activities in various stages of FC growth.

In the introduction stage, the principal activity involves importation of raw materials, followed in the growth stage by technology transfer, licensing, and franchising from a foreign business partner (Sarkar & Cavusgil, 1996). Johanson and Wiedersheim-Paul (1975) argue that internationalization is a consequence of developments in the domestic market, as FCs accumulate expertise from foreign alliances that help them boost their own technologies (Kock & Guillen, 2001). Another strategic purpose of such alliances is to compete more effectively with firms outside the relationship (Kock & Guillen, 2001; Walker & Poppo, 1991). The CEO of Vitro claims that international partnering and exporting helped the company grow faster and are crucial to future growth. Intensified competition in a maturing local market often forces FCs to seek new business opportunities abroad. Exporting can be the first step in the process; for example, Sabanci and Tata have trading companies in London. For most Korean FCs, exporting was a core business that grew rapidly in the 1970s and 1980s. FCs may initially use intermediaries such as import agents and sales subsidiaries, but they tend to assume the business themselves as they reach maturity.

Exhibit 2 Internationalization of family conglomerates

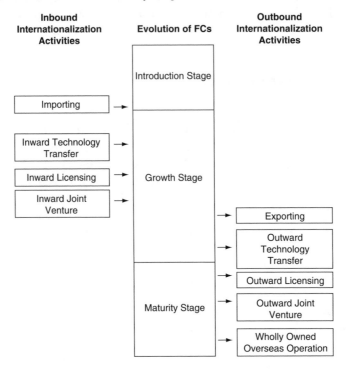

In the growth and maturity stages, FCs may become direct investors and increase their international holdings. Activities in foreign markets deepen, and major modes of entry are wholly-owned subsidiaries, turnkey projects, and joint ventures. Hyundai, Daewoo, and Samsung have a larger number of wholly-owned subsidiaries in foreign markets compared to Ayala in the Philippines, Astra in Indonesia, and Siam Cement in Thailand. In the late growth stage, the switch from exporting to direct investment in overseas operations is a crucial decision. Major obstacles to internationalization are lack of knowledge and resources. As FCs learn about foreign markets, the perceived risk of investment is reduced, and overseas expansion grows rapidly. Late in the maturity stage, FCs may increase the level of resources committed abroad and change the mode of market servicing. Licensing and joint venture agreements are examples of inter-mediate moves toward direct investment, such as wholly-owned subsidiaries.

Need for technology

Technology is not a main driver in the introduction and early growth stages of most FCs because the initial focus is on production capacity to meet customer demand. When foreign businesses enter the market, however, there is a pressure to adopt new technology in order to increase efficiency and remain competitive. FCs seek know-how and technology through licensing arrangements and joint ventures with foreign partners that can offer the latest technology. The following example reveals how Sabanci started producing synthetic fibers in Turkey (Sabanci, 1998):

> In Turkey, the industry was developing and the consumption of polyester fibers was increasing steadily daring the 1960s. Turkey was obliged to import them with its scarce foreign currency. Sabanci Holding started the idea of setting up a plant for the production of polyester thread and fibers. At that time, the most important problem was the foreign currency. Foreign currency for such plants was allocated by the Association of Chambers. When Sabanci Holding brought its proposal about the polyester fiber factory, it obtained a license for DM 220,000. Now another problem was to get a license. . . . It was the first time Sabanci bargained about a license. The managers did not even know either how to make a know-how contract or the procedures for paying for the license. Finally, Sabanci signed the licensing and technology agreement with ICI, the British firm, and the SASA company was established. ICI provided the machinery but could only provide short-term experts. Over time, Sabanci learned to train qualified people, increased the capacity of SASA, expanded its product lines and produced polyester filament yarn, and brought in new technologies.

In the maturity stage, FCs are more likely to start high-tech businesses based on their accumulated knowledge and to build their own R&D centers (Amsden & Hikino 1994; Kock & Guillen, 2001). Companies such as Alfa, Koc, and Mahindra & Mahindra are preparing to meet competition through rapid modernization and expansion of manufacturing technologies. Samsung and Hyundai are focusing on high-tech industry more than ever before.

How family conglomerates evolve

Our research reveals a typical growth pattern for FCs. At the introduction stage, a single founder with limited capital responds to a marketplace opportunity and creates an enterprise that fulfills an unmet need. The Koc Group in Turkey, for example, was an early mover in the period following national independence. Access to capital, government contracts, and lack of any viable competition were some of the factors that facilitated its growth. Siam Cement in Thailand benefited from similar circumstances.

During their rapid growth, FCs expand into related as well as unrelated businesses, building a network of affiliated companies (see Stage I and II of Kock & Guillen, 2001). Foreign alliances may be formed to counter foreign competition and secure technological know-how. As expansion continues in terms of number of industries as well as businesses, many FCs form or acquire financial institutions to meet capital needs. The content analysis also suggests that the second or third generation starts to take over the management of a company in the growth stage, where most FCs in this study were founded in the early 1900s.

Several studies have suggested that there is a positive effect of education and training on the firm's propensity to change and its growth (Datta & Guthrie, 1994; Davis & Harveston, 2000). As members of the second or third generation, who are usually better educated (have a college degree or MBA degree), become involved in the business, they tend to hire professional managers from outside the family (Jones & Rose, 1993). Therefore, the active involvement of the next generation with a higher-level education fosters transformation of the organization, and facilitates globalization activities of the FC (Cavusgil & Naor, 1987; Simpson & Kujawa, 1974). A new organizational structure may be needed to meet the challenges of expansion and global competition, and holding companies may be established to identify strategies and to control and coordinate activities.

In the maturity stage, diversification slows or ceases (see Stage III of Kock & Guillen, 2001), and FCs focus on competing with major domestic rivals and/or seek new business opportunities in foreign markets to gain economies of scale and scope. The usual pattern is to move gradually from exporting and/or importing of raw materials and components, to domestic joint ventures with a foreign partner, and/or to importing of subcontracted components, contract manufactured goods, and licensed or OEM products (Dent & Randerson, 1997). Finally, FCs tend to enter into cooperative agreements related to R&D, production, marketing, and purchasing (Luostarinen & Hellman, 1994). Some imitate world-class companies by creating wholly-owned subsidiaries and joint ventures in foreign markets. As technology becomes critical to retaining competitive advantage, they attempt to boost their own technological capabilities (Kock & Guillen, 2001) and fond R&D centers to compete globally.

Due to their management experience and capital resources, some mature FCs can be counted among the largest industrial and financial conglomerates, not only at home but also abroad. Because of the large scale of their business, these FCs may opt for strategies that focus on lower production costs, diversified product lines, and improved customer service. For instance, Vitro Mexican group seems to excel in cost efficiency, Mahindra & Mahindra in customer service, and the Koc Group in dealer networks to provide fast and high-quality customer service.

What does the future hold for family conglomerates?

Will FCs continue to prosper in EMs? The optimistic view is that the family influence will remain strong due to accumulated wealth and stockholder power (Chung, 2000; Hwang, 2000). Although ownership tends to become dispersed so that a single owner is unable to control the entire conglomerate, it is highly likely that the family as a collective owner can continue to exercise power through cross-investments. For instance, according to the Korean Fair Trading Committee, the average cross-investment within a conglomerate is above 35% among the 30 major Korean conglomerates, compared to average ownership by individual family members of around 3.3% (Donga, 2001). With this sort of arrangement, conflicts within the founder's family could weaken the collective ownership by a conglomerate. The recent financial crisis of Hyundai Group has proved the importance of collective ownership of founder's family through cross-investment. Even though some subsidiaries of FCs are becoming publicly held, the founder's family still has significant influence and control on management.

As the second or third generation inherits the business, more FCs are expected to hire professional managers, and family members are likely to play a less direct role (Hwang, 2000). The founder's death or transfer of power to the next generation often marks the transition to professional management and the addition of outsiders to the board. One may speculate that management of FCs will become more participative as well as more professional. For example, Koc in Turkey and Vitro in Mexico now include executives from Western companies on their board.

The pessimistic view is that FCs will face pressure from government as well as domestic and international markets to reduce the number of core businesses in an effort to improve market competence. Also, a leadership vacuum may occur in the second or third generation (Church, 1993). There is some empirical evidence in support of the common observation that "the first generation builds the company, the second preserves it, and the third squanders it" (Andrade et al., 2001). In addition, as the Hyundai and Daewoo cases illustrate, FCs seem to have some degree of vulnerability due to family ownership (Cabrera-Suarez, de Saa-Perez, & Garcia-Almeida, 2001; Hwang, 2000; Khanna & Palepu, 1999, 2000; Kock & Guillen, 2001; Schulze, Lubatkin, Dino, & Buchholtz, 2001) or the lack of professional management (Kao, 1993; Khanna & Palepu, 1999; Nachum, 1999). Founder family-oriented management decisions rather than market-oriented decisions may create greater vulnerability and inability to respond to changing market developments (Chung, 2000; Hwang, 2000). Even though an increasing number of FCs are hiring professional managers, the family influence on business operations can still affect strategic moves significantly (Drozdow & Carroll, 1997).

Loyalty to the founder family is a characteristic of the managers of FCs (Drozdow & Carroll, 1997; Hayashibara, 1997), but this is not always good for business. For example, the founder of the Samsung Group long dreamed of having an automobile manufacturing arm, a hope not achieved before his death, and the group continued to pour financial resources into the plan. The expansion was undertaken, even after his death, at high financial risk and despite government and industry concerns about overcapacity. The new unit was eventually taken over by a competitor during the restructuring that followed the Korean economic crisis.

Furthermore, FCs usually are less likely to experience pressure from third-party watchdogs such as investors, financial institutions, and government because these sources of external pressure have been internalized to some extent by having their own financial arm and/or networking with government officials (Dent & Randerson, 1997; Granovetter, 1995; Nachum, 1999). The protected and subsidized business environment to which they are accustomed is another source of FCs' vulnerability (Jones & Rose, 1993; Shin, 1993). As a result, FCs encounter significant challenges when they enter Western markets, causing them to adopt new ways of competing and managing.

Compared to most Western companies that have been professionally managed for decades, the senior leadership in FCs may be a major liability. Global pressures may accentuate their vulnerability and reduce FCs to smaller players in the future. Indeed, as local markets have globalized, the representation of family-owned businesses in the ranks of the top 100 companies has fallen sharply: from 71% to 57% in Mexico; from 51% to 34% in Venezuela; and from 24% to 19% in Argentina (Andrade et al., 2001). Deregulation and the advent of MNCs have spurred cross-border integration of economies and industries. FCs are definitely being challenged to match the multinationals' scale, brand recognition, cutting-edge management techniques, and deep pockets. To survive and thrive, FCs will also need stronger governance models that provide for a smooth succession of power across generations.

What Western companies should know about FCs

FCs represent both a promise and a challenge for Western companies (Prahalad & Lieberthal, 1998; Kock & Guillen, 2001). Strategic alliances have become an important tool for MNC entry into emerging markets, and in many cases the most likely partner is an FC. It is not critically important that the FC be experienced in the particular industry represented by the Western firm. The foreign partner is likely to seek the strengths that complement its own assets: local market knowledge and experience, established networks with suppliers and distributors, and government contacts (Kock & Guillen, 2001). Davidson (1980) notes the importance of long-term experience in a particular market; as familiarity increases, firms become more comfortable with local differences and more confident in their ability to capitalize on local expertise (Shetty, 1979). In other words, as the local FC partner assumes some of the country risks and reduces uncertainty, foreign firms become more willing to commit resources.

Strategic alliances between FCs and Western companies can take several forms, such as joint ventures, licensing agreements, distribution and supply agreements, R&D partnerships, and technological exchanges (Inkpen, 1998). The local market knowledge of the FC and the technical knowledge of the Western company may determine the type of alliance (Dawar & Frost, 1999). Modes of entry depend upon the partners' needs, as shown in Exhibit 3.

A Western company may form alliances in EMs for various reasons. It may be seeking a market for its products, a production site, source of materials, components, or technology. Product marketing, for example, requires warehousing, transportation, and retailing, and the FC may be able to supply facilities, vehicles, and a sales force. If the foreign company is interested in penetrating the market in a relatively short time, the business network and/or consumer recognition of the FC is very important (Arnold & Quelch, 1998; Ger, 1999; Kock & Guillen, 2001). A Western company may not be willing to license its technology at the initial stages of entry, so the appropriate partnership may turn out to be distribution and supply agreements. In this type of arrangement, learning is minimal by the FC, whereas the Western company is more active in acquiring local market knowledge.

In 1988, for example, Ford Motor formed a partnership with Kia to intro-duce the Sable into Korea. Ford was interested in Kia's distribution and after-service network; Kia wanted a premium model to complement its product line at the time when technology transfer for producing the car was too costly for Kia. In another case, Digital Equipment Corporation designated Tatung, a Taiwanese FC and market leader in computers, as the main distributor of its workstations and related client-server products. With this 1994 agreement, Digital took advantage of Tatung's local experience and distribution network, and Tatung gained the benefit of carrying a technologically advanced product ("Tatung as Main Distributor," 1994).

Exhibit 3 Appropriate market entry strategies for western companies in emerging markets

	High		
Family Conglomerate's Need for Technical Knowledge	Technology Licensing	Joint Ventures
	Wholly-owned Investment	Distribution and Supply Agreements
	Low		
	Low		High

Western Company's Need for
Market Knowledge

Depending upon the business scale of FCs and their unique relationship with the local market, Western companies should consider carefully whether a part-nership is the appropriate entry mode (Harrigan, 1984; Kock & Guillen, 2001). In the case of manufacturing, the Western company may want to protect its technical knowledge and property rights, in which case it will look for an FC whose need for technical knowledge is high. When the Western company requires market knowledge and the FC is interested in technical know-how, entry through a joint venture may be appropriate.

In 1997, Sabanci entered a 50–50 equity joint venture with Danone, a European leader in dairy products and owner of the Evian brand of bottled water. Danone brought ample technical knowledge in packaging and bottling, and a reputation for healthy and environmentally friendly products, but it lacked information on the Turkish market. Sabanci is a leader in Turkey with its bottled water, Hayat, and is knowledgeable about customers, retailers, and distributors. The collaboration with Danone to market Hayat made this brand the market leader within the first year. Danone then introduced its dairy products into Turkey through Sabanci.

Joint ventures have been used to exploit markets and technologies, and they can be very important in maintaining a firm's competitive advantage. Alestra is a joint venture in telecommunications formed by ALFA in Mexico, AT&T, and Bancomer-Visa. Through the collaboration, AT&T addressed a new market, and ALFA provided a network in Mexico and gained access to AT&T's advanced technical knowledge.

In other cases Western companies enter the local market without an ally and put pressure on domestic FCs. For example, India became a major export base for auto components when the economy was deregulated. The entry of multinational automobile giants forced Mahindra & Mahindra to meet the challenge through a rapid upgrade of manufacturing technology. The company built an R&D center to speed up the design of products to meet customer needs. It also formed a partnership with Peugeot, which licensed its technology, to manufacture diesel engines. In another case, Sabanci founded Temsa to provide boilers and ventilation and heating systems; later, it agreed with Mitsubishi Motors to produce buses in Temsa plants, using Mitsubishi engines.

A Western company may gain a good understanding of a local market through previous alliances and then pursue its own wholly-owned venture. For example, Ford Motor learned about the Korean market through its partnership with Kia and it launched a wholly-owned subsidiary, Ford Motor Company of Korea, in 1996. Similarly, BMW AG, the German automotive company, set up a wholly-owned operation in Indonesia, where market knowledge had been gained through an earlier partnership with Astra International ("BMW AG Forms Subsidiary," 2001).

Although FCs are owned and controlled by a family, there are other factors that shape a business. These include national culture and economic policies (Ward, 2000). The evolution of a family business is closely related to the local economic environment. The cultural context is an important determinant of types of ownership and the leadership vision of the family owners. FCs can provide real value to Western companies because they incorporate firm-specific advantages, such as market knowledge, government relations, and network strength (Manikutty, 2000). Western companies entering an EM should conduct an extensive investigation in order to assess the capabilities of the local FCs, as well as the national cultural and economic environment. When complementarities exist, a partnership may be viable.

Conclusion

Despite cultural differences in business operations—including government protection, availability of capital, and employee work ethic—family conglomerates in different emerging markets exhibit many common patterns of evolution. Market expansion strategies such as diversification and internationalization are widely adopted, and FCs benefit from and adapt to their business environment. They play a substantial role in local markets, and Western companies entering those markets should investigate their competitive advantages and market position. A collaborative partnership with an FC can reduce risks as well as the time and capital necessary for foreign market entry.

Family conglomerates have much to offer Western companies: a local business network, government contacts, knowledge of local markets, established channels, an agile decision-making process, and more. FCs also stand to gain from the new business opportunities and know-how that Western companies may bring to the arrangement. By identifying the complementarities that FCs offer. Western companies can enjoy more frictionless entry into emerging markets.

The phenomenon of family conglomerates has received relatively scant attention from business scholars. This is surprising, given their economic dominance in many emerging markets. In the present article, the authors attempted to partially fill this gap by providing a survey of their evolution and significance in a number of emerging countries. A content analysis of select FCs reveals common patterns and allow us to make some statements about their current and future role in such economies. Nevertheless, much more work is needed. Many questions remain unanswered in this context. What accounts for the relative success of some FCs while others in the same country seem to struggle? What are the dynamics of transforming FCs into more professionally managed businesses? How are traditional FCs coping with the globalization of markets and intense competitive pressures from multinational players? What are the principal success factors in FC-Western company partnerships? What lies ahead in terms of the ownership of these companies? These and similar questions begs scholarly research attention in the future. It is hoped that the present work stimulates the research community to initiate future projects designed to shed additional light on this phenomenon.

References

Amsden, A. H., & Hikino, T. (1994). Project execution capability, organizational know-how and conglomerate corporate growth in late industrialization. Industrial and Corporate Change, 3(1), 111–147.

Andrade, L. F., Barra, J. M., & Elstrodt, H. P. (2001). All in the Familia. McKinsey Quarterly, 4.

Arnold, D. J., & Quelch, J. A. (1998). New strategies in emerging markets. Sloan Management Review, 40(1), 7–20.

Ben-Porath, Y. (1980). The F-Connection: Families, friends, and firms and the organization of exchange. Population and Development Review, 6(1), 1–30.

Biggart, N. (1990). Institutionalized patrimonialism in Korean business. In C. Calhoun (Ed.), Comparative Social Research, vol. 12: Business institution (pp. 113–133). Greenwich. CT: JAI Press.

BMW AG forms subsidiary. (2001). Jakarta Post. Retrieved May 14, 2002, from http://www.thejakartapost.com

Cabrera-Suarez, K., de Saa-Perez, P., & Garcia Almeida, D. (2001). The succession process from a resource- and knowledge-based view of the family firm. Family Business Review, 14(1), 37–47.

Cavusgil, S. T. (1997). Measuring the potential of emerging markets: An indexing approach. Business Horizons, 40(1), 87–91.

Cavusgil, S. T., & Naor, J. (1987). Firm management characteristics as discriminators of export marketing activity. Journal of Business Research, 153, 221–235.

Chung, Y. P. (2000, September 19–20). Corporate governance system in Korea: What questions should we ask for future recommendations? Presented at the Transforming Korean Business and Management Culture Conference, Michigan State University, East Lansing, MI.

Church, R. (1993). The family firm in industrial capitalism: International perspectives in hypotheses and history. Business History, 35(4), 17–43.

Datta, D. K., & Guthrie, J. P. (1994). Executive succession: Organizational antecedents of CEO characteristics. Strategic Management Journal, 15, 569–577.

Davidson, W. H. (1980, Fall). The location of foreign investment activity: Country characteristics and experience effects. Journal of International Business Studies, 11, 9–22.

Davis, M. S. (1968). Entrepreneurial succession. Administrative Science Quarterly, 13, 403–416.

Davis, P. S., & Harveston, P. D. (2000). Internationalization and organizational growth: The impact of Internet usage and technology involvement among entrepreneur-led family businesses. Family Business Review, 13(2), 107–120.

Dawar, N., & Frost, T. (1999). Competing with giants: Survival strategies for local companies in emerging markets. Harvard Business Review, 77(2), 119–129.

Dent, C. M., & Randerson, C. (1997). Enter the chaebol: The escalation of Korean direct investment in Europe. European Business Journal, 9(4), 31–40.

Donga. (2001). Hyundai Group's financial crisis. Donga Daily Newspaper. Retrieved January 9, 2001, from http://www.donga.com/docs/issue.html

Drozdow, N., & Carroll, V. P. (1997). Tools for strategy development in family firms. Sloan Management Review, 39(1), 75–88.

Dyer, W. G., Jr. (1986). Cultural change in family firms: Anticipating and managing business and family transitions. San Francisco, CA: Jossey-Bass.

Emerging market indicators. (2001, August 25). The Economist, p. 82.

Emerging multinationals: Enter the Lippo-potamus. (1994, July 16). The Economist, p. 61.

Garten, J. E. (1997a). Troubles ahead in emerging markets. Harvard Business Review, 75(3), 38–50.

Garten, J. E. (1997b). The big ten: The big emerging markets and how they will change our lives. New York: Basic Books.

Ger, G. (1999). Localizing in the global village. California Management Review, 41(4), 64–83.

Granovetter, M. (1995). Coase revisited: Business groups in the modern economy. Industrial and Corporate Change, 4(1), 93–129.

Guillen, M. F. (2000). Business groups in emerging economies: A resource-based view. Academy of Management Journal, 43(3), 362–380.

Guillen, M. F. (2001). The limits of convergence: Globalization and organizational change in Argentina, South Korea, and Spain. Princeton, NJ: Princeton University Press.

Harrigan, K. R. (1984). Joint ventures and global strategies. Columbia Journal of World Business, 14(2), 36–64.

Hayashibara, M. (1997). From family business to multinational. Asian Business, 33(11), 19.

Hitt, M. A., Dacin, M. T., Levitas, E., Arregle, J. L., & Borza, A. (2000). Partner selection in emerging and developed market contexts: Resource-based and organizational learning perspectives. Academy of Management Journal, 43(3), 449–467.

Holsti, O. R. (1968). Content analysis. In G. Lindzey & E. Aronson (Eds.), The handbook of social psychology: Research methods, vol. 2 (pp. 596–692). Reading, MA: Addison-Wesley.

Hoover's Handbook of World Business. (1999). Austin, TX: Hoover's Business Press.

Hwang, I. (2000, September 19–20). Diversification and restructuring of the Korean business groups. Presented at the Transforming Korean Business and Management Culture Conference, Michigan State University, East Lansing, MI.

Hwang, I., Lee, I., Seo, C., Lee, B., & Han, H. (2000). Chaebol structure and chaebol policy: Evaluation and recommendations. Seoul: Korea Economic Research Institute.

Import-import. (1997, November 29). The Economist, p. 70.

Inkpen, A. C. (1998). Learning and knowledge acquisition through international strategic alliances. Academy of Management Executive, 12(4), 69–80.

International Directory of Company Histories. (1998). Chicago, IL. St. James Press.

Johanson, J., & Wiedersheim-Paul, F. (1975, October). The internationalization of the firm: Four Swedish case studies. Journal of Management Studies, 305–322.

Jones. G., & Rose, M. B. (1993). Family capitalism. Business History, 35(4). 1–16.

Kao, J. (1993). The worldwide web of Chinese business. Harvard Business Review, 71(2), 24–38.

Khanna, T., & Palepu, K. (1997). Why focused strategies may be wrong for emerging markets. Harvard Business Review, 75(4), 41–51.

Khanna, T., & Palepu, K. (1999). The right way to restructure conglomerates in emerging markets. Harvard Business Review, 77(4), 125–134.

Khanna, T., & Palepu, K. (2000). The future of business groups in emerging markets: Long-run evidence from Chile. Academy of Management Journal, 43(3), 268–285.

Kock, C. J., & Guillen, M. F. (2001). Strategy and structure in developing countries: Business groups as an evolutionary response to opportunities for unrelated diversification. Industrial and Corporate Change, 10(1), 77–113.

Lane, H. W., & Beamish, P. W. (1990). Cross-cultural cooperation behavior in joint ventures in LDCs. Management International Review, 30, 87–102.

Leff, N. (1978, July). Industrial organization and entrepreneurship in the developing countries: The economic groups. Economic Development and Cultural Change, 26, 661–675.

Lexis & Nexis Corporate Affiliations: International Public and Private Companies (Version 5). (2003).

Links with the first family. (1994, October). Asiamoney, p. 36.

Luostarinen, R., & Hellman, H. (1994). The internationalization processes and strategies of Finnish family firms. Helsingin Kauppakorkeakoulun Kuvalaitos, Helsinki, Finland: HSE Press.

Manikutty, S. (2000). Family business groups in India: A resource-based view of the emerging trends. Family Business Review, 13(4), 279–292.

Manila moves in on the family conglomerates. (1982, May 17). Business Week, pp. 51–53.

Mariussen, A., Wheelock, J., & Baines, S. (1997). The family business tradition in Britain and Norway, modernization and reinvention? International Studies of Management & Organization, 27(3), 64–85.

Markides, C. C. (1997). To diversify or not to diversify. Harvard Business Review, 75(6), 93–99.

Milgrom, P., & Roberts, J. (1992). Economics, organization, and management. Englewood Cliffs, NJ: Prentice Hall.

Mulholland, J. P., & Thomas, K. (1999, April-June). The price of rice. InsideIndonesia, 58. Retrieved May 14, 2000, from http://www.insideindonesia.org

Nachum, L. (1999). Diversification strategies of developing country firms. Journal of International Management, 5, 115–140.

Osborn, R. N., & Hagedoorm, J. (1997). The institutionalization and evolutionary dynamics of interorganizational alliances and networks. Academy of Management Journal, 40(2), 261–278.

Prahalad, C. K., & Lieberthal, K. (1998). The end of corporate imperialism. Harvard Business Review, 76(4), 68–79.

Principal International Business. (1998/1999). New York: Dun & Bradstreet Inc.

Sabanci, S. (1988). This is my life. Avon, Great Britain, UK: Bath Press.

Sarkar, M., & Cavusgil, S. T. (1996). The trends in international business thought and literature: A review of international market entry mode research: Integration and synthesis. International Executive, 38(6), 825–848.

Schein, E. (1983). The role of the founder in creating organizational culture. Organizational Dynamics, 12(1), 13–28.

Schulze, W. S., Lubatkin, M. H., Dino, R. N., & Buchholtz, A. K. (2001). Agency relationships in family firms: Theory and evidence. Organization Science, 12(2), 99–116.

Shetty, Y. K. (1979). Managing the multinational corporation: European and American styles. Management International Review, 19(3), 39–48.

Shin, Y. H. (1993). Modern form of capital accumulation: A study about the formation of Indonesian family conglomerates. Korean Political Science Review, 27(2), 251–274.

Simpson, C., Jr., & Kujawa, D. (1974). The export decision process: An empirical inquiry. Journal of International Business Studies, 5, 107–117.

Sorenson, R. L. (2000). The contribution of leadership style and practices to family and business success. Family Business Review, 13(3), 183–200.

Steers, R. M., Shin, Y. K., & Ungson, G. R. (1989). The Chaebol: Korea's new industrial might. New York: Harper & Row.

Tatung as main distributor. Dow Jones International News. Retrieved July 25, 1994, from http://www.wsj.com

Walker, G., & Poppo, L. (1991). Profit centers, single-source suppliers, and transaction costs. Administrative Science Quarterly, 36(1), 66–87.

Ward, J. L. (2000). Reflections on Indian family groups. Family Business Review, 13(4), 271–278.

Woodall, P. (1998, March 5). Survey: East Asian economies: How many paths to Salvation? The Economist, pp. S14–S17.

Wright Investors. (2000). Corporate information, Wright Investors' Service, Inc. Retrieved July 23, 2000, from http://profiles.wisi.com/profiles/Comsrch.htm

Daekwan Kim is assistant professor of international business and marketing in the College of Business at Florida State University. E-mail: dkim@cob.fsu.edu. Destan Kandemir is a doctoral candidate in the Department of Marketing and Supply Chain Management at the Eli Broad Graduate School of Management at Michigan State University. E-mail: kandemir@msu.edu. S. Tamer Cavusgil is University Distinguished Faculty and the John W. Byington Endowed Chair in Global Marketing at Michigan State University. E-mail: cavusgil@msu.edu.

Chapter 15

Transferring management knowledge to Russia

A culturally based approach

Executive overview

Russian managers entered the decade of the 1990s ill-prepared to manage their companies in the country's chaotic transition to a market economy. This article draws lessons for transferring Western management knowledge to Russian managers from programs conducted over a ten-year period by the Rayter Group, a cross-cultural training organization. The group's experience underscores the transitional nature of business values among Russian managers, including the need to recognize the barriers and potential opportunities that traditional culture and values can create, as well as the potential for newly developing ones to support the transfer of Western knowledge. These two sets of values must be understood and appreciated by those transferring knowledge through the design and execution of management education programs, as well as in other situations like joint ventures and parent-subsidiary operations. The lessons presented in this article are grounded in the context of a culturally based approach to transferring knowledge that includes the culture, values, attitudes, and behaviors of Russian managers. These factors affect the capabilities of both transferors and receivers of knowledge to engage in effective knowledge transfer. The article concludes with recommendations for knowledge transfer in Russia that may also be useful in other transitional economies.

A time of frustration

IN THE MID-1990s, the general director of a newly privatized Russian enterprise was frustrated that the trainers he had hired would not let him simply buy an off-the-shelf strategic plan. Under the former Soviet central planning system, he had always been given a plan for his enterprise developed by government ministries. Although the plan was often unrealistic, he found ways to meet the goals in order to receive bonuses for himself and enterprise workers. After the privatization of his enterprise in the early 1990s, he, like many other directors, had run their enterprises without plans, often with shortsighted actions that weakened their companies while adding to their personal wealth.

It was difficult to convince this CEO that his previous experiences would not work as the decade of the 1990s progressed and Russian companies were moving into a far more competitive situation. This idea frustrated the senior manager who had had quite a successful career under the old system, and his reluctance to change was a major frustration for the training team. They had to find a way to tailor training and development efforts to help the director and his managers be effective in the new Russian context.

A culturally based approach to knowledge transfer

Knowledge transfer has been described as "a process of systematically organized exchange of information and skills between entities."[1] Westerners often find themselves grappling with transferring knowledge in transitional economies, such as between MNCs and their subsidiaries, between joint-venture partners, and between trainers or consultants and their clients. To assist Western managers involved in these situations, we offer a culturally based approach to transferring management knowledge in Russia. It is based on experience from a decade of management training programs conducted by the Rayter Group, a U.S.– Russian cross-cultural organization described in the Appendix.

According to a culturally based approach, many barriers to knowledge transfer can be attributed to specific aspects of Russian culture, values, attitudes, and behaviors that affect managerial practices.[2] Culture has been described as "the collective programming of the mind which distinguishes one group or category of people from another."[3] Culture reflects "the ideas, values, norms, and meanings shared by members of a society and perpetuated through families and communities."[4] In a learning context, "culture shapes the processes by which new organizational knowledge—with its accompanying uncertainties—is created, legitimated, and distributed."[5] Values consist of global beliefs or abstract ideas that "transcendentally guide actions and judgments across specific objects and situations."[6] Values are derived from culture and play an important role in shaping managers' attitudes about work as well as the choices they make and the behaviors they engage in.

Our approach thus concentrates on the capabilities of the receivers, Russian managers, by focusing on the culture and values that underlie their attitudes and behaviors. We also address the absorptive capacity of receivers, "the ability to recognize the value of new information, assimilate it, and apply it to commercial ends."[7] Considered by some researchers to be a major influence on knowledge transfer,[8] its importance has also been noted in transitional economies, particularly between MNCs and their subsidiaries and between joint-venture partners.[9] The lessons learned from the Rayter Group's Russian training programs are presented as a four-step process of accepting, understanding, communicating, and implementing information. Correspondingly, the abilities of the trainers to transfer new knowledge depended on the cross-cultural nature of their teams.

Early attempts at Western knowledge transfer in Russia

Hundreds of market-oriented management training programs, from short seminars to full-scale MBA programs, were developed in Russia in the 1990s, often with Western input.[10] Many programs, however, failed to consider the difficulty of transferring knowledge in a transitional economy.[11] During the Soviet era, domestic management training programs typically emphasized knowledge of rules and procedures and discouraged creativity, innovation, and initiative.[12] Based on the Rayter Group's decade of experience in Russia, we conclude that effective transfer of Western management knowledge requires managers to engage in a four-stage process that includes accepting, understanding, communicating, and utilizing new knowledge.

The Rayter Group's approach to knowledge transfer

The Rayter Group employed a bicultural team of American and Russian facilitators who were able to draw on their respective backgrounds in the content of Western practice and the context of Russian business culture to offer an effective integrated approach to knowledge transfer for Russian executives.[13] (See Appendix for background details on the Rayter Group.) Such individuals and teams help ensure that the initial conditions of the knowledge recipients are well understood, and that trainers, as knowledge transferors, are capable of engaging in successful knowledge transfer.[14] Working as a bicultural team helped members be sensitive transferors of knowledge, helped the non-Russian trainers gain better understanding of the participants' culture and values, and allowed trainers to modify their knowledge transfer techniques appropriately.

The Group found that the managers' conflicting values could present barriers to knowledge transfer and limit their absorptive capacities to receive knowledge. Recognizing that the values underlying the managers' attitudes and behaviors had been formed primarily in the former Soviet system, the trainers incorporated specific elements from that system, such as negative motivation. Additionally, because most managers were not starting with a *tabula rasa*, to accomplish real change they had to go through a process of unfreezing the elements in their backgrounds that inhibited receptivity to learning market-oriented practices.[15] Over time, the Rayter Group team, particularly in its key strategic planning activities, focused more and more on utilizing management practices and techniques that reflected deliberate, linear processes. The explicit nature of these practices and techniques allowed an easier transfer of knowledge because they are akin to explicit knowledge that can be clearly expressed as data, universal principles, and other forms of specific information. In contrast, tacit knowledge is noncodifiable and is based in ideals, values, and emotion.[16] Such explicit techniques facilitated shared experiences between the trainers and managers, enabling the recipients to more readily implement both explicit and tacit knowledge. The trainers' use of learning-by-doing techniques and other creative processes made knowledge more understandable and actionable for the managers.[17] In the process, managers had to develop strategies and solutions reflecting their own priorities and values. The training approach thus accomplished the objective of utilizing managers' traditional and emerging values that supported the content and processes of knowledge transfer.[18]

A conflict of values for Russian managers

Since knowledge transfer is intended to affect attitudes and behaviors, cultural and value underpinnings need to be understood and incorporated in knowledge transfer activities. Recognizing that Russian managers' behaviors are affected by conflicting values, we discuss these two sets of values, those that most managers developed before the market transition, as well as emerging values that have the potential for better absorbing Western management knowledge.[19] This view on emerging values is based primarily on the GLOBE study, a multicountry survey that included the views of 450 Russian managers in the mid-1990s.[20]

Recognizing traditional Russian values as a foundation for knowledge transfer

The majority of managers who are still running most Russian enterprises tend to be older and have values from the Soviet period. This is especially true in manufacturing companies and enterprises located outside the major cities. In contrast, MNCs in transitional economies often prefer to hire younger people because they do not have to unlearn knowledge and undo values.[21] Most managers with experience in state-owned enterprises carry prejudices from their past, including avoiding risk and accountability, mistrusting others, and lacking initiative, and thus find it difficult to change their mentality, accept new ideas, and adapt to new work systems. A study of Russian managers cautioned Westerners not to underestimate traditional values, as well as history and past experiences, since all are of great importance to Russians.[22] For instance, the Communist Party railed against capitalism as being exploitive, saying that profits and competition occurred at the expense of the general population, and that maximizing profits was unethical.

In their previous careers, the managers involved in the Rayter Group's programs had been given objectives under the Soviet system that required meeting centrally mandated plans rather than operating profitably. These goals led them to focus on meeting planned targets and protecting their enterprises and positions. They were masters of circumventing rules and directives and worked in underhanded ways by hoarding materials and labor and concealing and manipulating information.[23] Their behaviors reflected a lack of trust, a disdain for measures and controls, real numbers, and truthful reports, as well as a lack of respect for laws they saw as senseless.[24] Their lack of trust, for instance, stemmed from the highly arbitrary, punitive conditions of the communist and tsarist periods.

Thus, Westerners must understand the managers to whom they are transferring knowledge and skills, and the managers must develop the perspective of learners, realizing that what was successful in the past is likely not appropriate for the new market-oriented conditions.[25] In fact, the most successful managers under the old system could well be the least successful under the new. Most of the managerial values developed during the Soviet period, and their attendant attitudes and behaviors, are antithetical to Western management practices and are potential roadblocks to successfully transferring Western management knowledge. Still, as the Rayter Group found, some Western knowledge and practices can successfully build upon this foundation.

Incorporating emerging values in knowledge transfer

Emerging values can also be viewed as facilitators of knowledge transfer in transitional economies. In the GLOBE study mentioned earlier, managers described nine aspects of Russian culture as they saw them at the time and as they thought they should be in the future. Responses for the former appear to reflect values originating in the earlier Soviet and even pre-Soviet or tsarist periods, while responses about the future seem to reflect the changing values that managers saw as being appropriate in a market economy.

The managers viewed the country's future orientation as being very short range, leading to a singular focus on short-term goals. However, they believed that it should become relatively long range over time. This trend could lead to a higher degree of acceptance for longer range strategic planning for enterprises, a key element of Western knowledge to be transferred during training. However, strategic planning must still be integrated with short-term goals like survival.

Uncertainty avoidance is a "society's reliance on social norms and procedures to alleviate the unpredictability of future events; the extent to which its members seek orderliness, consistency, structure."[26] According to the GLOBE managers, uncertainty avoidance was very low but should be higher in the future. This trend could be helpful for Westerners since it seems to indicate an increasing disposition for structure, formal rules, and procedures, all of which could facilitate transferring Western knowledge.

Russian culture has been remarkable for its tradition of extremely high power distance, described as "the degree to which members of the society expect power to be unequally shared."[27] The GLOBE managers confirmed this high power distance, but wanted power to be more equally shared in the future.

In the context of knowledge transfer, this trend toward a more equal distribution of power could lead to greater acceptance of individual responsibility rather than looking to a strong leader as the only source of power and responsibility. Still, the traditional Russian preference for a strong leader must be appreciated, and Westerners might have to recommend or institute top-down control techniques that Russians not only respect but also expect.[28] However, these techniques must be introduced and applied properly to facilitate a climate for eliciting opinions or sharing knowledge since these activities were not fostered during Soviet times.

Performance orientation is "the degree to which a society encourages and rewards group members for performance improvement and excellence."[29] As might be expected because of low motivation under the Soviet system, the GLOBE study managers viewed performance orientation as being quite low, but thought it should be high in the future. This trend could increase acceptance of accountability and responsibility for one's own performance.

Two other culturally based values could be important for transferring knowledge. In-group collectivism refers to "the extent to which members of the society take pride in membership in small groups, as opposed to the society at large," while humane orientation is "the degree to which a society encourages and rewards its members for fairness, altruism, generosity, care, and kindness."[30] The GLOBE managers assigned much higher scores to both characteristics as they looked to the future, indicating that these should be far more prominent. Together, these trends could pave the way for acceptance of teamwork, mutual contracts between managers, and pride in group accomplishments. Such characteristics were also noted as being important for Russian companies by the first Western CFO of Yukos, Michel Soublin (EfinancialNews.com, 2002).

However, such characteristics require interpersonal trust, which is also essential for knowledge sharing, and Russians have traditionally exhibited low trust. This characteristic has been found even among managers and coworkers who ostensibly share organizational goals.[31] It is particularly acute for senior managers who typically view sharing critical company information as a potential threat to company survival.[32] Thus, Westerners must work on building trust during knowledge transfer activities if they are to utilize the increasing importance of in-group collectivism and humane orientation.

Applying the culturally based approach to knowledge transfer

The Rayter Group training teams came to understand that they had to embed processes in their programs that fostered a more open culture, facilitated communication and team building, and also reflected their own appreciation of the managers' past experiences and operating circumstances. They realized that a culture of openness among managers and employees in Russian companies is essential when rapid change and learning are the goals.[33]

Understanding the cultural underpinnings of Russian managers' values, attitudes, and behaviors also offered clues on their thought and communication processes. It also became the foundation for techniques, such as strategic planning teams, that could be effectively included in training programs. The trainers also encouraged client firms to adopt appropriate and clear rewards that were consistent with the past experiences and values of the managers. The use of a rules-based, back-to-basics managerial approach, grounded in explicit knowledge, led to better acceptance, understanding, and communication of the knowledge transferred. This approach also fit well with work practices that still include steep hierarchies which discourage meaningful participation in decision making. One Russian senior executive coach similarly observed that a Russian CEO had asked why he should seek his managers' input in important decisions when he himself made the strategy, and their role was to carry it out.[34]

Consistent with earlier research, the trainers found that the strategic plans developed by the Russian managers, while being longer term, should also include clear, short-term tasks with realistic and measurable results.[35] Managers had become cynical toward long-term planning since the Soviet five-year plans were far from realistic. Still, strategic planning frameworks appeared to satisfy the need of many Russian managers for rational mental models to clarify managerial practices by presenting them pictorially and graphically.[36]

Another training component recognized the importance of bonuses and other material incentives, as well as punishments, that were part of the old system that still influenced many Russian managers.[37] As a result, several client firms adapted a three-step motivation policy in which punishments became increasingly severe (see Exhibit 1).[38]

Lessons for effective knowledge transfer in Russia

The four lessons below, learned during a decade of working with Russian managers, are based in knowledge-transfer theory as well as in the values-based approach discussed earlier. The lessons recognize that managers must be ready to accept new knowledge, comprehend it, communicate it, and implement it. Trainers, as transferors of knowledge, must in turn design programs to lead managers through the process in a way that accounts for the inherent conflicts in their values.

Lesson #1: Check the DNA

Efforts to transfer management knowledge are likely to be wasted on recipients who do not approach the process with a receptive attitude. It is crucial that they be capable of and open to acquiring knowledge.[39] Thus, the first priority must be to choose firms and recipients committed to learning and applying new management knowledge and practices. Over the past decade, the Rayter Group developed a "DNA" test for potential Russian training participants that has proven useful in judging their suitability for training and receptivity to market-based management knowledge and practices.

D is for Denial

To be able and willing to accept new knowledge, managers must have moved beyond many of their old Soviet-based values, attitudes, and behaviors. Most of the early participants in training programs conducted from 1993 to 1995 by the Rayter Group were still in shock from the immense political, economic, and social changes that had rocked the country. Some who visited the U.S. exhibited signs of depression and engaged in excessive drinking and withdrawal from their groups. Many feared that their enterprises would be permanently cut off from the resources provided by the state, forcing them to be totally responsible for their own destinies.

Many participants developed a protective cloak of denial. A deputy director of a large Soviet-era bank candidly stated in 1994: "The state is still my meal ticket, so I will appease them and you by pretending to take this training seriously. The system in Russia may be shifting, but it will not affect me directly. My world will never change." Although denial is not nearly as prevalent as it once was among Russian managers, it can still be found in large, industrial enterprises that are insulated from the economic and political reforms of the past decade. Thus, it is crucial to select training participants who no longer exhibit denial, and are thus open and receptive to new knowledge.

N is for Naiveté

The 1990s was a period when many enterprise owners and managers focused on immediate personal gain rather than building companies. They engaged in such self-serving practices as asset stripping and creating offshore companies to which they funneled their assets. This wholesale gutting of the country's industrial base has been referred to as the piratization of Russia.[40] From 1995 to 1998, the Russian economy appeared to flourish and requests for Rayter Group training programs increased. Money seemed to be no object for many Russian executives, but their attitudes caused the trainers to become increasingly pessimistic about the prospects for genuine reform in Russian companies. Many managers seemed interested primarily in family excursions to the U.S. and requested that the training organization develop connections and open personal bank accounts for them in the U.S. Such requests were denied, but the trainers took them as a sign that the accumulation of personal wealth had become the main objective of many Russian executives, even if it meant the death of their organizations. The trainers generally viewed participants' attitudes during this period as: "The state is no longer my meal ticket, so I must buy one. Don't bother teaching me anything, just sell me a plan for my company. I am ready to pay, and then you can take me shopping."

A fundamental test of their willingness to accept new knowledge was whether managers were ready to take personal responsibility for their learning rather than relying on answers provided to them, as was the case in the centrally planned economy. The idea, for example, that a one-size-fits-all plan could be applied to any organization had its roots in that environment, and illustrates the naiveté with which many Russian executives approached the transfer of management knowledge. It was not unusual, for example, for them to offer trainers large sums of money to provide copies of policy manuals and strategic planning documents of U.S. firms. While these offers were refused, many wealthy executives still believed they could make their organizations successful by simply copying Western business plans. As an example, one Russian executive told a U.S. trainer that her director general had threatened she would lose her job if her document-filled luggage going back to Russia weighed less than 100 pounds.

Over time, the trainers succeeded in convincing clients that solutions could not be bought off the shelf, but must evolve through a messy process centered on the unique realities of their own firms in the Russian context. As one trainer noted: "Russian managers must overcome their naiveté of believing they can buy answers to their problems. They must understand the necessity of working in their businesses and learning to build the bridge as they walk on it." In short, they had to be willing to accept responsibility and become personally account-able. Thus, the trainers had to be sure that the managers selected for training no longer displayed the naive attitudes and behaviors from earlier in the decade.

A is for Acceptance

Russia's devastating economic and financial crisis in August 1998 seemed to be the catalyst for a major shift in the attitudes and priorities of many Russian managers, including a much greater readiness to accept Western management knowledge. As the economic situation stabilized in 2000, managers showed a renewed interest in training, and their requests lacked the naiveté of the past. No longer distracted by easy money, they seemed ready to accept that acquiring knowledge in market-oriented management practices was their only real hope for survival.

By 2003, the Rayter Group's programs were conducted exclusively on site in Russia. Multiple training sessions at each firm averaged 12 hours a day, often six days a week for several weeks. In contrast to the past where they had initially seen the state as their firms' meal ticket, followed by the exploitation of their firms as their own personal ticket, Russian managers seemed to say: "I accept legitimacy as my ticket. I am ready to learn." The trainers understood the significance of this change and saw it as an indication of potential trust as well as an acceptance and willingness to be ac accountable. They sensed that the DNA of Russian managers had changed, indicating that they had let go of their denial and naiveté and had accepted reality. With this change in values, attitudes, and behaviors, more managers had now become candidates for receiving and accepting new management knowledge, while the trainers were better prepared to transfer that knowledge.

Lesson #2: Appreciate the mindset

When individuals are ready to fully engage in knowledge transfer, it is impor-tant to appreciate their mindset, and consider their cognitive capabilities and potential absorptive capacity. The trainers realized that the managers' abilities to assimilate and apply new knowledge still depended greatly on traditional values, knowledge, and experience, which could be a barrier to, or in some cases a foundation for, knowledge transfer. Earlier, many Western trainers had relied on a lecture format for knowledge transfer, while much of the knowledge was highly tacit and required direct interaction between the learner and the trainer. As one expert noted, application-based learning and critical self-reflection would have been more appropriate techniques in this context.[41]

These techniques are particularly relevant to transferring strategic management concepts and practices, which were the focus of the Rayter Group's programs. Strategic planning in the West is typically divided into process, focusing on how strategy is formed, and content, such as the Boston Consulting Group matrix or Michael Porter's generic strategies.[42] The trainers realized that the planning process used to develop strategic content was particularly important in Russia because, under Soviet planning, strategic content had been completely disconnected from the strategic process, with managers receiving plans from Gosplan and other central Soviet ministries. Thus, it is not surprising that Russian managers involved in earlier training programs wanted trainers to provide ready-made strategy content, but they were very apprehensive about getting involved in the strategy formulation process. Their resistance to taking an active role was understandable but must be overcome if change were to occur in their cognitive frameworks at a strategic level.[43] In short, their involvement and personal accountability were necessary for effectively transferring knowledge that could be understandable, sustainable, and actionable.

The time-consuming early meetings with managers provided additional opportunities for the trainers to better understand the mindsets of individual managers as well as the strategic planning groups. Since many managers had been appointed by their bosses, they were often reluctant to become actively involved in a process they viewed as personally threatening or just another "theater play." They also seemed to feel that the trainers were challenging their personal knowledge and experience, and some exhibited a fear of failure. Additionally, high-level Russian executives have generally been resistant to working in teams with lower-level managers, particularly if such interaction has the potential to threaten the prevailing order and power structures.[44]

Such reluctance, however, usually faded after a few days in later programs because the top management of client firms had already passed the DNA test, which suggested that their values and attitudes had been modified and their behaviors would likely be cooperative. Enthusiasm for the planning process seemed to grow, as did trust and personal bonding between the trainers and managers. Occasionally, however, resistance to participation did not diminish and led to a form of psychological warfare, which one Russian trainer called "*lomat' golovy*" or "breaking their heads." Exhibit 2 provides an example of how entrenched such resistance could be among some managers, and describes a solution.

The training group's approach to strategic planning was based on the principles of rational-analytical decision making that underlie most prescriptions in strategic management.[45] That approach emphasizes explicit frameworks and tools for developing strategies that facilitate the transfer of tacit, actionable knowledge. This is in contrast to the incremental model of strategy, which depends less on analytical frameworks, is more reactive than proactive, and evolves in a fluid, less deliberate process of emergent action and learning.[46]

The rational-analytical model has been criticized in the West for placing too much emphasis on controlled, intentional thought processes based more on conscious skills than intuitive skills. It as also been criticized as oversimplifying the strategy process and placing too much control in the hands of the CEO, who emerges as the principal strategist while relegating others to subordinate roles.[47] However, such characteristics make the rational analytical approach particularly appropriate when transferring knowledge to Russian managers because it satisfies their need for a rational, intentional framework that offsets their current deficiencies in intuitive skills.[48] The rational-analytical approach also allows for the dominant planning role to be reserved for the owner or director general, a reality compatible with Russia's traditionally hierarchical organizations. The trainers thus incorporated managers' prior experiences and cognitive capabilities when designing and implementing programs to help the managers understand and apply newly acquired Western management knowledge.

Lesson #3: Get them talking—up, down, and across

To ensure that the managers would understand and leverage their new knowledge, the trainers had them communicate extensively with other participants as well as with the trainers themselves. This was not as straightforward as it might seem, since serious internal barriers of organizational structure and politics, as well as those related to cognition and behavior, often impeded the process. Russian managers have traditionally been suspicious and prone to secrecy after years of operating within the punitive and shortage-ridden Soviet system. Additionally, although groups were often cohesive within themselves during that time, managers were unaccustomed to sharing knowledge horizontally due to the extreme emphasis on vertical hierarchy and formal power. Many senior managers also held the expectation that they must always appear more knowledgeable than their subordinates in order to maintain their formal power in the hierarchy. Thus, many mid-level managers seldom participated in important decisions, leading them to see little value in sharing knowledge across their organizations or with lower hierarchical levels.

The trainers took such values, attitudes, and behaviors into account and utilized them as foundations for the techniques they introduced. For example, the strategic planning committee emerged as a vehicle that recognized the Russian tendency to develop strong attachments to groups.[49] As an integral part of the new management practices, that committee became the core liaison in a new matrix structure, commonly used in the West, that facilitated the development, implementation, and control of strategies in the Russian firms. Since the success of the committee depended on members' willingness to share information across functions and departments, it served as a knowledge-sharing device that helped overcome many barriers of the old Soviet model.

The strategy matrix structure introduced to the Rayter Group's client firms supplemented the old functional structure and built upon the traditional desire of Russian managers for models that clearly illustrated the explicit planning process they were to follow. Specifically, the strategic planning committee created the overall strategy and assigned each strategy to one committee member ultimately responsible for its accomplishment. Only board members, owners/directors, or deputy directors were assigned responsibility for an overall strategy. If a strategy had three underlying goals, deputies or department heads were assigned direct responsibility for these goals, including developing a detailed action plan for each goal. These goal-level managers had responsibility for the people assigned to specific tasks within each of the action plans, typically mid- to lower-level managers or key support staff across different departments in the organization. Each task had a specific, measurable outcome and a relatively short deadline for completion. The rules and procedures for implementing the action plans were not negotiable once signed as an executive order by the owner/director general. This was in keeping with many Russians' strong preference for rules set by superiors.

The matrix structure created conditions in which managers and their subordinates operated within two hierarchies: the traditional, vertical departmental structure, and the new multidirectional structure that flowed vertically and horizontally to fulfill specific strategies. In contrast to other techniques that built upon traditional values, attitudes, and behaviors, this arrangement was a radical change for most Russian managers since it fostered new, transparent, and interactive behaviors. Implementing such structural reforms, and reinforcing them with formal rules and procedures, has proven to be essential for information sharing to occur in Russian firms. The new emphasis on knowledge sharing must also have the unequivocal support of the director general because Russian firms are still driven primarily by a tight form of authoritarian control wielded from the top.

Lesson #4: Call for action

Once the trainers were satisfied that managers had accepted new knowledge, internalized and understood it, and communicated and shared it, they encouraged them to apply it in their organizations. In the Soviet system, focusing on problems rather than encouraging actions toward solutions, was raised to an art form. Managers typically avoided problems because they had little if any power to control or remedy the situation. There was no reward for being assertive or outspoken, and risk-taking behavior was seen as reckless and self-serving, rather than something of value to the enterprise. Managers understood that the safest route to success was to maintain a low profile and draw little attention to themselves. This approach reflects a still-prevalent Russian workplace attitude that it is better to find someone to blame than to find a solution.

As a legacy of the Soviet system, Russian executives had become masters at hiding mistakes and omissions behind layers of organizational ambiguity and inefficiency. Thus, newly acquired management knowledge and practices would adhere only with the "glue" of the monitoring and control devices used to ensure individual accountability. The trainers found that a combination of carrot and stick was essential to promote action.

As a result of the newly devised strategic plans, managers' individual goals were based on their departmental roles, as well as on their responsibilities assigned within the strategy matrix at the general strategy, goal, and task levels as appropriate. Yet, without individual consequences tied to individual responsibilities, personal accountability for accomplishing goals was unlikely. To address this challenge, client firms were encouraged to link individual performance directly to compensation systems.

Compensation management has been one of the most challenging areas for Russian managers after the government-controlled compensation system was abandoned in the post-Soviet era.[50] In the early 1990s, the training group encouraged executives to adopt a pay-for-performance policy, but the idea was generally resisted as being too radical. In Soviet times, bonuses had been a component of compensation, but were tied to group and enterprise results rather than individual performance. By the mid-1990s, however, some Western firms operating in Russia had begun to employ Management by Objectives to determine bonuses for Russian employees based on a percentage of salary.[51] To help clients link pay with performance, the trainers worked with them to build a motivational approach compatible with Russian business culture that they called the Three Strikes program (see Exhibit 1). In this case, the trainers sought to build upon traditional Russian values, attitudes, and behaviors to help ensure that the newly acquired knowledge would be implemented effectively.

The trainers also realized that in this transition period they had to build upon newly emerging values, attitudes, and behaviors. They found that executives who took an active role in creating protocols and control measures to monitor performance developed more effective communications in their firms. Employees were more likely to realize there was no longer a place to hide and that excuses would no longer be tolerated. The training group's experience indicated clearly that the link between performance and compensation was a key to promoting individual accountability and effective actions, something not thought possible under the Soviet economic system.

Recommendations for effective knowledge transfer

Knowledge transfer between Westerners and managers in transitional economies can occur in different situations. While the focus of this article has been on the interaction of Russian managers with Western trainers, such transfer also occurs in Western subsidiaries in Russia, cross-national joint ventures, and Western companies with Russian employees. Drawing upon the four lessons learned in this training experience, the following recommendations are offered for Westerners who would engage in knowledge transfer with Russian managers, or possibly in other transitional economies since conflicting values are also found in those situations.

Assess the capability of knowledge receivers as well as knowledge transferors

As Lesson #1 suggests, it is important to develop techniques such as the DNA approach to ascertain the readiness and willingness of managers to engage in meaningful knowledge transfer. A suitable DNA means that managers have the absorptive capacity for accepting new knowledge. Unless they exhibit this DNA, any efforts to introduce new knowledge will likely be futile. Additionally, the knowledge transferors must themselves be ready to engage in an open process that requires them to adapt their own approaches to knowledge transfer.

Ensure the sustainability of the transfer

Lesson #2 underscores the need for Westerners to appreciate the mindset of knowledge receivers and take pains to test their understanding and internalization of the knowledge imparted in the transfer. Even if the receivers appear willing and able to accept new knowledge, the transferors must do their best to understand the values, attitudes, and behaviors that can inhibit or facilitate receivers' genuine understanding and internalization of new knowledge. It is unlikely that knowledge acquired will be sustainable unless it is built upon more deeply felt values, attitudes, and behaviors.

Understand the need for continuous communication

Lesson #3 noted that it is imperative that the knowledge transferred be disseminated in many directions to ensure that it can be leveraged within an organization. When managers discuss and communicate the knowledge they receive with trainers and people in their organizations, they are likely to develop a true understanding of the usefulness of their newly acquired knowledge. Additionally, the knowledge can be leveraged among others in their firms, thereby providing greater benefit and broader utilization.

Develop techniques that facilitate implementing newly acquired knowledge

Lastly, the call for action in Lesson #4 emphasizes that all of the earlier steps are a prelude to the implementation of actionable knowledge in organizations. It is not enough that managers accept, understand, and communicate their newly acquired knowledge. They also must be able to take actions based upon it. To do so requires their deep involvement in the knowledge-transfer process, which in turn requires that knowledge transferors develop techniques that demand such involvement. Clear models and explicit techniques are critical to the process of transferring tacit knowledge in transitional economies like Russia since managers have shown the need for very clear guidelines to bring new knowledge to an actionable state.

A continuous process

The difficulty of transferring knowledge in transitional economies like Russia is demonstrated by the fact that it took the better part of a decade, and the constant involvement of the training teams with Russian clients, to develop a process for creating new organizational cultures and management practices. Transitional economies are marked by tumultuous change, uncertainty, and confusion. The trainers' appreciation for the situation faced by Russian managers was essential to developing approaches that built upon their culturally based values, attitudes, and behaviors. The trainers used traditional Russian values as well as newly emerging values as foundations for introducing appropriate techniques to encourage learning and create receptivity for knowledge transfer. The trainers also learned that effectively transferring management knowledge in transitional economies like Russia required going back to the basics of Western management practices, and emphasizing explicit mental frameworks in their programs.

The lessons learned in Russia during the decade of the 1990s, as well as the recommendations drawn from them, might need to be revisited over time as cultural foundations moderate and new values replace some of those from a previous era. Also, greater experience with a market economy and Western management techniques might lead to different approaches to effectively transfer knowledge in transitional economies like Russia. However, such changes will likely come slowly, and these lessons and recommendations should serve well for the foreseeable future.

Exhibit 1 *The Three Strikes motivational program*

The Three Strikes program developed by Russian managers in the training sessions initially focused only on those who held key responsibilities in implementing a new strategy. For example, Birusa in Krasnoyarsk sought to develop a quality control program in product design. The goal-level managers and the deputy director responsible for this strategy followed rules created by the strategic planning committee to facilitate their group meetings. One rule required that any documentation to be shared at weekly meetings be provided to all members at least 24 hours in advance. Failure to do so triggered the first strike, calling for a 50-percent cut in the person's monthly bonus. If the individual failed a second time, the second strike occurred, resulting in the loss of an entire monthly bonus. A third-strike offense triggered termination procedures conducted in accordance with Russian law.

Although such practices may seem harsh, the Three Strikes program was so successful that five client firms expanded the system with a policy called extraordinary guarantees, a form of contractual agreement between individuals whose work is highly interdependent. For example, in a Richel scrap metal operation in Chelyabinsk, the head of the receiving department was required to have enough cash on hand to pay drivers delivering loads of scrap metal. He and the chief accountant made an extraordinary guarantee agreement whereby the chief accountant had to process Receiving's requests for funds within 24 hours. Likewise, the head of Receiving had to provide Accounting with receipt documentation from the drivers within 24 hours. If either manager failed to live up to the extraordinary guarantee, it triggered the first strike. Although the Three Strikes approach is punitive in nature, firms which used it in conjunction with extraordinary guarantees found that individuals tended to increase their communication and began viewing each other as internal customers to whom they were accountable.

Exhibit 2 *A solution to resistance to training*

An example of resistance to training occurred in a firm we call Old Guard that involved a battle of wills between trainers and participants. In the first visit to Old Guard, a trainer spent six days mired in mental combat with 15 top managers who had selected themselves for the strategic planning committee. Although Old Guard no longer held a monopoly position, and the owner of the company was present at all meetings, 12 of the 15 executives refused to believe that their organization's future required customers as the focus of its strategic plan. One executive adamantly stated: "We do not plan for customers. We plan for us. They [customers] will take what we give them." After a week without progress, the owner disbanded the committee and followed up by interviewing every other department head and middle manager in the company with the assistance of the trainer. The following week, the owner selected a new strategic planning committee based on individuals' competence and openness to organizational change.

The new committee created original organizational strategies over a period of six to nine months in multiples planning sessions working "hands on" with trainers. The approach to knowledge transfer was deliberately linear and highly structured to appeal to Russians' preference for clearly defined, short-term tasks in the context of a longterm planning process.

Appendix: Background on the Rayter Group

In 1992, the first author of this article formed a partnership with Gregory Rachmilevich Rayter, founder of the Russian Personnel Management Association (RPMA). The network of participants in this cross-cultural partnership included associates of RPMA with backgrounds in Soviet-era personnel management and management academics and practitioners based in the Dallas, Texas area. The goal of the partnership has always been the transfer of Western, market-based practices tailored to the unique cultural circumstances of Russian organizations.

By 1993, the group began offering training programs in two phases. The first phase provided intensive two-week seminars on-site training in Russian firms. As of 2004, the Group's client list had grown substantially and included firms from a wide variety of regions and industries in Russia and Ukraine. The industries included banking, manufacturing, energy, chemicals, food, and pharmaceuticals with such leaders as Avtovaz and Gazprom. The terms of Rayter Group contracts are negotiated with owners and/or director generals of client firms on a case-by-case basis and typically include eight to ten weeks of direct contact with firm participants, spread over four to six visits, with the total program spanning six to nine months. The program includes assistance in developing and implementing strategies, as well as altering organizational structures and policies to support new strategies. After an initial consulting contract is completed, firms often hire the Group on a retainer basis to ensure sustained commitments to, and implementation of, new strategic initiatives.

Notes

1   Wang, P., Tong, T.W., & Koh, C.P. 2004. An integrated model of knowledge transfer: From MNC parent to China subsidiary. *Journal of World Business*, 39(2): 168–182; quote from page 173.

2   See for example Elenkov, D.S. 1998. Can American management concepts work in Russia? A cross-cultural comparative study. *California Management Review*, 40(4): 133–156; Fey, C.F., & Denison, D. 2003. Organizational culture and effectiveness: Can American theory be applied in Russia? *Organization Science*, 14(6): 686–706.; Holden, N.J., Cooper, C.L., & Carr, J. 1998. *Dealing with the new Russia: Management cultures in collision*. New York: John Wiley & Sons.

3   Hofstede, G. 1993. Cultural constraints in management theories. *The Academy of Management Executive*, 7(1): 81–94. Citation from p. 81.

4   Hofstede, G. 1980. *Culture's consequences: International differences in work-related values*. Beverly Hills: Sage, 21.

5   DeLong, D.W., & Fahey, L. 2000. Diagnosing cultural barriers to knowledge management. *The Academy of Management Executive*, 14(4): 113–127. Citation from p. 126.

6   Rokeach, M. 1968. *Beliefs, attitudes, and values*. San Francisco: Jossey-Bass.

7   Cohen, W., & Leventhal, D. 1990. Absorptive capacity: A new perspective of learning and innovation. *Administrative Science Quarterly*, 35: 128–152.

8   Gupta, A., & Govindarajan, V. 2000. Knowledge flows within multinational corporations. *Strategic Management Journal*, 21: 473–496.

9   Tsang, E.W.K. 2001. Managerial learning in foreign-invested enterprises of China. *Management International Review*, 41: 29–51; Wang, P., Tong, T.W., & Koh, C.P. 2004. An integrated model of knowledge transfer from MNC parent to China subsidiary. *Journal of World Business*, 39(2):168–182.

10   Kozlova, T.V., & Puffer, S.M. 1994. Public and private business schools in Russia: Problems and prospects. *European Management Journal*, 12(4): 462–468; Aganbegyan, A.G. 2004. Corporate governance and business education. In D.J. McCarthy, S.M. Puffer, & S.V. Shekshnia (Eds.), *Corporate governance in Russia*. Cheltenham, U.K., and Northampton, MA: Edward Elgar.

11   Hollinshead, G., & Michailova, S. 2001. Blockbusters or bridge-builders? The role of Western trainers in developing new entrepreneurialism in Eastern Europe. *Management Learning*, 32(4): 419–436.

12   Puffer, S.M. 1981. Inside a Soviet management institute. *California Management Review*, 24: 90–96.

13   Michailova, S. 2000. Contrasts in culture: Russian and Western perspectives on organizational change. *The Academy of Management Executive*, 14(4): 99–112.

14   Gupta & Govindarajan, 2000.

15   Lewin, K. 1951. *Field theory in social science*. New York: Harper & Row.

16   Nonaka, I. 1994. A dynamic theory of organizational knowledge. *Organization Science*, 5: 14–37; Roberts, J. 2002. Questioning the role of information and communication technologies in knowledge transfer. *Technology Analysis & Strategic Management*, 12(9): 429–443.

17   Roberts, 2002.

18   See Grant, R. 1996. Toward a knowledge-based theory of the firm. *Strategic Management Journal*, 17: 109–122; Haridimos, T., & Vladimirou, E. 2001. What is organizational knowledge? *Journal of Management Studies*, 38(7): 973–993; Spender, J.C. 1996. Making knowledge the basis of a dynamic theory of the firm. *Strategic Management Journal*, 23: 835–854; Lane, H.W., Greenberg, D., & Berdrow, I. 2004. Barriers and bonds to knowledge transfer in global alliances and mergers. In H.W. Lane, M.L. Maznevski, M.E. Mendenhall, & J. McNett (Eds.), *The Blackwell handbook of global management: A guide to managing complexity*: 342–361. Oxford: Blackwell.

19   Puffer, S.M., McCarthy, D.J., & Zhuplev, A.V. 1996. Meeting of the mindsets in a changing Russia. *Business Horizons*, November-December: 52–60.

20   Gratchev M., Rogovsky, N., & Rakitski, B. 2001. *Leadership and culture in Russia: The case of transitional economy, www. haskayne.ucalgary.ca.*

21   Vikhanski, O.S., & Puffer, S.M. 1993. Management education and employee training at Moscow McDonald's. *European Management Journal*, 11(1): 102–107; Wang et al., 2004.

22   Michailova, 2000.

23   Lawrence, P.R., & Vlachoutsicos, C. (Eds.) 1990. *Behind the factory walls: Decision making in Soviet and American enterprises.* Boston: Harvard Business School Press.

24   Puffer, S.M., & McCarthy, D.J. 1995. Finding the common ground in Russian and American business ethics. *California Management Review*, 37(2): 29–46; Puffer, S.M., & McCarthy, D.J. 1997. Business ethics in a transforming economy: Applying the integrative social contracts theory to Russia. *University of Pennsylvania Journal of Economic Law*, 18(4), 1281–1304.

25   Holden, N.J. & Cooper, C.L. 1994. Russian managers as learners. *Management Learning*, 25(4): 503–522.

26   Hofstede, 1980.

27   Ibid.

28   Michailova, S., & Husted, K. 2003. Knowledge-sharing hostility in Russian firms. *California Management Review*, 45(3): 59–77.

29   Javidan, M., & House, R. 2001. Cultural acumen for the global manager: Lessons from project Globe. *Organizational Dynamics*, 29(4): 289.

30   Javidan & House, 2001.

31   Abrams, L.C., Cross, R., Lesser, E., & Levin, D.Z. 2003. Nurturing interpersonal trust in knowledge-sharing networks. *The Academy of Management Executive*, 17(4): 64–77; McCarthy, D.J., & Puffer, S.M. 2003. Corporate governance in Russia: A framework for analysis. *Journal of World Business*, 38(4): 397–415; McCarthy, D.J., & Puffer, S.M. 2004. Gaining legitimacy: Management's challenge in developing and transitioning economies. In H.W. Lane, M.L. Maznevski, M.E. Mendenhall, & J. McNett (Eds.), *The Blackwell handbook of global management: A guide to managing complexity*: 423–441. Oxford: Blackwell.

32   Mikhaylenko, A. 2004. Private enterprise owners and corporate governance. In D.J. McCarthy, S.M. Puffer, & S.V. Shekshnia (Eds.), *Corporate governance in Russia*. Cheltenham, UK: Edward Elgar.

33   Fey, & Denison, 2003.

34   Mikhaylenko, 2004.

35   Michailova, 2000.

36   Puffer, S.M., & McCarthy, D.J. 2001. Navigating the hostile maze: A framework for Russian entrepreneurship. *The Academy of Management Executive*, 2001, 15(4): 24–36.

37   Puffer, S.M. 1997. Soviet and American managers' reward allocations: A dependency approach. *International Business Review*, 6(5): 453–476.

38   Lawrence & Vlachoutsicos, 1990.

39   Hamel, G. 1991. Competition for competence and interpartner learning within international strategic alliances. *Strategic Management Journal*, 12: 83–103; Lane, P.J., Salk, J.E., & Lyles, M.A. 2001. Absorptive capacity, learning, and performance in international joint ventures. *Strategic Management Journal*, 22: 1139–1161.

40   Goldman, M.I. 2003. *The piratization of Russia.* New York: Routledge.

41   Meyer, K.E. 2002. Management challenges in privatization acquisitions in transition economies. *Journal of World Business*, 37(4): 266–276.

42   Huff, A.S., & Reger, R.K. 1987. A review of strategic process research. *Journal of Management*, 13: 211–236; Fahey, L., & Christensen, H.K. 1986. Evaluating the research on strategy content. *Journal of Management*, 12: 167–183.

43   Uhlenbruck, K., Meyer, K.E., & Hitt, M.A. 2003. Organizational transformation in transition economies: Resource-based and organizational learning perspectives. *Journal of Management Studies*, 40(2): 257–282.

44   Michailova & Husted, 2003.

45   Hofer, C.W., & Schendel, D. 1978. *Strategy formulation: Analytical concepts.* St. Paul: West.

46   Quinn, J.B. 1980. *Strategies for change: Logical incrementalism*. Homewood: Irwin; Fredrickson, J.W. 1983. Strategic process research: Questions and recommendations. *The Academy of Management Review*, 11: 280–287.

47   Mintzberg, H. 1990. The design school: Reconsidering the basic premises of strategic management. *Strategic Management Journal*, 11: 171–195.

48   May, R.C., Bormann-Young, C.J., & Ledgerwood, D.E. 1998. Lessons from Russian human resource management experience. *European Management Journal*, 16(4): 447–459; Warner, M., Denezhkina, E., & Campbell, A. 1994. How Russian managers learn. *Journal of General Management*, 19(4): 69–88.

49   Michailova & Husted, 2003.

50   Shekshnia, S.V. 2003. *Kak eto skazat' po-russki? Sovremennye metody upravleniia personalom v sovremennoi Rossii.* (How do you say that in Russian? Modern management methods in today's Russia). Moscow: Zhurnal Upravlenie Personalom.

51   Puffer, S.M., & Shekshnia, S.V. 1994. Compensating local employees in post-Communist Russia: In search of talent or just looking for a bargain? *Compensation & Benefits Review*, 26(5): 35–42.

Ruth C. May is an Associate Professor of Global Business at the University of Dallas. She has played an active role in training and consulting for Russian and Ukrainian companies since 1993 and has published numerous papers and articles on Soviet/Russian management. She received her BA from the University of Southern Mississippi, her MBA from Millsaps College, and her Ph.D. in strategic management from the University of North Texas. Contact: *rmay@gsm.udallas.edu*.

Sheila M. Puffer is Professor of International Business at Northeastern University in Boston. She is a past editor of *The Academy of Management Executive*. She has authored more than 100 publications, and was ranked in a recent study as the #1 scholar in business in Russia. She received her BA and MBA from the University of Ottawa, Canada, and her Ph.D. in business administration from the University of California at Berkeley. Contact: *s.puffer@neu.edu*.

Daniel J. McCarthy is the Walsh Research Professor and Co director of the nationally ranked High-Technology MBA Program at Northeastern University in Boston. He is the author of more than 60 publications, including the co-edited *Corporate Governance in Russia* (Elgar, 2004), and was ranked in a recent study as the #2 scholar in business in Russia. He received his AB and MBA from Dartmouth College and his DBA from Harvard University. Contact: *da.mccarthy@neu.edu*.